PRAISE FOR *MISERERE MEI*

Klepac's astute and precise reading of Rouault's dark images lead us into the actual darkness of the world. After vivid descriptions of his own experiences with street boys, the homeless, and prisoners in Romania, Russia, and the Czech Republic, Klepac guides readers into a study of their own inner abandonment and forsakenness. A deep meditation on many levels.

BR. PAUL QUENON, OCSO

Trappist at the Abbey of Gethsemani in Kentucky since 1958, where Thomas Merton was his novice master

This publication shows how poignantly relevant Rouault's art is to the lives and sufferings of real people then as well as today.

DR. SOO KANG

Professor of Art History, Chicago State University and author of *Rouault in Perspective* and coauthor with Holly Flora of *This Anguished World of Shadows: George Rouault's Miserere*

This book is a spiritual journey that goes deeply into Rouault's art--exposing the depths of despair, loneliness, and hope. And Rouault's visionary art gives Joel Klepac eyes to pay attention to his own life as a therapist, missionary, and spiritual director. The result is a moving meditation on the darkness and light that keeps company with all of us who seek to follow Christ.

WILLIAM DYRNESS

Senior Professor of Theology and Culture, Fuller Theological Seminary, Pasadena, California. Author of *Rouault: A Vision of Suffering and Salvation* and, most recently of *Facts on the Ground: A Wisdom Theology of Culture* (2022).

A unique and influential book! This is a powerful journey of self-discovery from multiple perspectives, beautifully interwoven. Joel is masterful in bringing together in his writing his artistic vision, missionary heart and his Internal Family Systems (IFS) wisdom.

IOANA POPA

MD, BCC, MTS, certified Internal Family Systems Practitioner, Team For The Soul®, Coaching, Consulting & Spiritual Care

Part art encounter, part memoir, part theological reflection, and part contemplative meditation, Miserere Mei shows the formative power of art to reveal, comfort, and disrupt. In doing so, Klepac brings new life and vibrancy to George Rouault's artistic contribution in the modern world.

WESLEY VANDER LUGT
Director of the Leighton Ford Initiative in Theology, the Arts, and Gospel Witness at Gordon-Conwell Theological Seminary and author of *Beauty Is Oxygen: Finding a Faith that Breathes*

Joel Klepac has embraced the vocation of holistic and integral healing, bringing deep wells of compassion to work with street boys in Romania, families in crisis, college students navigating stormy waters. That vocation manifests here as well, now gently taking readers below the tumult on the surface and into depths where an almost startling stillness is both stark and profoundly calming. The meditations on the haunting work of Rouault and on Joel's own remarkable life journey never trivialize or avoid the misery that is our inescapable human experience, but they invite readers into currents that can carry us to new depths of reflection, insight, experience, calm. Plunge into these living waters and you may be surprised where they carry you.

RICK AXTELL
Professor of Religion and College Chaplain, Centre College

In *Miserere Mei*, Joel gently facilitates a healing conversation with the reader's many parts using the tools of Internal Family Systems. Joel's wisdom and lovely heart is evident on every page. If you are looking for a thoughtful and artfully written guide to your healing journey, this will be a great resource.

DAPHNE ECK COPPOCK
MSW, LSWAIC

In *Miserere Mei*, Joel Klepac provides a captivating journey of self-discovery and spiritual reflection through the art of George Rouault. Klepac's work draws his readers into the scriptures through a sense of wonder, showing how beauty and suffering are not exclusive terms. The book is a remarkable testament to the transformative power of creativity and faith, and an invaluable resource for seeing how art allows us to explore the depths of divine life, beauty, and love.

JONATHAN POWERS
Assistant Professor of Worship Studies, Asbury Theological Seminary

From the earliest known cave paintings to modern art in the Louvre, art continues to have the power to touch people's hearts and minds. One of the best examples of the power of art can be found in the artwork of Georges Rouault. Joel Klepac has written a thought-provoking book on the art of Rouault that can help readers go deeper in their faith and find inner healing for their soul.

WINFIELD BEVINS

Director of Creo Arts, Artist-in-residence at Asbury Seminary, and author of Ever Ancient, Ever New: The Allure of Liturgy for a New Generation

I'm grateful for Joel Klepac! Joel is a lover of art, a lover of Christ and a lover of people. The material he brings to these reflections may begin with the "canvas" of Rouault, but it is then enhanced by a poignant combination of the mind of a therapist, the memory of a missionary, as well as the graceful touch of an artist in his own right. Joel's reflections are powerfully, and sometimes painfully, personal. They are all richly beneficial.

RICK DURRANCE

M.Div, D.Min, Rector of Wilmore Anglican Church

MISERERE MEI

A JOURNEY OF SELF-DISCOVERY
THROUGH THE ART OF GEORGES ROUAULT

JOEL KLEPAC, MA, LMFT

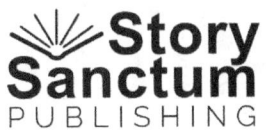

Story
Sanctum
PUBLISHING

Cover image: Head of Christ, c. 1937. Georges Rouault (French, 1871–1958). Oil on canvas; framed: 128.9 x 99.1 x 8.9 cm (50 3/4 x 39 x 3 1/2 in.); unframed: 104.8 x 75 cm (41 1/4 x 29 1/2 in.). The Cleveland Museum of Art, Gift of the Hanna Fund 1950.399 © Artists Rights Society (ARS), New York / ADAGP, Paris.

Interior plates: Miserere, Plates 1-33, c.1914-1918. Georges Rouault (French, 1871–1958). Aquatint with sugar lift, drypoint, burnisher, roulette; 22 3/4 x 16 1/4 inches. Bowden Collections © Artists Rights Society (ARS), New York / ADAGP, Paris.

Other interior images: c. 2023. Joel Klepac. Oil on canvas.

Cover design and interior formatting provided by Casselberry Creative Design.

Unless otherwise indicated, all Scripture references are from the KJV.

Content warning: This work contains stories involving suicide and self-harm related to the lives of children living on the street. If you feel at risk, please seek help; call or text 988 to speak with a professional mental health clinician. This book is not intended as a substitute for professional counseling.

All of the events in this memoir are true to the best of the author's memory. Some names and identifying features have been changed to protect the identity of certain parties. The author in no way represents any company, corporation, or brand, mentioned herein. Therapeutic process stories are based on author's own personal therapy and not on client narratives.

Story Sanctum Publishing.
First Edition.

ISBN: 979-8-9886653-3-5

to my wife
who has been with me through it all
and to my children
who inspire me to tell stories

TABLE OF CONTENTS

INTRODUCTION
Arriving at Rouault's Doorstep

A simple wooden cross was attached to the front wall in my childhood church, a perfect lower case "t" that stood isolated, suspended around two-thirds of the way up. In the back corner was a small, glassed room with a few cribs and bright-colored Noah's Ark wallpaper. More than that, I remember the solid, smooth feel of the oak pews we sat in or crawled under. In the "under pew" world was a deep cadmium red and black maze of octagon and square patterns in the carpet. The edges of the pattern were soft and varied and had a swirly flowery thing in the middle of the octagons. It had a mesmerizing effect. The Russian word for beautiful comes from their word for red, and as a young kid trying to make it through a church service, I think I felt this to be true. If nothing else, the carpet told me that this was a special place, and that we were people worthy to walk on red carpet, like royalty in fairy tales. Other than this abstract aesthetic religious experience involving the carpet, my growing-up church spaces were sparse and only theologically meaningful by accident.

Our next church met in a middle school cafeteria: cement block walls, ceiling tiles, movable chairs, polished concrete floors, lots of wires, microphones, music stands, and a preaching pulpit. There were two tables set up on either side for families to go to during the music to take communion. The right-side table had the grape juice, and the left side table had the wine. We used the tiny plastic disposable wine cups and tore off pieces of homemade bread that was usually on a large silver platter. Nothing in the aesthetic arrangement gave the sense of the sacred. Closing one's eyes seemed the best way to worship.

As a 16-year-old, I began playing guitar; the first song I learned to play and sing was Keith Green's version of "Create in Me a Clean Heart, Oh God," a protestant song version of Psalm 51 (Psalm 50 in Orthodox Church), the first line of which is the reference for the title of Rouault's series *Miserere et Guerre*. Playing and leading people in singing songs like these became a big part of my religious identity – helping people experience the presence of God, to experience, compassion and repentance that might bring them to fuller expressions and actions of care for others. The focus was on emotional authenticity and entering into a sacred space of the music, eyes closed.

Studying painting in college, I began to be attentive to visual aspects of everything around me. Naturally, my church spaces became the victims of a growing artistic snobbery. As I learned more about color, line, and form, I became painfully aware of how little attention was paid to these very real elements we move through every day. Everything could be seen from an aesthetic perspective. I quickly realized that this aesthetic aspect of life, which was becoming a source of fascination, was more or less ignored entirely by my small local religious community. There was little or no awareness of some of the great religious aesthetic traditions of medieval and Renaissance churches.

These dynamics left me feeling orphaned, becoming aware of color, line, shape, and form in a subculture which could only tolerate visual representations of verbal doctrines. Having never been in a church which seemed to take aesthetics as important, I doubted whether one could truly be a Christian and truly be an artist. This dilemma found an initial answer in the biography of the life and work of Georges Rouault (1871-1953), widely respected in the 20th-century art world and who was also a deeply religious Christian family man whose life might have been regarded by me at that time as "truly Christian."[1] He wedded authentic aesthetic values with a rich spirituality in a way I had doubted was possible from my limited perspective, and now I had a hero who held together spirituality and aesthetics without compromising either.

In 2004 my family and I traveled from Romania, where we were living at the time, to visit extended family in the Cleveland area, and I was able to get to the Cleveland Art Museum. I was indignant that Rouault's *Head of Christ* (c. 1937) was not on display.[2] On our way out the door, I inquired at the desk whether there was any way to be able to see the painting. I pulled out my sob story of living in Romania and not being able to get to the museum normally.

The kind folks asked their management what could be done. They arranged for me to return in two days, when they would pull the painting out of storage. Upon returning, they took me back to a large office area with a sea of desks. Against the back wall was the painting on a cart, with a folding chair placed in front of it. After spending about 45 minutes in front of the painting, I was invited to the print room. Once there, they gave me latex gloves so I could handle the prints graciously brought to my table.

Upon seeing my enthusiasm, the print curator brought out a large flat box on a cart. It was a full set of Rouault's *Miserere* (1948). The attendant opened the box and invited me to look through the entire set one by one. I had seen ten or twenty, but seeing them all in context, in order, on a table in a quiet room was startling. It was a sacred encounter with a piece of the soul of Rouault.

I brought into that quiet space of the print room visions of kids I was working with who lived on the street in Romania. Rouault had a way of holding that pain and brokenness, sitting with it, and seeing light beyond it without hurrying out of the darkness.

Twenty years later, I am a marriage and family therapist still fascinated with the inner life. By means of his work, Rouault continues to sit in the ashes with parts of myself I would rather disown; he points to people in our lives who are suffering and says, "Look at that sacred being in front of you."

The following reflections through the *Miserere* series are not intended to be scholarly arguments, but rather expressions of my relationship with the work of Rouault. I hope to be true to the spirit of Rouault and somehow testify to the power of art to transcend time and place, race and religion, ideology, and every form of difference imaginable; to speak to the shared experiences of humankind. And despite the very real and beautiful differences found in the human community, through empathy for the other, we can render those differences impotent to cut off our sense of belonging to one another.

Just over 100 years have passed since this work was completed. The elapsed time has not diminished the power of this work to connect with core human experiences, both the darkness and the unconquerable light.

Saint Isaac the Syrian in the 7th century described "hubba Šapya" as a love that "cannot be obtained by deeds of philanthropy or, in general, by human effect; it is a gift which we receive directly from God." Isaac's teaching on how the love of neighbor is acquired can be outlined as follows: a person withdraws himself from his neighbor for the sake of life in solitude and stillness; through this he acquires an ardent love of God; and this love gives birth in him to the "luminous love" (hubba šapya) of humanity.[3]

Many marvel at the reclusive habits of Georges Rouault. He generally came out of his studio only to eat and to be with his family or a few close friends. One wonders whether the luminous love for humanity spoken of by St. Isaac the Syrian was not present in Rouault. The way he viewed people is manifest in his depictions of them in his art. His luminous love seems to be seen in his gracious approach to the characters surveyed over his career.

Jacques Maritain (1882-1973), an eminent Catholic philosopher and close friend of Rouault, wrote that there was in him, "like a spring of living water, an intense religious sentiment, the stubborn faith of a hermit... which made him discover the image of the divine Lamb in all the abandoned and rejected for whom he felt a profound pity."[4]

And if, "The world's worst evil is the fear of loving,"[5] perhaps Rouault intends an exorcism of fear by his escapades through the darkest parts of the human experience. My hope is that the reader will make their own inner connections with these pieces and make steps towards more freedom from fear to spending more time in the state of compassion.

These reflections follow the movements of the first 33 prints of the *Miserere* series rather than in chronological order. For clarity and context, I have included here a very brief biography of Rouault and my own life.

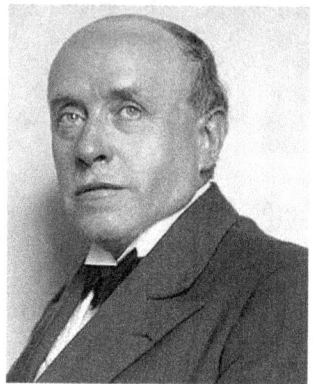

Georges Rouault [6]

Georges Rouault's History Timeline

Rouault was born May 27th, 1871, in Paris, and enrolled in the School of Fine Arts in Paris in 1889 to study painting with Gustave Moreau, also the teacher of Henri Matisse. In his mid-twenties he converted to Catholicism, and in his forties World War I began. In that period, he began his *Miserere* series. The complete series includes 58 prints in the final presentation and was shown for the first time in 1948. The work is a meditation on a religious and spiritual journey of repentance from an artist who lived in Paris through two world wars. [7]

Personal History Timeline

Most of these reflections draw on experiences during my time living in Romania between 2000 and 2009. There are several that go back to growing up in northeast Ohio until graduating high school in 1993, to a 5-month time in Murmansk, Russia in 1993-1994, and a 6-week trip to India in 1998, after college and before Romania. Since Romania, I attended graduate school, obtained a masters in marriage and family counseling, and started practicing in 2012 through the present. More recently, becoming an Internal Family Systems trained therapist added a lens through which to see human functioning in a more granular way.

Methodology

This writing project began as a way to dive deeper into Rouault's work, and to reflect on the inner connections made with parts of myself and the stories that have stayed with me over the years. I approach Rouault as a therapist of the soul, guiding the viewer through inner territories. What began as a couple of reflections on my favorite pieces turned into working with the first 33 pieces.

I don't come to this work as an art historian. However, as an artist myself, I started each reflection with a look at what was there in the print, what some of the historical, cultural, or theological elements there were that seemed apparent and important. I then sat back and entered the piece with an open heart, noticing what personal memories were evoked by the themes being presented. By the end of each meditation, I tried to bring together some of the personal themes, and themes that seemed apparent from an art critical analysis of the elements of the piece. I do not claim to hold any definitive interpretations or meanings for Rouault's work, only an honest desire to look deeply into the mysterious mirror of darks and lights that illuminate human experience.

I hope that you would not stop at reading these meditations, but that you would be open to unearthing your own connections with these fundamentally human themes.

What is Internal Family Systems?

Internal Family Systems (IFS) is a current evidence-based mental health therapy. While this book is not intended to replace therapy, it is based at least in part on some of the assumptions of IFS. It evolved out of family systems theories applied to the inner world of the individual. Initially, Richard Schwartz, the developer of the model, was working with folks with eating disorders and noticed them talking about "the part of me that binges" and "the part of me the restricts" and "the part of me that purges." He took the intuitive leap and began to facilitate sessions like he would with a family, engaging each of the parts and trying to understand the motives and fears of each one. He was surprised to find how much therapeutic movement could happen through work with these parts.

Schwartz began to discover that there were at least two kinds of basic parts that all people seem to have and that simply get exaggerated in response to trauma. Some have a protective role and others seem to hold overwhelming emotion for the system. There are many ways to get to know these parts of us, and it was in this frame of mind that I began to consider how Rouault's *Miserere* series might help us understand and get to know parts of ourselves as they resonate with parts of us longing to be seen and heard.

Schwartz was surprised to find that as clients differentiated parts and explored them, there emerged some core spiritual qualities that didn't seem like the protective or exiled parts. This spiritual core, he found, had qualities like compassion, connectedness, calm, curiosity, and openness of heart among other things. Finding this in even the most traumatized clients led him to his own awakening to spiritual realities he had denied for so long. When asking his clients what this was, clients would say, "That's just me." For lack of a better term, he settled on calling it "Self" or "Self-energy." The state of being "in the heart" in Eastern Orthodox spirituality, or similar states described in the major world religions came to be seen by Schwartz as the true therapist that can heal and guide the individual. In Rouault, this state seems evident in his compassionate posture towards humanity.

The guided meditations included in this book are geared in part to help the reader find that state of compassion or being "in the heart" when addressing their own parts evoked in the meditations. (See Video "Intro to Internal Family Systems (IFS) by Dr. Richard Schwartz" for a more complete introduction to IFS.) If you find it difficult to approach your parts with openness of heart and some base level of compassion, it is better to wait or work with an IFS guide.

Guide and Cautions for Levels of Engagement

While this is not intended to replace mental health therapy, these images, themes, and narratives can be evocative and distressing, with stories involving suicide, self-harm, and abuse. Some readers may come to this book with a trauma history. The higher the level of trauma history, the more caution is advised, including working with an IFS therapist and gauging the level of intensity for engagement with the work. It is important to find your window of tolerance, enough emotional engagement but not overwhelming emotional engagement. Rouault's images and themes are intended to get us in touch with parts of us that are often underground and overlooked. For spiritual and psychological growth, some people need increased intensity to get in touch with disowned parts of themselves. Others get flooded easily with intense emotion and need lower intensity in order to get the growth and healing needed. Please honor your inner system and your needs for safety and stretching appropriate to your current growth. In other words, ask yourself, where is that level of emotional intensity that is enough in order to learn and grow and where is it not so overwhelming to the point of shutting down or feeling emotionally flooded. There are at least three levels of intensity you may engage in this book. I ask you to engage at the level that is right for you.

Lowest level of intensity - simply spend time with the images, reading each chapter and skipping the meditation at the end of the chapter.

Medium Intensity - spend time with the image, read the text, and journal around the written guided meditations.

High Intensity - spend time with the text and listen to the audio guided meditations, pausing as you go to do your inner work. (This is only recommended for those high-level spiritual practitioners or folks very familiar with Internal Family Systems parts work, or under the direction of an IFS therapist or IFS practitioner.)

There are some stories involving suicide and self-harm related to the lives of children living on the street. If you feel at risk, please seek help; call or text 988 to speak with a professional mental health clinician (psychologytoday.com – Find a Therapist).

It is my deepest desire that these meditations would be a springboard for your personal growth. Often, when things get intense, we need a guide to help us find our way through our inner system to find healing and peace. While there are many evidence-based therapies that are highly valuable to this growth, I would recommend finding a therapist trained in the Internal Family Systems model as you will see discussed below. Also, the guided meditations follow the IFS model and you can bring unfinished work to an IFS therapist to naturally continue if needed. You can search for a trained IFS therapist here: **ifs-institute.com/practitioners**. For more information about Internal Family Systems, please visit **ifs-institute.com.**

Following each chapter is a guided meditation meant to offer the reader another opportunity to explore their own inner system of protective and exiled parts evoked by Rouault's images, the narratives, and reflections. While some of these meditations touch on exiled parts, they stop short of the complete witnessing and unburdening process needed for more complete healing. This should be done with an experienced IFS practitioner or IFS therapist. To listen to the guided meditations, you can either scan the provided QR code or go to **tinyurl.com/rouault-meditations**.

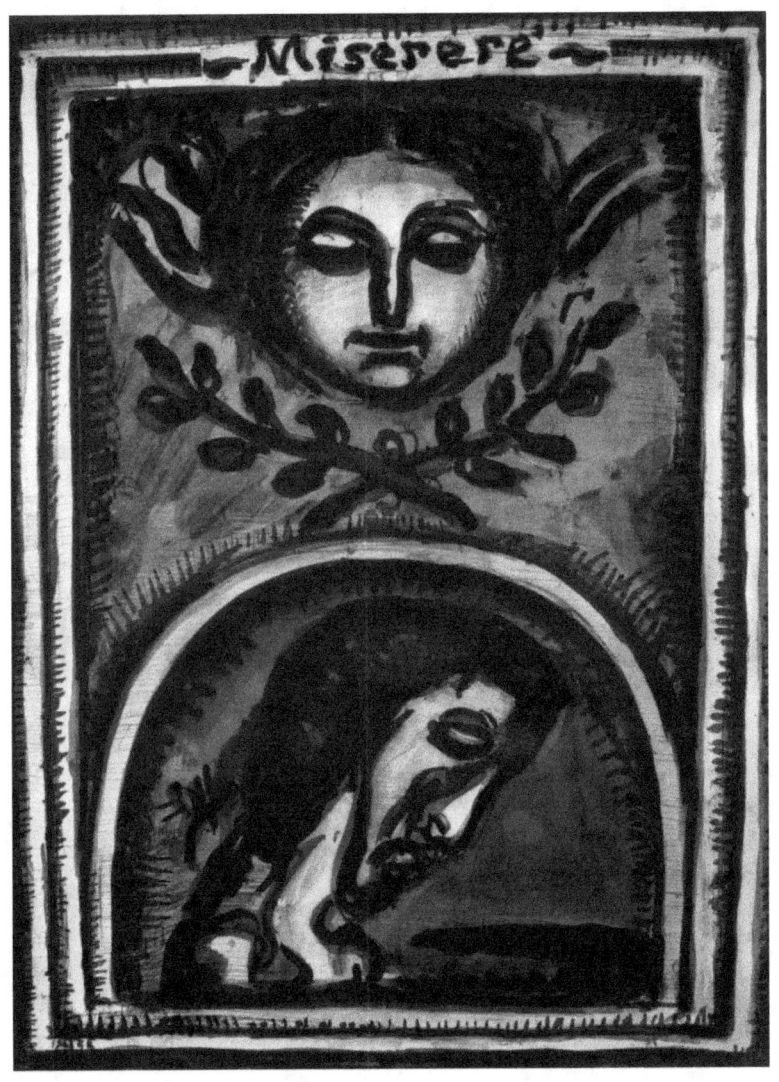

Plate 1

PLATE 1: MISERERE MEI

"Miserere mei, Deus, secundum magnam misericordiam tuam"
"Have Mercy on Me, O God, after Thy Great Goodness"

The first song I learned to play on guitar in my attic bedroom as a sixteen-year-old came from the words of Psalm 51 "Create in me a clean heart, O God."[8] The opening piece of Georges Rouault's *Miserere* series presents the viewer with a print with three internal frames. The third drawn frame creates an arch over the downturned profile of a head in the bottom center of the picture, separating it from the winged face above. Another two branches separate the faces which are reminiscent of laurel used in martyrs' crowns. The top face is a disembodied countenance recalling decorative images of the sun with a face. The "Winged Sun" suggests the Hebrew connotation of the image with Hebrew seals recalling scripture as in Malachi 4:2: "*But unto you that fear my name shall the Sun of righteousness arise with healing in his wings*" (KJV).

The original prints are large format, over 2 feet tall (25.88 inches). This makes the head of Christ in the full format images in rough proximity to a life-sized human head. These pieces are very much a one-to-one encounter, image with viewer, person to person. From a couple of feet away, they fill the viewer's field of vision almost completely, as would looking out of a large window. Small digital reproductions really don't do justice to the encounter with the images in person.

The profile head is very close in imagery to the next plate in the series, a downturned head of Christ, also at the bottom of the picture plane. It is in contrast with the neutral face, not happy or sad or anxious, but present, watching as the sun looks down upon the realm below.

Rouault had written poetic lines on separate pages from the prints and later the publishers placed them below the prints. I will refer to them as "associated stanzas" or "poetic lines" in order to respect Rouault's desire to allow the prints and poetry to have some separation and not function like titles in a traditional sense. They function more like a call and response, a litany related but separate celebrants, both helping on the journey of repentance. The language of titles moves us into rationalizing that tends to take us out of our bodies and more visceral awareness. By presenting them separately here, I hope the reader will take time with the images before reading the associated poetic stanzas on the following page.

The word "Miserere" – translated as "Have Mercy" – conjures the penitential psalm from the Catholic liturgical cycle and daily prayers, and the most used psalm in Eastern Orthodox Christianity. I will just refer to this psalm as the *"Miserere Psalm"* or Psalm 51 to avoid the numbering confusion.

In the Catholic Church, the Miserere Psalm is revered and placed in the prayers of repentance and absolution. In the Eastern Orthodox Church, it is prayed at least three times a day in full monastic life. It retains importance in Jewish practice as part of many feasts and ritual practices.

Contrasted with the Suffering Christ in the bottom of the image in Plate 1, the face at the top is placid like the sun. In this we may see the passionlessness of the Godhead in the passion of Christ, the divine apatheia of God.[9] According to this theology God does not react, but only acts. God does not move out of anger, sadness, or emotive force, but out of voluntary compassion, out of the depths of his mercy, out of His being as love. He is not moved to compassion, because He is and always has been essentially compassion. His nature is manifest or revealed, but not changed. It is interesting how the science of compassion in the social neuroscience literature is reflecting this same dynamic, that true compassion actually has to have a passionless aspect to it.[10] There has to be enough detachment and differentiation for room for the other person's experience and then compassionate action; compassion without compulsion.

The winged sun face above Christ also recalls the words from heaven at the baptism of Christ, "Behold this is my son with whom I am well pleased." Eastern iconography of the baptism of Christ emphasizes the unveiling of the three persons of the Trinity – the voice of the Father, the Spirit in the form of a dove, and the Son. A similar kind of trinitarian view of the work of Christ may be seen here, the action of Christ's compassion seen in the context of the trinity, mutual submission in love. The Christ in this work begins in the state of eternal belovedness.

Romania, August 2003 - *Journal entry*

"Worked on the *Danube from the Balcony* painting idea this morning. I couldn't bring myself to put a boat in it. Not yet at least. It's dark and mysterious and the river is a wild gurgling mass with banks at the bottom and top of the canvas. I couldn't help but think of Phillip Sherrard material about the interconnectedness of divine spirit and matter.[11] The picture is of the *material* – bottom of the painting, the near shore of the river, and the *spiritual/divine* – the distance at the top more surreal to the sky. The river

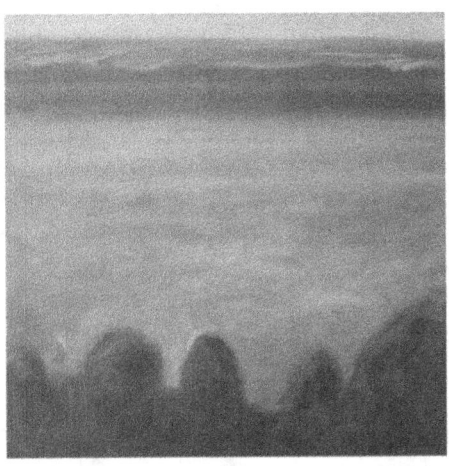

is this present, yet flowering mass which connects the two, but really there is land under the water which actually physically connects the shores as well as becomes a vessel for the uncrossable river. This is the connected mass, yet non-confusion of the banks of the river, the spirit and the flesh are just as real, it is only perspective which transfigures the spirit to a less solid appearance, though it is just as concrete. The river is very material, but it flows, moves mysteriously, has unexplored depths, is dark yet luminous, life-giving yet sucks the living into its depths and consumes life; it is beautiful and ugly, cleansing yet dirty, and full of illness and disease being carried down river. One can speed along its surface or fight to exhaustion and still move down river. Birds swim in the air above and fish fly through its murky currents eating the dead and the living, cleaning and carrying the disease of the waste..."

I believe that Rouault saw an interpenetration of the transcendent and the immanent, the spiritual and the material. The historic debate about the use of images, the iconoclast controversy between east and west were understood as being tied to the theology of how God could be fully God and fully human in Christ. Language that emerged from platonic roots, "commingled but not confused," became key to holding the tension of difference in unity, in Trinitarian theology, in incarnational theology (how Christ can be God and human at once), but also extends into understanding of how an image or icon can be intimately commingled with God without being God. It applies to anthropology as well: God is in our neighbor while not confused with actually being God. As seen in the creation theology: God is commingled with the tree or ecosystem without being the tree or ecosystem. Quite literally, "as you do it to the least of these you do it to me" (Mt 25). In other words, God's energies animate all things, while His essence is still something separate, outside of all created things, Being before being, intimately commingled without confusion. Another term sometimes used is panentheism, God in all, without confusion with created things.

Thomas Merton's famous vision echoes Rouault's vision on the divine shining through humble vessels:

> *"In Louisville, at the corner of Fourth and Walnut, in the center of the shopping district, I was suddenly overwhelmed with the realization that I loved all those people, that they were mine and I theirs, that we could not be alien to one another even though we were total strangers. It was like waking from a dream of separateness, of spurious self-isolation in a special world, the world of renunciation and supposed holiness. ... This sense of liberation from an illusory difference was such a relief and such a joy to me that I almost laughed out loud. ... I have the immense joy of being man, a member of a race in which God Himself became incarnate. As if the sorrows and stupidities of the human condition could overwhelm me, now I realize what we all are. And if only everybody could realize this! But it cannot be explained. There is no way of telling people that they are all walking around shining like the sun."[12]*

Rouault found a way to show the world this radiance through his graphic medium.

So perhaps Rouault here, in a visual shorthand, in this opening image signifies the immanent Christ and the transcendent sun. The arch enclosing Christ becomes his being God, cramped in the space of human flesh. The layers of reality converge in His incarnation; spirit and flesh meet.

Gregory of Nyssa espoused the idea of the "whole humanity," the first creation of humankind, not just of the individual first human, but the whole humanity created across time. Christ being the head of that "whole humanity."[13] It would be understood that we are in a redemptive process of healing and reconciling the whole humanity, including cultures, nations, families and neighborhoods; but also our inner communities, our inner parts and especially those parts of ourselves that have been barred from the table, often our pain or trauma-holding parts.

I don't know how much Rouault may have thought in these terms, but the spirit of the Miserere Psalm is one of self-reflection, seeing one's own brokenness. I don't read finger-pointing in Rouault's work, but compassionate holding of those people in our world and those parts in ourselves that are in need of presence, healing, joy, truth, restoration, deliverance, and reconciliation. Although it is a reach perhaps, I see in Rouault's work a seeking of all lost parts of humanity, something akin to the whole humanity of Nyssa.

Rouault has been criticized for the darkness of his images, most poignantly by Léon Bloy, his mentor, perhaps one of his most brutal critics. I believe his move towards the dark was his instinct towards this kind of reconciliation. The more we see ourselves in our neighbor, the more we sense our shared humanity.

I end this section with the Miserere Psalm and invite you to consider entering into the spirit of Rouault's *Miserere* series with an openness to consider your own personal growth and healing. Whether you are religious or not, Christian, Hindu, Buddhist, or atheist, read it as it feels comfortable and helpful to your inner system as you long for healing and belovedness.

Psalm 50/51 Miserere Mei...

"Have mercy upon me, O God, according to thy lovingkindness: according unto the multitude of thy tender mercies blot out my transgressions.
Wash me thoroughly from mine iniquity, and cleanse me from my sin.
For I acknowledge my transgressions: and my sin is ever before me.
Against thee, thee only, have I sinned, and done this evil in thy sight:
that thou mightiest be justified when thou speakest, and be clear when thou judgest. Behold, I was shapen in iniquity;
and in sin did my mother conceive me.
Behold, thou desirest truth in the inward parts:
and in the hidden part thou shalt make me to know wisdom.
Purge me with hyssop, and I shall be clean:
wash me, and I shall be whiter than snow.
Make me to hear joy and gladness; that the bones which thou hast broken may rejoice. Hide thy face from my sins, and blot out all mine iniquities.
Create in me a clean heart, O God; and renew a right spirit within me.
Cast me not away from thy presence; and take not thy holy spirit from me.
Restore unto me the joy of thy salvation; and uphold me with thy free spirit.
Then will I teach transgressors thy ways; and sinners shall be converted unto thee. Deliver me from bloodguiltiness,
O God, thou God of my salvation:
and my tongue shall sing aloud of thy righteousness.
O Lord, open thou my lips; and my mouth shall shew forth thy praise.
For thou desirest not sacrifice; else would I give it: thou delightest not in burnt offering. The sacrifices of God are a broken spirit:
a broken and a contrite heart, O God, thou wilt not despise.
Do good in thy good pleasure unto Zion: build thou the walls of Jerusalem.
Then shalt thou be pleased with the sacrifices of righteousness,
with burnt offering and whole burnt offering:
then shall they offer bullocks upon thine altar."

GUIDED MEDITATION

Take a moment to find a place to be still and quiet. See if it feels ok to close your eyes and count 5 breaths.

As you find yourself feeling settled inside, just check and see if it feels ok to proceed with the meditation to explore more of the inner dynamics happening as you read this chapter. Do you have the emotional space in your life right now? Please honor your need for less emotional intensity and come back to the meditation later if that is what is needed. If you feel ok, go ahead and continue on in the meditation.

Start with just noticing any body sensations that arose as you read and that you are feeling now in your body. Often there may be a tightness in the chest, gut heaviness, lightness or tingliness. What do you notice?

In what ways does the first line, "Have mercy upon me, O God, according to thy lovingkindness" resonate with you or annoy you? Make room for whatever reaction you may have.

Spend a few minutes noticing what it may have felt like to receive mercy in your life or to give mercy. See if you can focus more on the experience of mercy giving or receiving vs thoughts and ideas about mercy.

To engage with the high intensity level audio version described in the introduction, scan the QR code or visit tinyurl.com/rouault-meditations.

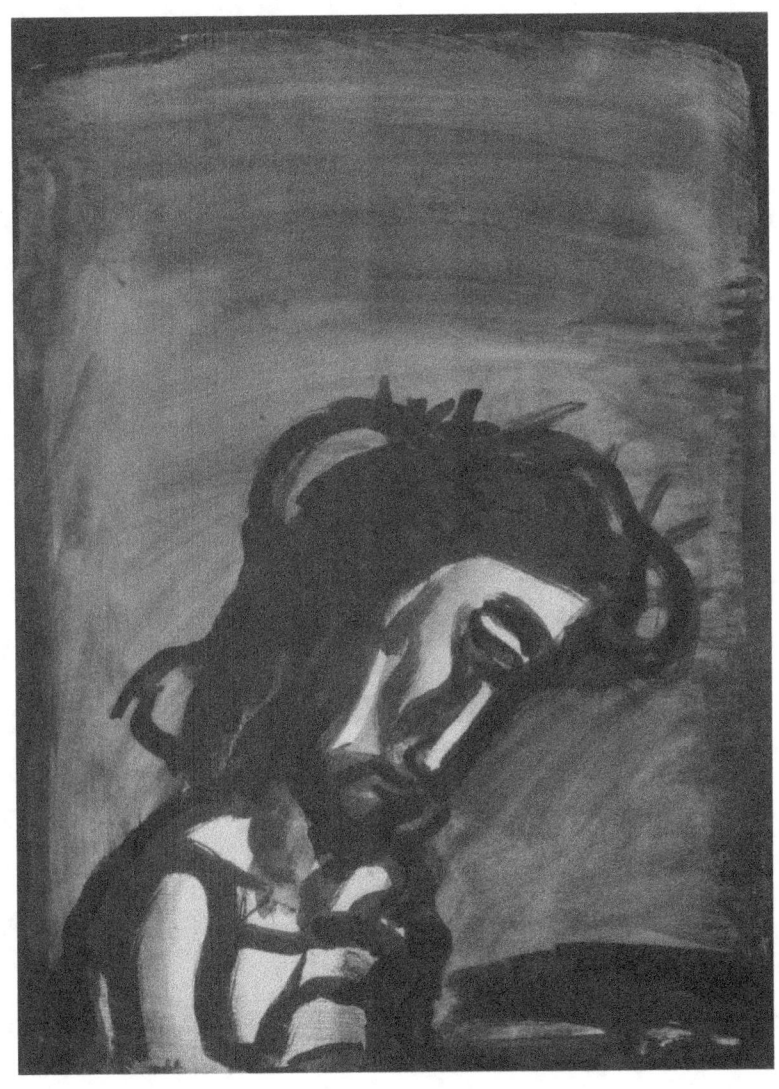

Plate 2

PLATE 2: CHRIST REVILED

"Jésus Honni…"
"Jesus Reviled…"

The poetic phrase "Jesus Reviled…" is the entry point Rouault offers to this image in Plate 2 of the series. The bleak landscape puts Christ down. Visually His head rises only to the middle of the picture plane, face glowing brightly, contrasted by black hair and crown of thorns. His is the downcast face, bearing the burden of suffering. It echoes the introductory image in Plate 1 of the series. The reviling words or blows from beatings, presumably, are in the air, as if the atmosphere were pressing down upon Him. We are not sure if it is over, or just a pause for the next blow to land. His face is down, and the divine head gazes at the earth below in a simple gesture that is the whole Philippians 2:5-11 "kenotic hymn" in a single image, self-emptying song of the early church services. It is as if Christ from all time intended to empty Himself, in order to suffer with all and to raise all flesh in the resurrection.

In the early church writers, Christ found His way down to earth, became flesh, went down to His death, and then immediately went down to Hades to conquer "death by His own death," as the Eastern Orthodox Paschal Hymn declares, "Christ has trampled down death by death and upon those in the tombs bestowing life." Right out of the gate, Rouault's Christ is one who joins humanity in the exiled places of shame.

Here Christ takes on flesh, identifies with humankind and all its humiliation, not just in general, but specifically with all those poor and oppressed, outcast and forgotten. He endured the active shaming of the crowds and the guards. Part of the death He was to conquer once and for all was the death of being reviled, demeaned, diminished, disrespected, or being stripped not just of clothes but of dignity, of being recognized in His and our humanity. While being reviled in this image, He is seen in a moment of taking on the shame of humankind. In this He is pictured as a radiating light in the darkness, divine light shining through reviled flesh. The unconquerable image cannot be overcome any more than the sun can be extinguished by clouds. So, too, those stripped of humanity by judgement, blame and criticism, stripped of humanity with the most ordinary of linguistic devices, a label like "blasphemer," or any other label we might choose to justify the removal of empathy and compassion.

Romania, 2006

Ion asked me to go with him to visit some relatives of his, knowing that his uncle had become a Christian some years ago. He is always dying for the chance to talk about his new faith with "his people," Roma.[14]

We entered the courtyard through a big metal gate to find his aunt lying on a couch moved outside to enjoy the summer air. It was a regular living room couch that they would put a tarp over at night. She was resting her Sunday away when we walked in. She didn't immediately recognize Ion, but with a few words in Roma (Romani language), her face lit up. Roma are divided up into different tribes, of which Ion is from the "skirt-wearing" tribe. It was evident that we were on Roma territory as soon as we walked in, as we were greeted by ladies wearing beautiful bright colored and layered skirts, long braided hair, and patterned scarf head coverings. One of these women made sure we had stools to sit on so that Ion could tell us his story.

He told the aunt how he chose to be in the family of God, and through faith in Christ his life is changed. Without pausing, he told how he could now read the Bible and write, how he was going to school and getting his birth certificate. "God is in my life." He would go on as long as he could about his new faith, about not being on drugs or alcohol for a year and four months. She motioned to one of her stepdaughters who had been listening in, "His face is changed, isn't it? He looks good." Then without a blink she turned to him and asked, "So why don't you find a girl and get married?"

It seemed clear to me that without the evident change in his face from what it was a couple years ago, they would have probably been impatient with all his preaching. The same thing happened each time a new person entered the courtyard; strange looks, "Who is this?" "Oh yeah, that kid who would beg from everyone," "That messed up kid who lived down there," and then, "He looks good," "He is different." This always prompted Ion to another sermonette.

Ion did have very yellow skin before due to his chronic illness and bad blood tests. However, that alone didn't account for the awe in his relatives' eyes when they saw him and he claimed, "Christ has done a miracle in my life."

As things often happen, this little visit occurred on Transfiguration Sunday. In Romanian, the Transfiguration is referred to by the ordinary words, "the changing of the face." The Eastern Orthodox understanding is that the transfiguration was not so much a light show, as it was the scales coming off the Disciples' eyes; they saw Christ as He always is. The veil came off and they really saw Christ. As Ion's aunt and other relatives asked him, "Why don't you find a girl and get married," they were acknowledging that they had finally seen Ion not as "street trash," a "beggar" or a "pest," but as an eligible bachelor. They saw him with new eyes. They saw beyond the labels.

The religious systems labeled God in Christ as bad, worthy of capital punishment. In the end it was the religious systems that were shown to be faulty, defunct, and impotent to discern the divine dignity in the human frame. Religion crucified God, putting to shame all human systems of righteousness.

In Rouault's image depicting Christ being reviled, beaten, we are placed in a front row seat to God in the position of the abused outcast. By extension, there is a divine identification with all outcasts, all those reviled, all those who are stripped of the dignity of being seen as divine beings in human flesh. The indignity experienced by Ion was not foreign to Rouault's Christ reviled.

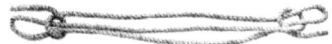

In some way, there is a part of each of us that carries shame. A part that holds the pain of being reviled. Other aspects of ourselves fill the mind with self-criticisms, beatings that last years, "If only I…," "I should have…," "I can't believe I am such a …". Rouault's Christ is inside there sitting in the ashes with that part that continues to be reviled in us. The part often waits for healing, for a kenotic descent into the depths of the human psyche to reach down and speak dignity back in, to bring understanding and self-forgiveness. Our severe hatred for our neighbor or enemy is only a reflection of our hatred for these inner parts in isolation, tortured by our own fierce guards hurling insults. Rouault's Christ is reviled again any time we revile ourselves, our neighbor, or our enemy.

Kentucky, 2021

Focusing on my caregiver part, doing Internal Family System Therapy parts work, I notice that some memories drive my inner caregiver (the aspect of my internal system focused on caregiving as a way to protect from other intense feelings). The histories of abuse people close to me had suffered left me feeling there was no room for me to care for my own parts that held loneliness and hurt. The voices of social justice leaders who highlighted the cruel realities of the world's poor rang in my head and reinforced this idea. How could you not sell everything and care for the poor, the war victims, children, women caught in the sex trade, human trafficking, and the list went on and on (and still does).

But the conclusion for my caregiver part was, as with my family and so with the world, "There is no room for me to dare to take up room or attention, the suffering is so great out there." "Only a terrible person would nurture their own pain, stand up for their own needs." I am sure that this was a big part of my attraction to Rouault early on, that he was fitting the narrative of my caregiver part, sacrificing all for the suffering world. It is a black and white world with which my inner part resonated. Unfortunately, care for others was framed in total opposition with care for self. The extreme of caregiving for me was about finding a way to be seen and to belong, to be accepted, to have a role that allowed me to matter and be valuable to others. While often looking very compassionate, it has been often driven by a fear of being lost and alone if I were to ever lose my role as caregiver.

I honor the caregiver part and all its intentions for me, to help me belong and have a valuable place, and then speak to its fears by letting it know about those in my life now who love me and support me regardless of being a caregiver 100% of the time.

Going deeper into the caregiver's concerns, I see a real fear that if the caregiving is peeled away, somehow I will not be loved and valued. Caregiving hides this shame, this fear of being unlovable or lost if not for extreme caregiving. That part in me now gets to hear from the voice of love, "You are good enough," "You are beloved," "Nothing you do can add or take away from your belovedness." And, "Love and give freely, without compulsion or necessity, no need to prove or earn anything, you are already seen, heard and valued." And, "Let the shame wash away, and feel the refreshing waters of fidelity, solidarity and connection."

I encourage the reader, caution the reader, to enter into these waters, not to pile on more shame of what you have done or not done, criticizing yourself, but rather to honor those parts of you that have been trying hard, to see and address your fears that are the barriers to your compassionate core self-leading.

GUIDED MEDITATION

Take a moment to find a place to be still and quiet. See if it feels ok to close your eyes and count 5 breaths. Check and see if you have emotional space to sit with this meditation.

Are there self-labeling habits you have that limit your freedom, limit your creativity, and limit your being fully alive? Can you notice and acknowledge that critical part of you, that part that reviles other parts of you? Can you just get curious about that critical part for a few minutes? What can you notice about that critical part? Does it have a tone or flavor or quality you can discern? If you can approach this critical part with curiosity and openness, ask it what it is worried about happening to you if it were to relax and not criticize you so much?

Is there an underlying intention in the critic that you can appreciate? If it feels ok, just ask that critical part what it would need to be reassured of in order for it to not feel the need to cut you down like it does? See if there is a way you could honestly reassure that part. Are there needs that are met in your life now that maybe weren't met when the critical part ramped up in your life?

See if you can't spend a little time appreciating the positive intention of the inner critic. And maybe it is possible to negotiate with it to find less distressing ways to meet that same goal if it is not met already. As in the example above, my inner critic was trying to make me good enough, and it can calm down when I remind it of the people who accept me as I am.

When this inner reflection feels complete for you, take a few moments to return your attention to your breath and to the space around you. Perhaps spend some moments reflecting on the experience and take any notes on things you would like to explore further later or insights you want to hold onto.

To engage with the high intensity level audio version described in the introduction, scan the QR code or visit tinyurl.com/rouault-meditations.

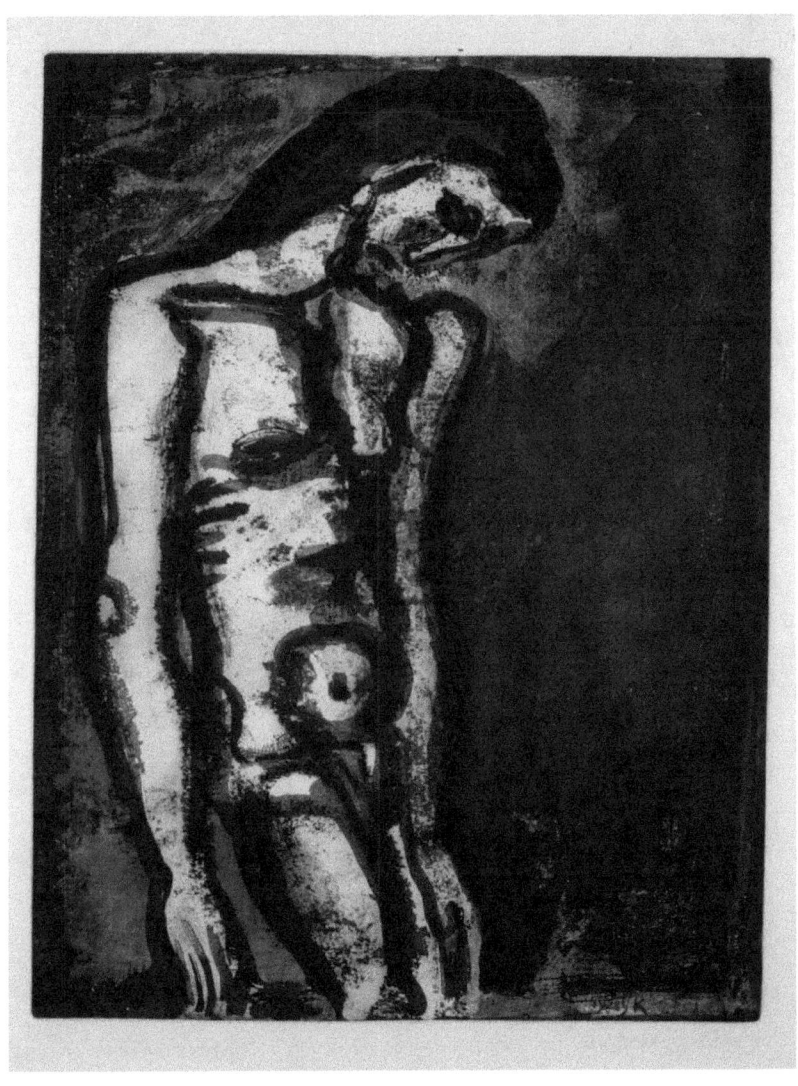

Plate 3

PLATE 3: FOREVER SCOURGED

"toujours flagellé..."
"forever scourged..."

"Forever scourged..." builds Rouault's vision of Christ as one who suffers with all who suffer. In Plate 3, "forever scourged...," we are quickly in the deep end of suffering. Presented as a naked figure, Rouault conjures the passion of Christ, the beatings or scourgings in full swing. Christ's worn-out body stands at an angle as if in mid-fall or being held up by some unseen post. The composition ends at the fingertips, creating strong downward vertical lines of two arms and body.

As in Plate 2, there is a downward visual movement, the head and face echoing the head from Plates 1 and 2, eyes closed, face to the ground. There is no horizon, only an ambiguous sky presumably, dark enough to set off the body of Christ in contrast, making His flesh the strongest highlight in the piece, also outlined in black contours. The black hair is almost a strange shape on top of His head, as if a black weight stands on His head, weighing him down. Though the landscape offers almost nothing in terms of imagery or anchoring, its bleakness and the fact that Rouault was working on it during the duration of World War I lead me to associate this scourged body of Christ with the desolate warscape, the trenches, smoke, and gas.

In "forever scourged...," Christ is identified with suffering; there are none who suffer without Christ suffering with them. Christ's passion and death connects God to all human suffering. Rouault builds on his specific Catholic visual language of the passion of Christ, being scourged, tied to a post and whipped with brutal numbers of strikes. There is a sense of unending suffering.

Rouault was not merely attempting to describe a historical religious story; he was connecting at once the sufferings of humanity in war times to Christ's suffering, the constant bombings, the bringing back of the bodies of the dead, the loss, the desolation of centuries of work, destruction of farmland, homes, and livelihoods. Rouault recounts each atrocity, however small or large, as another blow to Christ, "forever scourged." A hundred years after he created this piece, we can list the atrocities of the past century. From our own inner parts suffering to a whole people suffering genocide.

As long as humanity suffers, Christ is scourged.

Romania, 2001

The Beatings Never End

they're here again out from the rain
but they are all wet beatings never end

hole in her shirt girl cries for tea
fills it with sugar but can't forget dad

no job and no power no hope to hold
anger within and family together

the girl plays while mother grips
exhaustion, pain and a cup of coffee

the streetlight burns and the kid whines
mom closes her eyes to look for something

Although we crossed paths with this woman in Romania, it is the story of women across the globe, enduring one episode after another of abuse, feeling trapped, helpless, caught in the dilemma of feeling, "the devil you know is better than the devil you don't know."

"Lord, have mercy," "Christ is reviled," and now "forever scourged" in Rouault's litany. While a specific historical context spurred Rouault to create these images, his method of connecting with the inner realities opens them up to general archetypes, to common human experiences. While we may consider the violence of war as the scourging of Christ, we may also consider the violence done to ourselves in the internal war that many of us fight "forever."

As with women trapped in domestic violence, relationships are characterized by both a very real external war as well as an internal war. The victim feels stuck and is of course ravaged with the internal war even more than those loved ones that can see it. This stuck-ness often leads to returning over and over again, much to the dismay of loved ones. The internal war sounds like, "Is what he says true? Am I worthless? Would anyone else ever love me?"

So it is with all of us to a lesser degree, living between external violence and internal violence. Violence at its basic level is any diminishing of the basic dignity of the person.[15] Rouault, in his close-up of abstracted single figures, plays with both the internal and external aspects of human experience.

Romania, 2005 - *Excerpt from letter to supporters*

Two of the boys arrived at the Friday evening meeting in the street with news of Robert having fallen from the fifth floor of an apartment building. It was not clear if he had committed suicide, if he had been pushed, or if it was an accident. He was alive when they took him to the hospital, but died soon after. I can't imagine what his last hours were like.

Two years before, Robert came into Lazarus House to live with us. A few months before that, he began expressing an interest in getting off the streets after having been on the streets almost three years. In the process of trying to understand his intentions and willingness to work to come off the streets, I discovered some of the complex causes for his arrival on the streets. He had learned to cope with the streets and rejection from his family by huffing a glue bag, smoking, and cutting his arms to release the anxiety that would often build up in his blood vessels.

Robert was a survivor and a victim of his own survival methods, as many of our boys were. He tended to be quiet and withdrawn. When he moved into our home, he did whatever we asked, he made small talk, enjoyed playing cards, and with a little conversation, it was obvious that he was very intelligent. He is the kind of kid who has learned to be invisible. Ironically, after only six days with us, he disappeared after telling us that he was going to the outhouse in the church courtyard. We didn't hear anything from him for a couple of months. Now he acted embarrassed. While he was with us, he had difficulty with attention and receiving affection, though he obviously enjoyed it, playing *Uno* around the dinner table and watching movies together.

I don't know yet if it was suicide or homicide, and this has left the question in my mind about whether even if it was suicide, are we all guiltless in his death. Many speak ugly things against children living on the streets. They suffer abuse and neglect; they manipulate people to get needs met and are used to being manipulated and used to meet the needs of others. The overall message these kids get from society is, "Go away, out of sight, we wish you were dead." Most people don't verbalize these things, but some are so bold. Often the most bold are the same ones that matter the most to these boys. Robert may have thought he was doing all those people a favor.

Robert was always very reluctant to talk about God, unlike many of the other boys. Often they confess to Christ and pray to get through the long nights, but Robert never tried to give any such impression. I always got the sense that he was on his own, even if his little brother was around, and I think he felt that if there was a God, He didn't do him any good anyway.

My wife and I were on a date one day in the summer before his death and ran across Robert and his brother. We caught up a little as he casually told us about being strangled, showing us the scar on his neck and about his time in the hospital. During the conversation I had the impression that he was checking in with his parents. Even though he only stayed a week with us, he still felt a connection to us, like we knew him and he us, and that it was important that we knew certain things about him.

Though he had left, we had invited him into our lives and still had not rejected him. He had a crooked smile, bright eyes, a soft voice, and gentle presence. We will miss him.

"Lord, remember all those who have fallen asleep in the hope of the resurrection and eternal life. Forgive all their sins committed in knowledge or ignorance. Let them enjoy Your eternal blessings in the Light of your presence; grant them peace, refreshment, fellowship with your saints, and life that never ends. Have mercy on us, for You are full of grace and love mankind. Amen."
-- from the Eastern Orthodox Prayer Book

There seems to be no hard line between the outer scourgings and the inner ones, and the inner ones are often perhaps more deadly. In this image Rouault begs us to see all scourging, all suffering, as the suffering of Christ. When we find we have done the "scourging," the words of King David who just sent a man to his death, "Have mercy on me, O God," seem fitting. Rouault challenges us with the brutal, bloody reality that there is not a beating or scourging that is not felt by Christ, either inflicting pain on ourselves through denigrating self-talk or self-harm or the dehumanizing of others through words, actions, or inaction. "As you have done it to the least of these, you have done it unto me" (Matthew 25).

GUIDED MEDITATION

Take a moment to find a place to be still and quiet. See if it feels ok to close your eyes and count 5 breaths. Check and see if you have emotional space to sit with this meditation.

How does the image of Christ "scourged" connect with your experience? Do you have shame or guilt that comes up around things you have done or not done to others? Do you feel the pain of internal self-scourging, parts that work hard to make you feel bad to protect you from further missteps? And when there are shaming parts there are parts that receive that shaming. Can you acknowledge those places, too?

Let's start with the scourging part, the part that shames you. Can you notice any scourging part in you that directs its energy towards you or others? Can you just be curious about why this part feels it needs to do this? Are there times in your life when the harsh self-scourging part started getting more active to protect from something ever happening again, from ever feeling a certain way again? Can you appreciate the intention of the scourging part even if its strategy has felt very destructive? What would it need in order to relax and consider a new alternative to protecting you? See if you can address those things in a new way.

Can you just notice the shame-holding parts inside of you, the part that holds the pain of the inner scourging? For now, just see if you can acknowledge it and let it know you see it there. If it feels honest, send it a message that you will work to heal it when you can get to it safely.

To engage with the high intensity level audio version described in the introduction, scan the QR code or visit tinyurl.com/rouault-meditations.

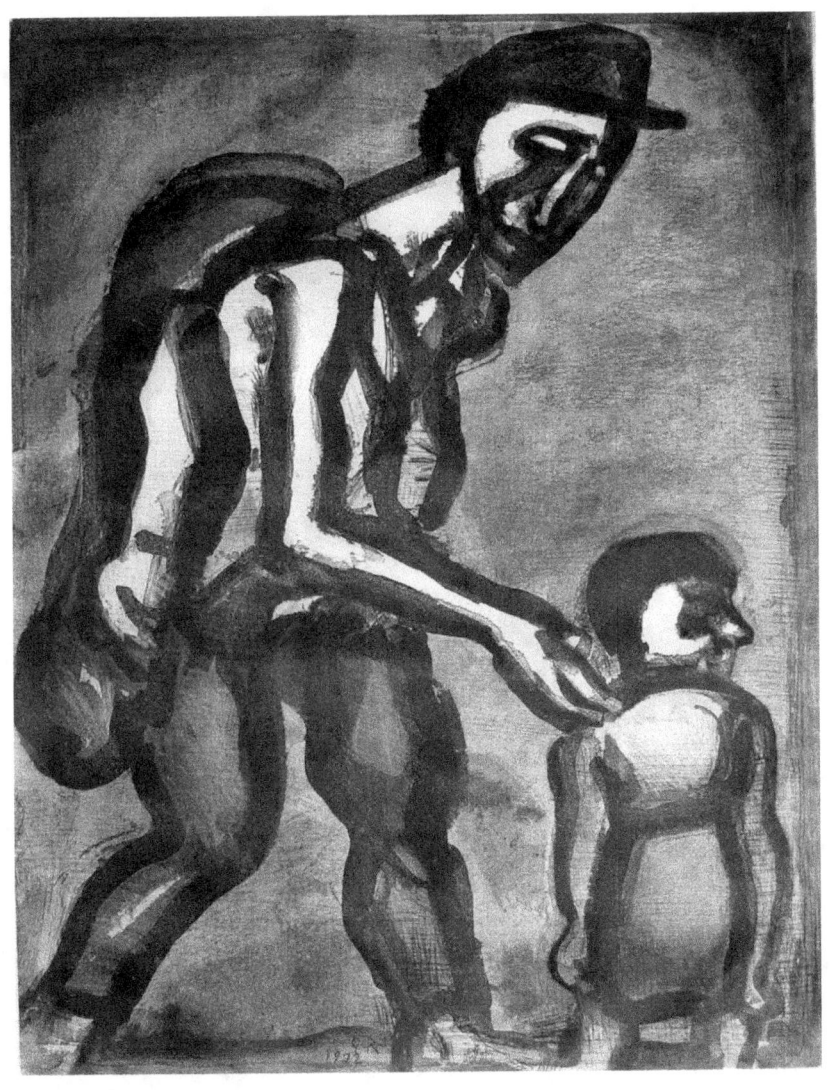

Plate 4

PLATE 4: TAKE REFUGE

"Se réfugie en ton coeur, va-nu-pieds de malheur"
"Take refuge in your heart, barefooted waif of misfortune"

"Take refuge in your heart poor wanderer (or "barefooted waif of misfortune")," says the poetic stanze connected with this piece, 4th Plate in the *Miserere* series. A person wearing a hat, carrying a burden, and coaxing a child on. The refugees radiate the warm light through the black and grey modulated tones. The child seems to be warily looking in the direction the adult is directing, fearful of what lies ahead, almost saying, "Will it be better, really?" The weight of the burden feels enormous, and to carry it for an undetermined distance, demoralizing. It is already hard enough, and now to coax a child into going on. The gaze of the child begs the viewer to wonder about what is outside the picture; the adult in motion has a foot outside of the frame. They don't have a home in the representation of their exile. There is no rest, no peace, no security, no home.

Between 1914 when he began work on the series, and 1948 when the series was finally exhibited, Rouault must have encountered countless refugees living in France during two world wars. In them Rouault seemed to see light, illumination of all poor wanderers – and perhaps he plays with the resonance between inner and outer realities, how the actual refugee reflects in inner condition of longing for a homeland. He could have sung, "I am a poor wayfaring stranger," the old American Spiritual in the same spirit.

Rouault recognized the spiritual or psychological truth that in some sense all humans are refugees between birth and death, between families of origin and their found families and communities; between stages of psychological and spiritual development, the transient nature of our existence seemed apparent to him. And yet, in humankind's exile there is a luminosity shining throughout the transient state. At once the image captures compassion for both the refugee wandering through the fields and towns of France seeking comfort and rest, as well as his own heart's desire for a place of belonging.

Rouault lived in this dual reality, which was also seen by Maritain in his understanding of poetry bridging two realms.[16] This can be seen in a religious or spiritual way, but also through a poetic lens of bridging macrocosm and microcosm. Modern psychology recognizes the universe outside in relationship to the universe inside.[17] The ancient theology of Maximos the Confessor articulated microcosm and macrocosm.[18] It could also be thought of as one reality refracted in two directions but inherently interpenetrating one another; there is not hard division.

Murmansk, Russia, 1993

A man walked by, above the arctic circle outside of Murmansk, Russia. He looked like he had come from some ways off, and I knew the 45 minutes he had to get to the bus, canvas-grey backpack bending him over as he silently walked by, twilight barely lighting his way, the Tuloma River in sight. I didn't imagine him as a refugee, but Rouault's image conjures the similar feeling of heroic feat of survival that I saw in this man's rugged face. So Rouault's wanderer seems steeled for the journey, yet complicated by the misunderstanding of the child, not understanding how to hold a vision of the unseen and exhaust oneself in its pursuit. "Seek refuge in your heart."

Romania, 2001

In the months following our miscarriage, I felt like I was wandering through a bombed-out city, hoping for a solid structure to find a new spiritual home. In the middle of my 30-minute walk to the day center where I was working was the city's Romanian Orthodox cathedral. I was feeling the weight of the burden of death and destruction in the world, now felt deeply in my own loss. It now seemed that the suffering of the poor, the refugee, the enslaved, the oppressed was amplified in my awareness. I almost tripped over a dead dog hiding under the curb. It felt like everything was dark, death and misery.

If I – a white American male, who could fly home to relative affluence at any time – felt so horrid, how much more those who suffer these things alongside structural injustice, poverty, and oppression? Nose-ground and blamed for their own suffering, how do they do it? I thought it before now, but I felt the suffering in some small way.

I stepped into the cathedral to find a mostly empty space. A priest was at the back chanting a service for the dead as part of a funeral remembrance service. I moved toward the front and found a flip-down seat to the right of the nave. The great iconostasis stood in the center front of the church, in front of the altar area rising up 40 feet, bearing a full array of icons, patron saints, Christ and the Theotokos;[19] above them the 12 feasts of the church depicted the 12 apostles, the last supper, and a cross above it all. This symphony of images was all framed in a seamless, sculpted, gold-leafed frame. The remaining walls in the vast space were covered with frescoes depicting layers of the cosmic scheme, from the great Pantocrator in the dome down to the local Romanian saints that stand practically shoulder to shoulder with the faithful who stand for services in the open space. All of this was still stunning to me, but no longer unusual.

In the backdrop of my emotionally demolished state in this light-filled space was the single voice of the priest in byzantine tone, chanting with such ease that it sounded like breathing. The quarter tones find their way back to the root, ascending, descending, winding around each other in the great echoes, old notes resonating with the newer and newer; rising, falling, creating a chorus out of a single voice. Like a bird in the eaves of a great skyscraper I sat still, blending into the side of the church. I felt spent. No youthful optimism, no notions of being able to save anyone. The dead dog I saw earlier made visible my worn-out, tired state. I was headed to work, but was struggling to face the community down the hill.

I sat for some time in that timeless space and lost myself in the spinning universe, bathed in song, in light. All at once, like the knife to the throat of a goat, it pierced me. This was the answer to the pain. This holy place bent time so that the present moments here are also the end of the story, beauty consuming everything. The ugly, distorted, death stink would be, or is, made powerless. The light comes on, darkness is defeated, love consumes the pain, it is righted. It wasn't a denial of the pain, but a taste of the end of the story in which I was not the center, my faith was unnecessary to make it come to pass; I was but a witness to a rising sun, with only the power to open my eyes and let the light flood in.

This makes it sound like it was an intellectual thing. It was the piercing of a knife – quick, sharp, decisive. This was a taste of the consummation of all things by beauty and love. "Seek Refuge in your Heart, Poor Wanderer."

It is as if Rouault sees the human heart as an organ of hope, a place to find refuge and comfort. In the work of Internal Family Systems among other psychotherapies, we find the struggle in clients to transition from finding their peace through changing circumstances to shifting to an internal orientation. Clients often come into therapy for ideas on how to change the people around them, to seek an ally who will collude with them in the idea that the solution is to change the environment: if only people were nicer to me, if only I had the right job, if only I had married the right person. What we find is that peace comes in becoming one's own "primary caregiver," finding one's way to meet our inner exiles, inner wanderers who have been shut out in their shame.

When we can connect with those places that hold the painful shame, the toxicity is drained away and now there is a new way to offer our exiled parts refuge in the compassion of the core self. There is an inner homecoming of sorts that happens when these wound-holding parts of ourselves are seen and heard and welcomed by the powerful, calm, and compassionate core self. Without understanding any of the contemporary developments of clinical psychology, Rouault seemed to get, in some way, that finding home and peace is a move within the heart.

GUIDED MEDITATION

Take a moment to find a place to be still and quiet. See if it feels ok to close your eyes and count 5 breaths. Check and see if you have emotional space to sit with this meditation.

Are there parts of you that have felt like a refugee? Can you gently connect with the parts of you that have felt homeless, alone, or wandering? See what words connect with your experience and try to let go of the others. Maybe there are parts that periodically struggle to figure out who you are and where you belong?

As you identify with the poor wanderer, perhaps the adult or the child in the Rouault image, how do you feel toward that part of you? Can you make room for your compassion to see this aspect of you with gentleness? The seeking-longing-suffering on the journey part? Can you comfort this part of yourself with your own words? Something like, "Of course you feel alone and afraid, and now you are loved and accepted here as you are, you are seen and heard even in your wandering, your longing is evidence of the home waiting for you."

What, from your compassionate wisdom, would you give this child, dragged along, not knowing the context, the bigger picture? What is that lost child needing to know from you now? Does it know you have survived up till now? See if you can just sit with this child as you would your own child giving them your presence and attention and a deep awareness of being held and seen. Can you help this child feel found in your compassionate presence now? If this connects for you, try to stay with it and not hurry away.

When this inner reflection feels complete for you, take a few moments to return your attention to your breath and to the space around you. Perhaps spend some moments reflecting on the experience and take any notes on things you would like to explore further later or insights you want to hold onto.

To engage with the high intensity level audio version described in the introduction, scan the QR code or visit tinyurl.com/rouault-meditations.

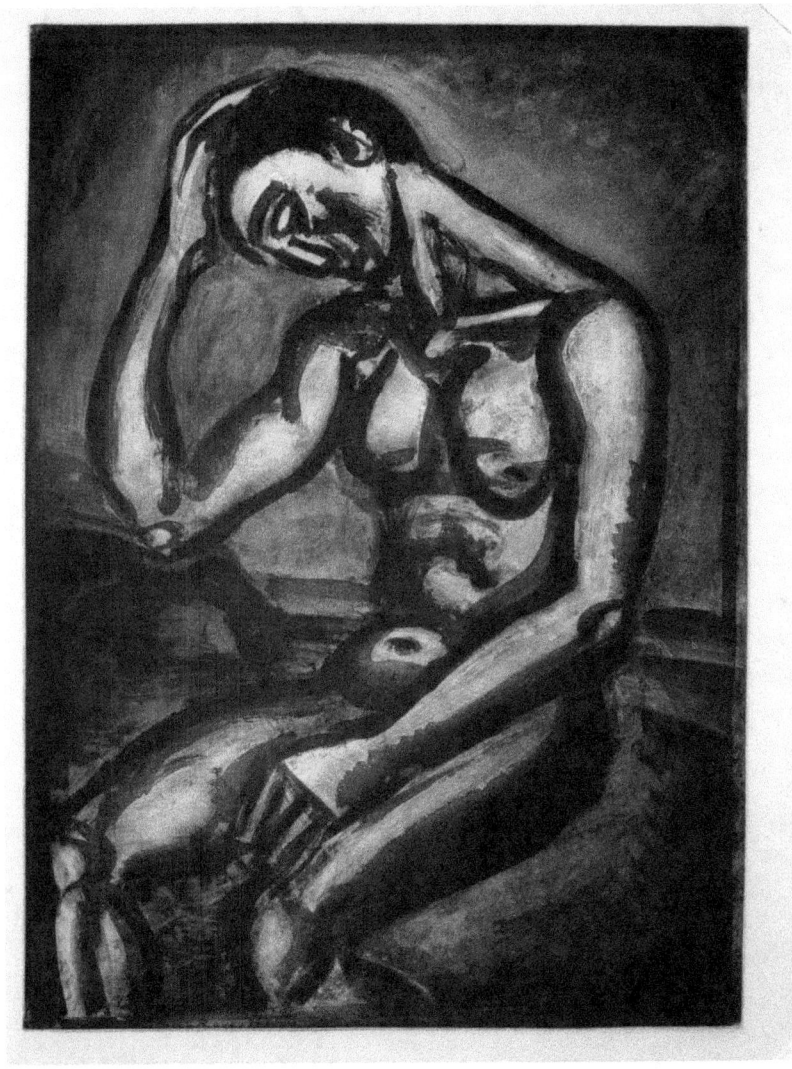

Plate 5

PLATE 5: ALONE

"Solitaire, en cette vie d'embûches et de malices"
"Alone in this life of pitfalls and malice"

A solitary seated figure holds its head with the right hand. Its body curves from the elbow of the right hand up to the head, continuing the curve over the head down the neck and left arm, then around to the hip and upper leg. The holding of the head turns the attention of the figure inward, focusing on the overwhelming internal experience of "alone." The figure is without covering, naked, vulnerable. Psychologically, the figure's external state mirrors the internal state alluded to in the associated poetic line, "Alone in this life of pitfalls and malice." It is unclear if the figure sits in an external space or in an interior room; however, the figure seems overwhelmed with the internal experience, oblivious to the external surroundings, as if the person shuts out sources of more pain from "pitfalls or malice."

The ambiguity of language in the stanza generalizes to all sources of human misery; the "pitfalls" point to pain brought on by one's own attempts at life and the "malice," pain from others. By doing this, Rouault stays in a compassionate position toward the seated figure, a generic victim of life. Rouault does not label his figure with a sin, but empathically resonates with its suffering of aloneness. There is a subtle but inherent generosity in this perspective of human suffering that distinguishes Rouault from the blame and shame systems which label persons in relation to how they uphold institutional ideals. Rouault gives us humankind, often suffering in a psychological loneliness, yet radiating light.

Romania, July 2007

He sat in front of me telling me about the fresh wounds. They were up and down both arms. It turns my stomach even now. A shaving razor was taken and swiped across, making railroad tracks from the bottom to the top of both forearms. They were fresh, barely coagulated, clean and deep cuts, all self-inflicted.

He told me the story,

> "It was dark. I felt awful, lonely, and sad. We were all there underground, under the elementary school in the hot water duct

tunnels where we always go when we are tired. Monkey had a radio, and we were listening to the mourning music, and you know how it is. You think about how nobody loves you, how you are alone in the world. How the darkness is your only friend. I saw my aunt pass the street corner today and she wouldn't even turn to look at me. And I was hungry, and I missed my mom who hasn't come out in a month. I am the scum that covers my skin. I am an animal, trash, and a bum just like they say. I'll never escape this glue-bag huffing. I am stupid. The music kept playing and my insides turned towards the day I was beat up when I wouldn't leave, the night the new man moved in with mom. Someone went out for a razor and the 'old man' cut himself first. He was drunk already. My head was pounding; the bag (for huffing glue) makes me feel better but gives me huge headaches. My inside-out stomach was unbearable. It is like I have a bicycle pump hooked to my big toe and someone is pressurizing my blood. The razor is the only way I know to relieve the pressure. A couple of cuts feel good; relief, clear clean pain, not the crappy awful dark mush of hellish feeling. If I don't, I will pop and explode all over the sewer walls."

The fires they build fill the dark underground channels with smoke and their faces with ash and black smoke residue. Their eyes come out like Ethiopian men's eyes in the dark, lights shining around their pupils."

As he told me the story, I just stood awestruck at his chiaroscuro radiant—sounds contradictory eyes, with their thin glossy surface reflecting the street lights. In the midst of the horrific suffering with loneliness, he still bore a radiance and vibrancy that was undeniable.

February 2021

I just heard that another one of the boys, who was now probably in his late 30's, froze to death on the street alone.

"Alone in this life of pitfalls and malice," we are people walking out of the sewer with blackened faces and dried blood on our arms. We are survivors of our own self-hatred in the sunlight of God's blanketing acceptance. We are drunk, with glue-stained lips after our deep deathly hangover sleep, staggering out into the morning light.

By offering an ambiguous figure – no room for blame, shame or distancing ourselves from this figure – Rouault mirrors our inner state, coaching us along the Miserere Psalm's journey. Who has not felt existentially alone at some point or another? Who does not have parts of themselves that are difficult to acknowledge, accept or connect with? Inner parts that feel utterly alone and overwhelmed when outer circumstances conspire to trigger them. Rouault puts a mirror up to the exiled parts that hold our aloneness. How many activities and noise-making devices do we use to shut out this inner part that holds the feelings of aloneness? But not only the pain of being alone, but alone in pain. With the pain of aloneness is the reality that we are made for community.

Loneliness is a hunger that says we are made for more than food. We yearn for communion, fraternal connection, and unity because we are made for it. Perhaps Rouault is seeing the essential suffering of humankind here in this stark figure who is alone. This aloneness is our most grievous suffering: working over the years with suicidal people bears this out. The person who is contemplating killing themselves, almost always feels this desperate aloneness.

This image embodies Rouault's courageous descent into his own aloneness, giving form to it, so that the viewer can no longer be isolated in their aloneness.

The inner experience of loneliness carries fear and hopelessness, saying things like, "Will I ever connect, will I be alone forever?" Fear of further pain of loneliness may energize parts of us that seek desperately to connect, to impress, to serve others, to be seen and desired. Even caregiving, acting out of a place of loneliness, carries an implicit fear: "What if I am not needed? I must prove my value by my service, or none will care for me." This kind of action starts with a deficit to be filled, a canyon to be crossed at all costs, "My caring action will solve my loneliness." True life-giving compassion is impossible when fear dominates the internal experience. One serves and becomes bitter at lack of recognition when strategies for becoming worthy of love fail to fill the pain of loneliness.

Stillness, silence, and solitude in the "perfect love that casts out fear" become the home base from which one may enter into compassionate action energized by love. The starting place is agape and apatheia, compassion and contentment. This kind of "contribution to the wellbeing of others" is like sharing a flame, lighting the candle of the other, which does not diminish the giver in the giving.[20]

While this vision may be clear, the struggle to get there is difficult. Our feelings of loneliness are a gift of information that illuminates our fearful parts that need healing. These parts need to know that before you were born, before you ever did anything, you mattered; you bore a radiance that has never, nor will ever, increase or decrease, regardless of action or inaction.

We may encounter others who will tell us, directly or indirectly, that we matter, they "love us no matter what;" that they "want to be with us," and "know us." Often it does not feel safe to acknowledge this. A protective part inside tells us to reject this affirmation, "They are just saying that to be nice." So the biggest barrier to embracing our unshakable belovedness is our own protective fear of what would happen if we accepted and believed. Feeling lonely, then, is often not a matter of what others do or don't do, but our inner experience of blocking the acceptance of our essential belovedness.

There is another part in us that is often shoved down: inconvenient intense feelings of hopelessness, the feeling that people will never be safe enough to be allowed into our pain; fear of rejection, of people seeing our shame, terror that we are truly unworthy of love and kindness. A part of us holding the pain is locked in our inner castle turrets, prisons, and basements, locked and sealed away.

Rouault gently offers an image that may resonate with many of our own parts that feel locked away, "Alone in this life of pitfalls and malice." Transformation involves a recovery of these lost alone parts into communion with the rest of the inner system. Paralleling the inner experience, cultural and global transformation also involves recovery of these lost people into community with the rest of our beloved body of humankind.

GUIDED MEDITATION

Take a moment to find a place to be still and quiet. See if it feels ok to close your eyes and count 5 breaths. Check and see if you have emotional space to sit with this meditation.

What parts are stirred in you when reading this chapter? Can you connect gently with those parts of you that are awakened, perhaps a caregiving part, a fearful part, a part feeling the aloneness, regrets? Maybe sense worry parts about not having been there for someone who hurt themselves?

As you look at the figure representing this exiled aloneness in the Rouault image, how do you feel toward him? Can you connect with your compassion for this figure of aloneness, of internal suffering? Do your internal parts that feel alone feel seen in this figure?

What do you wish your part that bears this pain of aloneness could hear or could come to be aware of? Can you gently speak your compassionate wisdom to this part of you that holds that pain of loneliness? Can it hear of its essential belovedness?

Do you notice any resistance to believing in your essential belovedness? Can you just be curious about the parts that are worried about really accepting this truth? Can you just ask them what it is they are afraid of happening if you were to accept you are loved? If you can offer this belovedness to the part, take time to do that. If there is resistance to doing that, just acknowledge those resistant parts, knowing they have good intentions as well.

When this inner reflection feels complete for you, take a few moments to return your attention to your breath and to the space around you. Perhaps spend some moments reflecting on the experience and take any notes on things you would like to explore further later or insights you want to hold onto.

To engage with the high intensity level audio version described in the introduction, scan the QR code or visit tinyurl.com/rouault-meditations.

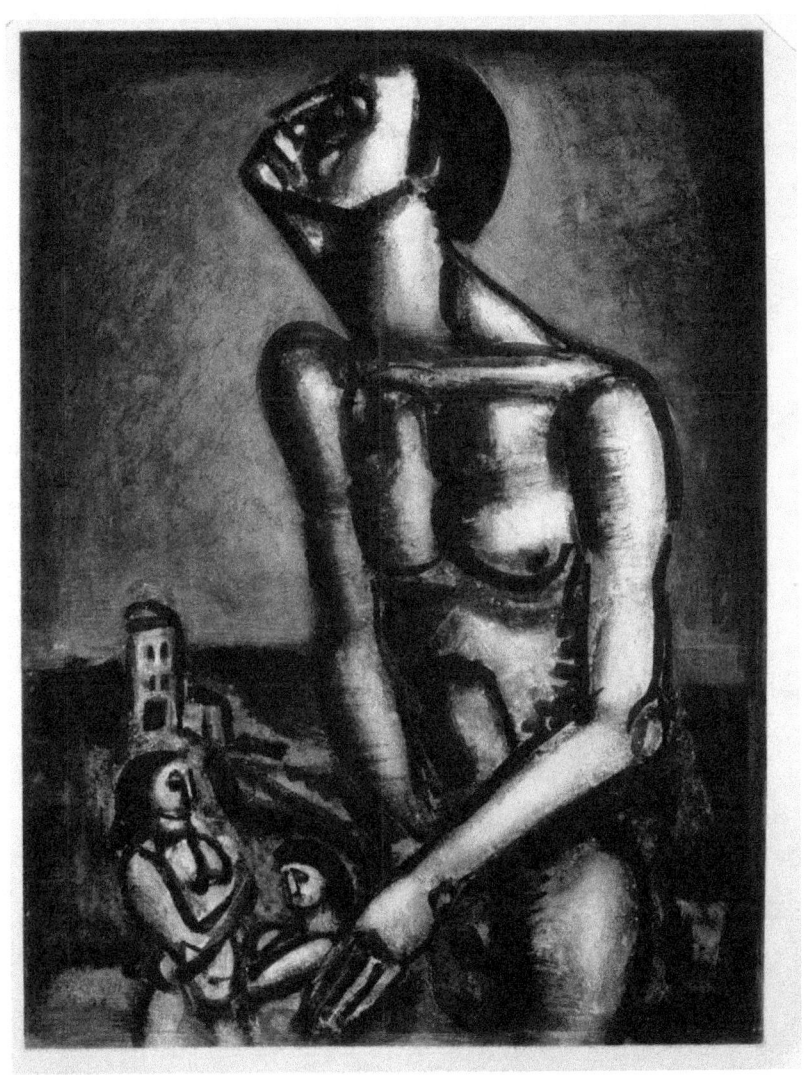

Plate 6

PLATE 6: CONVICTS

"Ne sommes-nous pas forçats?"
"Are we not convicts?"

In "Are we not convicts?" Rouault shows a foreground torso from the hip up, a naked figure with face to the sky with what looks like closed eyes. He stands in the exterior landscape with a structure at the horizon, with four windows and a large lower-level door. Small, distant female nude figures seem to be interacting with each other. The large primary foreground figure seems to be holding the wrist of his left hand with his right hand.

One wonders about who might the "convicts" be that captured Rouault's imagination? Were they war criminals or those suffering the treatment of the criminal justice system of his time? One wonders at the two women: are they loved ones, or are they convicts as well? Are they onlookers? And then there is the structure in the background: is it a courthouse, a jailhouse, or just an ordinary home? Rouault seems to leave these all ambiguous to some degree though I wonder if those living in his time would have picked up enough cues to connect it with their contemporaries' treatment. However, the simplicity helps the image carry across time and across levels of reality, from the interpersonal to the intrapersonal, our inner experience. Rouault's poetic line associated with this plate challenges the viewer to not see a case to point a finger at, but rather to consider how the presented "convicts" are a portrait of the inner state of the viewer. "Are we not convicts" generalizes the guilt of humanity. But what guilt?

Rouault's association with Léon Bloy and his Catholic faith suggests he is referring to human guilt before God. His stanza echoes the words of Christ, "He that is without sin among you, let him first cast a stone at her..."[21] It seems that what Rouault may be getting at is not so much a theological statement about the status of humankind before God, but rather a challenge to the viewer to consider compassion for the convict much like Christ. We are challenged to consider the other with empathy, as if we were the convict.

Romania, 2005

Trembling in the December cold for a little more than an hour, a good Romanian friend and I waited to be admitted into a juvenile detention center in Craiova, in western Romania, to visit a 16-year-old boy we had been working with. We knocked at the large steel door around ten in the morning. Snow was coming down as a result of the steam from the cooling tower across the street. Knocking on the door again. Finally a tiny door the size of a half dollar opened, and an eyeball appeared looking down at us and up the sidewalk. Then came the door the size of a piece of notebook paper. It had bars in it spaced just right, so only our identity documents could be passed through.

Waiting with us was a psychologist on her way to do a series of evaluations on the kids. A few months prior a dozen kids were protesting and set one of their mattresses on fire. A couple of the kids died of smoke inhalation before they were evacuated. This lady was the first part of an initiative to improve the emotional climate of the detention center. She mentioned that there was no therapy available for kids locked up. They only had psychological evaluations once a year to track their development. After some time in an unheated waiting room, we were allowed in to visit the young man who was a loud little kid when I had last seen him. He wore a thick, light blue buttoned down smock thrown over his clothes instead of the orange they wear inside. He mumbled through a Kleenex, in soft tones, looking at us as if we would understand him whether or not we heard his words.

Later he said, "Pray that everything would be good, go really well.' He told of how his dad taught him to pray, saying he would accidentally interrupt his dad making the sign of the cross and praying the 'Our Father.' I could imagine him in a little one-room house with his father, where there is little privacy and little chance of private prayer. Finally, one day his dad asked him if he knew the 'Our Father' and taught him to pray it. He wanted us to know he tries to pray still, at every meal. The theme repeated over the two-hour visit was his desire to get his life started again when he gets out in a couple of months: to get a job, to finish school. Intently looking me in the eyes for the first time in an hour, he asked about the boys' home and how it worked.

The next week I went to a court hearing for another boy. In a knee-high pen he waited with about twenty young men standing and waiting their turn to be addressed by the judge. They all had to wait as the non-incarcerated brought complaints before the judge of electricity being turned off. As I waited in the smoke-filled lobby, a group of kids who lived on the streets entered. If I hadn't known them all personally, I wouldn't have guessed that they lived on the streets. Some were related to the young man being tried, and others were just along to exchange smiles with a buddy they haven't seen for some time.

The startling thing for me was how casually these kids swam through the courthouse smoke; they knew the rooms, the place to look up their friends' names on a list, and they were at home in the system. I wished it was from the secondhand smoke, but my head and gut ached seeing this whole other level of life these kids endure. In *True Notebooks*, Mark Salzman tells his story of his teaching in an Orange County juvenile detention center. He quotes the nun who heads a program. "Look at this place—it's awful! It's falling apart, it's depressing, it's unsafe. What message does that send to these kids? That we simply want to dispose of them. It's obscene. It is unconscionable that we aren't willing to do better than this! We have given up hope on rehabilitation. That says more about us than it does about these children." I felt sickened at the narrow options left for these kids.

First, they are greeted into the world by parents, often loving, but not ready to be parents, without the resources, living with untreated trauma or otherwise unsupported to care for an infant and all it entails. Often due to lack of parenting education, children are neglected and malnourished. Parents fall prey to abusing alcohol, hard labor jobs, and relationships stressed to the breaking point.

As I heard on a bus the day before, a lady commented to her friends, "Today we eat, tomorrow we starve, the next day we have money, the next we are left hungry, and the next we get a break, and the next we have no food on the table again, that is just the way it is, no matter who is elected."

Often the kids are expected to take care of themselves at an early age, and many find the streets a reasonable option when thinking of the father or mother becoming a monster awakened by alcohol in the evening, or to a cold quiet house where a parent is passed out in bed all the time. These kids are survivors, walking the tight rope balanced between survival on the streets and jail. The clear message to these kids is that they are hopeless and primarily a problem to be solved by politicians or the police. This was my experience in Romania, but the story resonates still across the world. These are our world's "convicts."

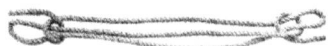

"Are we not convicts" begs the viewer to deconstruct the artificial barrier of blame that cuts off our natural compassion by putting people in separate categories away from ourselves. By othering the "convict," we attempt to exonerate ourselves. We don't usually think of the convict as a kid, but in reality, even the 80-year-old prisoner was a kid with a history begun in innocence.

If Rouault were titling the print today it might have been, "Are we not all felons." Rouault's love is a radical compassion, beyond the status quo system where with the right label we feel relieved of our burden of compassion: "They are beyond compassion," "They are just felons," or whatever other dismissive label.

I have experienced in consultation with staff in a community mental health center lots of compassion for clients until suddenly someone offers the diagnosis "Borderline."[22] A room of therapists hear, "Oh another Borderline," let out a sigh, and the empathy leaves the room. Likewise with the label of "felon."

Rouault is asking a lot of his viewer. He makes us squirm and look for excuses about why we should not be lumped in the same category with people we have shut our hearts off to. In doing so, we not only cut ourselves off from our compassion for the convict, the addict, the felon, the borderline, etc., but we cut ourselves off from our own internal "convicts."

The psychological distance between ourselves and others is always the exact distance we are separated from our own inner aspects. We distance from those parts of ourselves we have locked away and try to forget about, those wounded parts, the desperately angry parts, those parts that would love to get revenge, recover dignity through some desperate act, or in short, the shame-holding, shame-hidden parts that believe that somehow at our core we are flawed, bad and forever broken.

This is perhaps the beauty of the mystics who, cultivating compassion over a lifetime of prayer and service, come to the conclusion that they are surely "the worst sinner on earth." By starting as the least, the mystics open themselves to communion with all: no one is below them, no one needs to be shoved down to preserve some perverse illusion of self-righteousness. St. Isaac the Syrian described the result of ascetic struggle as the experience of "luminous love for all humanity."

"Are we not convicts" challenges the viewer to transcend the barrier of labels to find ourselves in a common humanity with every convict. In Rouault's vision there is no us and them, only us. The path of the Miserere Psalm is a path that leads to union with the whole humanity.

GUIDED MEDITATION

Take a moment to find a place to be still and quiet. See if it feels ok to close your eyes and count 5 breaths. Check and see if you have emotional space to sit with this meditation.

What parts of you resist identifying with the felon, the convict? What parts hate the "convict" part of you whether innocent, accused and hurt. Is there a part that can identify with the convict, perhaps a part that felt stuck and without options but to violate the boundaries of others?

What parts block self-compassion and self-understanding for your parts that bear the blame, shame or humiliation? Can you ask the critical parts to give some space for compassion for this short time? If so, can you acknowledge your accused convict parts and hold them with neutrality, moving toward holding them with compassion?

If you were at peace with your convict parts, would you be more open to demonstrating compassion to the persons convicted of crimes in your outer world? How much of your striving and achieving are parts desperate to prove you are not bad? Can you address those parts with a deeper basis of worth of the human person, that is unchangeable and given?

Often for true self forgiveness we need a deeper understanding of the dynamics contributing to the moral injury, the transgression. We are not looking for excuses, but a deeper understanding so that the offending part won't feel it has to jump in destructively.

Is there any insight you can use to offer both understanding for the convict part as well as a new plan for not being in that kind of situation again, or addressing your needs before they get to an extreme point?

When this inner reflection feels complete for you, take a few moments to return your attention to your breath and to the space around you. Perhaps spend some moments reflecting on the experience and take any notes on things you would like to explore further later or insights you want to hold onto.

To engage with the high intensity level audio version described in the introduction, scan the QR code or visit tinyurl.com/rouault-meditations.

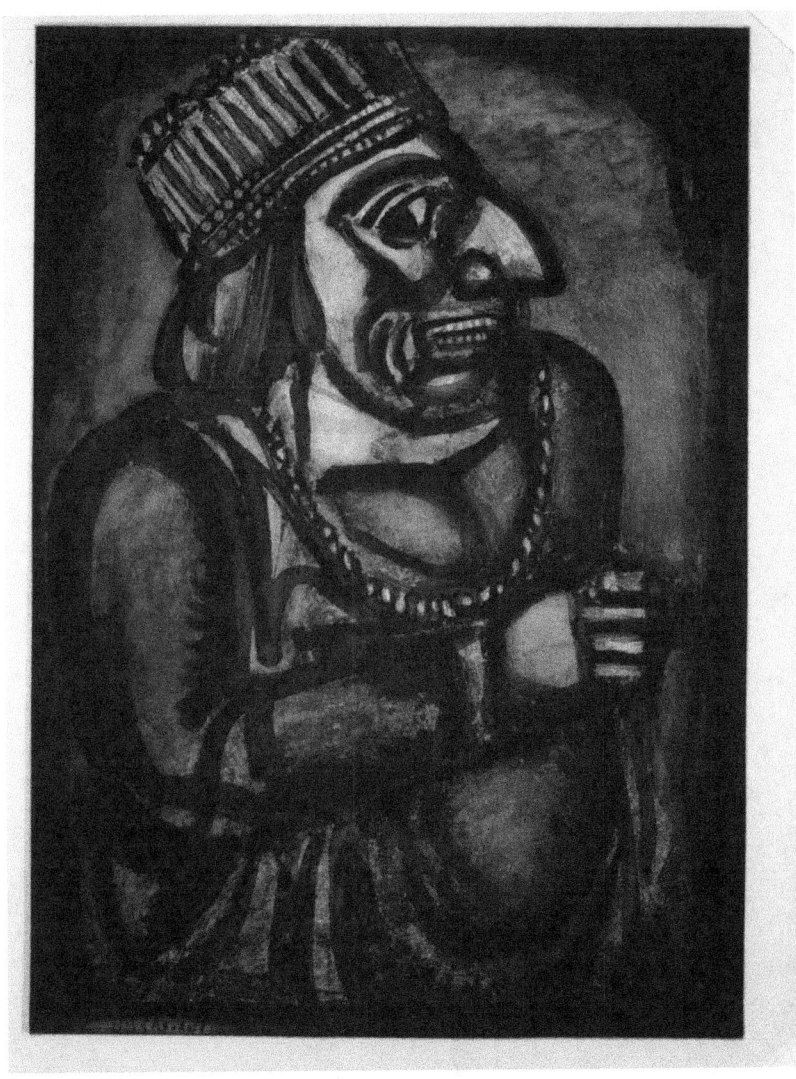

Plate 7

PLATE 7: KINGS

"Nous croyant rois"
"Believing ourselves kings"

A grossly exaggerated wealthy person looks at the viewer out of the corner of his eye in the plate seven. The torso of the figure up close encroaches on the space of the viewer, as if a person were peering into a window up close. We are not seeing him across the room, but at the distance of having a conversation with him. Keeping in mind the scale of the originals, the head of the figure is close to life-sized. This person wears a crown of some kind and necklace, and looks at the viewer out of the corner of his eye. In contrast to the naked torsos in previous images, this person is lavished with thick robes. Perhaps referencing portraits of royalty that fill wings of art museums, Rouault gives us a grotesque caricature of the wealthy. We also get to see articulated teeth, the apparatus for devouring a more subtle version of Francis Bacon's *Three Studies for Figures at the Base of a Crucifixion* (1944) where humanity is reduced to beasts of consumption.

In the spirit of the associated poetic line, Rouault begs us to consider the dissonance between outer forms and inner realities. Images of refugees, or the solitary figures, invite the viewer to consider their own impoverished parts. In contrast, now he asks us to see our own delusion of control, power, wealth or perhaps high standing. Using the word "believing," he more directly points to the prophetic nature of the print, pointing out the error in belief. Rouault seems to balance human perception against the existential realities of death, suffering and limitation.

The position of king is only a parody of God, who has the ultimate power, though He is seen to operate from compassion in Christ. Much as Rouault saw the feeble parody of judges in the light of existential reality, so with the rich here: in our temporary insulation from the reality of our human frailty, the delusional hope of untouchability, the power to achieve and hold love and safety.

The teeth and eye, the sideways glance, conjure the fear inherent in the delusion of power. To "believe ourselves kings" is to believe there is a distance between us and our fellow humans; the fear that others are just waiting to dethrone us from our position. Here is another source of human isolation. Self-enthronement is but the delusion of separateness, which Rouault challenges in his deep empathy brought to all his figures. In the context of the Miserere Psalm, I doubt that Rouault was hoping we would see anyone but ourselves in this image. The illusion of power is a pitiable state.

Romania, 2003

I grew up working alongside my father, painting homes for some of the wealthy elite families in Cleveland, Ohio. It was an experience of touching up baseboards in country clubs, spending weeks matching antique bricks to complete a new million-dollar addition in order to be sure it fits with the rest of the home, messing with slate roofing, asking butlers where to find a bathroom, or changing 10 foot light fluorescent bulbs 50 feet up in the air which illuminated a single clay tennis court.

I never thought of our family as poor, but compared to these places we worked I certainly felt like I was from a different class living in a different universe. We were trained to never speak of the wealth, to pretend it was normal to have the top car in every make in the same color filling 5 garages: white BMW next to white Mercedes next to white Porsche next to white Alpha Romero next to a white Lamborghini!

In Romania, we had recently moved into a different apartment. This one had one bedroom, besides the living room. We brought Iulian over to see it one day, as we had been escorting him to his 4th grade class each day for a few weeks. Left to his own devices, he never managed to arrive at school. Even when our community began to accompany him to school, it was understood that if you ever let go of his hand he would run, and you may or may not catch him.

He of course wanted to see our new apartment. When we moved our scant belongings into it. I thought of friends' home in the US and how simple this little place was: low cost, small footprint. I certainly had some pride about how simply we were living.

Iulian walked in and began his numbering of rooms. "One room" was the entryway, about 3ft by 5ft, "two rooms" pointing to the closet in the entryway, "three rooms" pointing into the kitchen, "four rooms" eyeing the balcony enclosed with glass, a 3-foot by 15-foot space for drying clothes, "five rooms" walking into the living room, "six rooms" pointing out the bedroom, "seven rooms", noticing the transition between living, bedroom and bathroom, "eight rooms", pointing out the closet next to the bathroom, and "nine rooms" finally counting the bathroom.

As he walked through my house scandalized by my wealth of rooms for just two people, I could not help but think of his apartment: one room full of beds and a second smaller room with a makeshift stove top and small table for eating, washing and everything else. Bathroom was shared with others in the house that was turned into separate dwellings. Water was in the shared courtyard below. This space was shared by varying numbers of people, but at least by his family of 5. My self-righteousness was shredded for a moment, at least. Suddenly, I was the guy I had judged all these years for conspicuous wealth in the face of poverty.

Some years later, my father's customer with all the cars mentioned above called him on when his own father was on his death bed. Of all the people of power and influence he could have called, he called his painter who tried to see him as just another person. In that space he seemed to just want a human connection, a friendly person without strings or complications, just a human connection.

"Believing ourselves kings." Death defies our perception of being kings. So we like to talk about how people close to death only regret not spending more time with loved ones. In the end there is no satisfaction in wealth and power, it is a failed attempt at security and connection undone by death every time. Every time.

Rouault sees light in us even with our delusional self-perception as "kings". He says "our" not a finger pointing "their." He includes himself, discloses himself in the prophetic statement. A part of him believes he is a king. This part is fearful and delusional, but still a part of the common human experience. So, to "believe ourselves kings" must in some way be about our delusion of separation from those around us, the accompanying fear of being uncovered, having our sins shouted from the housetops and losing our place. Death defies all hierarchy, all division, all sense of self-importance. Death doesn't care.

And then there are those teeth in the print. They almost echo visually the repetition in the crown and in the necklace. Perhaps Rouault had in mind Isaiah 3:15, "What do you mean by crushing my people and grinding the face of the poor?"[23] Rouault asks us to consider whether we are forsaking the poor, neglecting their care, perhaps even hiding behind a constructed personal righteousness, a narrative that makes me good and deserving and justifies not lending compassion to the poor and marginalized.

"Believing ourselves kings," we grind the faces of the poor, and when part of us feels entitled, and above the riff raff, are we not also neglecting aspects of ourselves, our stories, our wounds that need attention, care, understanding? Parts of us that feel utterly powerless? Often the inability to extend compassion for the poor is a symptom of not being able to be kind to oneself. Inner tyranny breeds outer tyranny. Rouault doesn't let us off with finger pointing and locating the "bad element" outside of ourselves. He challenges us to see our power and privilege as something to gladly relinquish, for our delusion of separation is but gaudy polyester children's dress up clothes and plastic pearls.

GUIDED MEDITATION

Take a moment to find a place to be still and quiet. See if it feels ok to close your eyes and count 5 breaths. Check and see if you have emotional space to sit with this meditation.

Check inside and see if you connect with your own inner parts attached to strategies for security, for choice, for power and reputation? Can you connect with any of you experiences which may have amplified this self-vow to protect these interests at all costs? What are these parts afraid of happening if you were to hold more loosely control over your security or your relationships?

Do you have space to appreciate the inner motivations of this protective part to keep you safe and connected? Can you approach these fearful parts with gentleness and compassion? If you can just take a moment to let them feel understood by you. Understanding is not agreement with the strategy.

Try to ask the part, if you really understand their concerns would it be willing to relax some and allow you space to make a choice informed by more than this fear? To perhaps consider sharing power and control with others? Could the part allow you to listen longer to others in your life, being more vulnerable in hearing the perspectives and needs of others?

Ask the part if it be nice to relax the guardedness in order to create more space for authenticity and trust in relationships?

Can you listen to the parts of yourself hidden by the delusion of power? Can you attend to those parts of you that feel helpless, and offer them any hope you have of a benevolent Power outside yourself? Just a simple acknowledgement that a part of you feels helpless can calm some of the tension around those feelings.

When this inner reflection feels complete for you, take a few moments to return your attention to your breath and to the space around you. Perhaps spend some moments reflecting on the experience and take any notes on things you would like to explore further later or insights you want to hold onto.

To engage with the high intensity level audio version described in the introduction, scan the QR code or visit tinyurl.com/rouault-meditations.

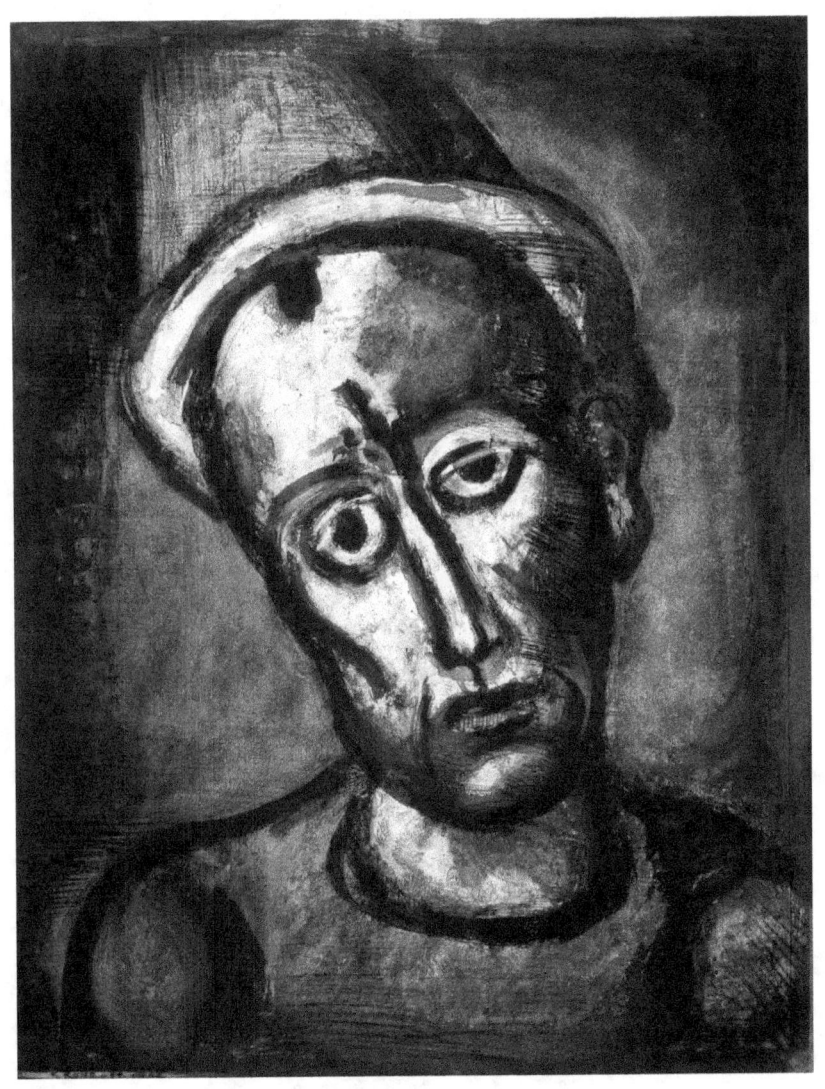

Plate 8

PLATE 8: MASKS

"Qui ne se grime pas?"
"Do we not all wear masks?"

"Do we not all wear masks?" depicts a clown with tilted head wearing a simply composed hat. The face is the brightest white in the composition, betraying the melancholy expression. We are presented with a face in an iconographic space. As in Eastern Orthodox icons, the portrayed figure engages the viewer directly, something like an ancient version of the mockumentary. It is intended to be a personal encounter. The eyes of the figure swell with the struggle for authenticity. The makeup is thick and the barrier feels impenetrable. It feels like an open question: will the viewer of the collected prints, upon examining themselves as reviled, scourged, a convict, a refugee, be willing to acknowledge authentically the resonances in their own soul to these archetypal forms? Do we not all wear masks? Psalm 51 – the overarching title of the series – in verse 6 says, "Behold, thou desirest truth in the inward parts: and in the hidden part thou shalt make me to know wisdom."

Rouault wrote of his own transformative encounter with a clown that formed his poetics, "All of us clowns more or less we all wear a spangled costume, but if we are caught by surprise the way I caught that old clown, oh then who would dare to claim he has not moved deeply by immeasurable pity? My failing if it is one in any case it is the source of immense suffering for me is never to let anyone keep on his spangled costume be king or emperor what I want to see in the man facing me is his soul and the more exalted his position the more I fear for his soul."[24]

I was riding on a bus one day. I had just bought a rabbit skin hat to try to blend in with folks in northern Russia, and to keep warm. Feeling insecure about being an American in Russia, being an 18-year-old a long way from home; and in 1993 the closest communication was to go on an hour and a half trek to the city where a Norwegian company had a hard line tapped into Northern Norway. We could send a fax to the US for a fee. This was how I communicated with my parents that I had arrived safely, after about a month since leaving home. Fitting in felt important, and barely speaking any Russian increased my sense of vulnerability.

We rode the bus from the closest town to the lodge where we were staying, and when we got off the bus someone realized they had not recognized me on the bus as "that new American." If I kept my mouth shut and wore my hat I could hide and that felt good. This time I was hiding my identity under a hat.

Years later, visiting one of the youth we were working with in Romania in a juvenile detention center, we were let into the courtyard of the center when they were transferring some people from one bus to another. Lining the edges of the courtyard getting ready for the bus transfer were half a dozen people dressed in all black, with balaclavas on and holding automatic weapons at the ready. The firearms were intimidating, but it was the masks, the anonymity that amplified the terror. They created a mystery and a distance that still haunts me today. It was something about the covered face that blocks the face, our primary instrument for connecting with one another. By our mother's face that we are drawn into being, we find ourselves and our personality, our value. The covering of the human face is a radical impoverishment of connection.[25] The ski masks intentionally protected the anonymity of the guards from potential retaliation if something were to happen. Likewise, we use psychological masks to protect ourselves.

Doing some of my own inner work I find a clown-like part in me that compels me to hide what may bring criticism or rejection. It dreads vulnerability that might lead to hurt, but also loves the chance to connect with others. My wife has pointed out that I get sarcastic when I am meeting someone new. It is as if this joker comes out, dying to impress. I want to belong and be loved by everyone, and this part believes it would be best if everyone thinks I am funny and smart so they will want me around. It is a mask. My wife sees through it and pities the lengths I can go to win some approval and avoid rejection before feeling securely connected with someone.

Rouault places a mirror before the viewer and asks about our masks. Thomas Merton made famous the concept of false selves.[26] Perhaps more difficult to deal with are the masks of false selves that we use to hide from ourselves.

Perhaps self-righteousness is among the potent forms. The formula might be, "Since I do/don't do X, that must mean that I am in the good category." I have labeled myself in the good category, helped often by the group I am part of who reinforce the categories of good people and bad people. This labeling is a mask that detaches one from being attentive to what is actually needed in the moment. Labeling oneself "a good parent" is actually not helpful in being present and attuned with your children and can get in the way of being an effective parent. The self-deceptive masks create a block to presence and attunement to self and others.

Other masks are designed to hide our pain. Will I be accepted if I were to show or acknowledge my suffering? Would people love me as I am if they knew? Can I trust to that someone>\?others to tread with care if I open up to someone safe? Underneath these masks, is the desire to connect, to belong, to be safe.

In this case I believe Rouault is asking us the question, "do we not all wear masks," inviting us into self-discovery.

Zen wisdom says that to name a thing is to already falsify it.[27] Pure experience is a sacred encounter. To speak of it, is to exponentially depart from its essence, as it might be to tell someone about a transcendent experience. It quickly diminishes in potency with each word. It might be noted here that I feel the discomfort around writing many words about and responding to the work of Rouault. His work was meant to be an experience in and of itself. To speak of it, to try to nail it down too precisely would be to kill a butterfly while trying to see it more closely. At some level his work should be just encountered. The more words, the more scientific or historical clarity, the more we place a mask on the work. The raw beauty is covered over with ideas of what we want the work to say, or hope it says, and sometimes perhaps avoiding a direct encounter that may delight or horrify us. This writing perhaps is a demonstration of my guilt at masking the work in my words. So please spend time just sitting in front of these pieces with an ear to your inner world and an eye to the undulating surface before you. Make room for an intimate encounter, naked and without masks.

Kentucky, March 2020

As I write these reflections during the global COVID-19 pandemic, we have quite literally been all asked to wear a mask, and now it is suggested to "double mask." The first time going out in public wearing a mask felt wrong. To have one's face covered, hidden in that way, felt somehow dishonest. All my middle school appearance insecurities began to surface again: fears about being accepted wearing a mask or not wearing a mask, which kind of mask feels ok to wear and with whom. A whole new consciousness of masks developed in my inner world.

After months on end of grocery shopping and doing all of public life behind a mask, I was amazed to find how normal it became. Then the flip happened at the almost startle reaction to seeing people unmasked: fear, judgement, and delight and being able to see directly a fuller expression of another person's immediate reactions on their whole face. We have become aware of the beauty and gift of being unmasked with one another, to be transparent and authentic to one another in a way we never realized was so magical.

Maybe this new revelation of what we have always had without knowing it, being present and unmasked, might increase our hunger to learn to be "unmasked," authentic and present with others in our lives. The fear of contributing to the spread of a virus has driven our covering up our faces. This outer reality begs the question Rouault was asking a hundred years ago: what fears are keeping us hidden, even when it is safe, even when we are with people we know are emotionally nurturing? When will we unmask and fully be together?

GUIDED MEDITATION

Take a moment to find a place to be still and quiet. See if it feels ok to close your eyes and count 5 breaths. Check and see if you have emotional space to sit with this meditation.

How am I hiding behind masks, which disconnect me from really encountering self and others? Can you identify any masking parts of you? Protective parts that are masters of hiding your vulnerable places?

What are these protective parts trying to avoid thinking about, talking about? If you can identify a masking part can you approach it with openness and curiosity? If so, can you ask that masking part what it is afraid would happen if it let down the mask a little more? Can you notice the positive intention of the masking part? If so can you offer some appreciation for its intention to help protect you in the way it does?

If there are any ways that the masking parts concerns are either outdated for your life now, or not as necessary with certain safe people in your life now, can you update the masking part?

Is there someone you could be more vulnerable and authentic with, share my struggle, my suffering in a way that feels relatively safe?

Are there people I avoid because they bring up vulnerabilities in me I am hiding from? Is there any willingness to work towards healing your shame, guilt, hurt so I don't feel like I need to avoid vulnerability in others?

When this inner reflection feels complete for you, take a few moments to return your attention to your breath and to the space around you. Perhaps spend some moments reflecting on the experience and take any notes on things you would like to explore further later or insights you want to hold onto.

To engage with the high intensity level audio version described in the introduction, scan the QR code or visit tinyurl.com/rouault-meditations.

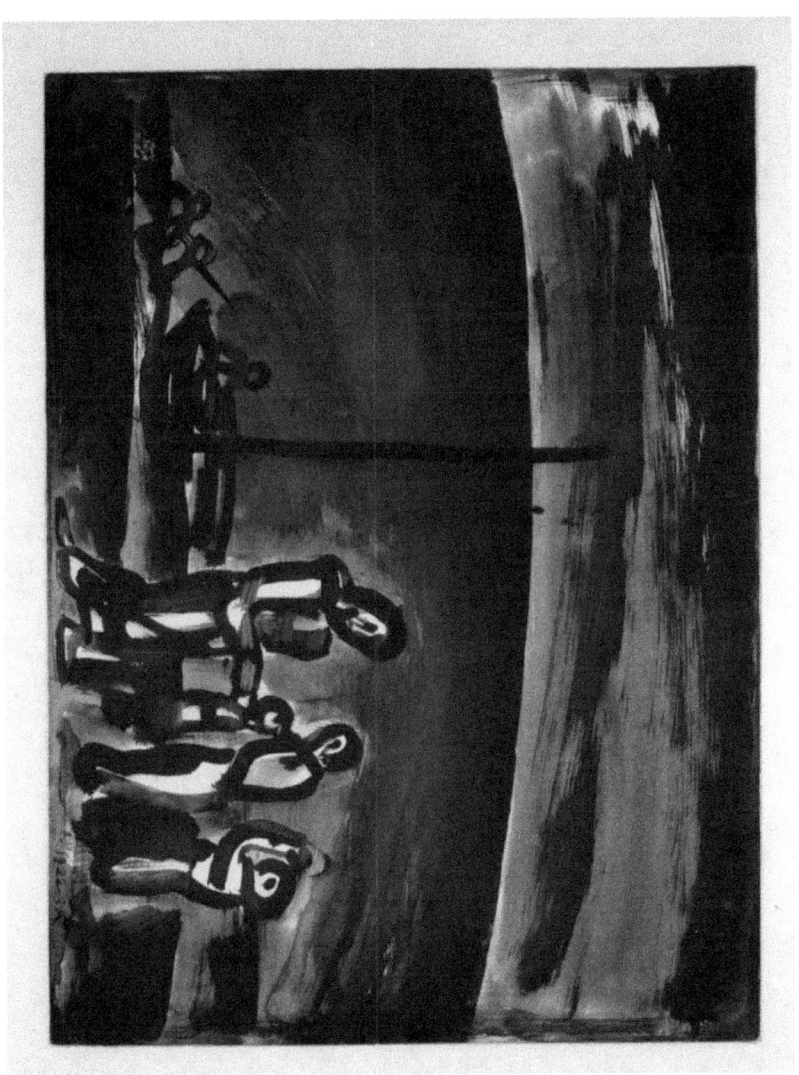

Plate 9

PLATE 9: BEAUTY ON THE WAY

"Il arrive parfois que la route soit belle..."
"Sometimes the road is beautiful..."

The bend of the earth and a seascape set off the space with light coming over the horizon. A boat in the middle ground at the edge of the water begs the question of whether the group of travelers are coming or going. Someone still on the boat, perhaps its pilot and one who conveyed the group across or will carry them. The sail of the boat is down. It is unclear if the grouping of figures is a family, a group of children, or perhaps Christ with children, refugees or travelers. The group of figures take the brightest values in the picture plane; they radiate light from within their black frames.

"*Sometimes the way is beautiful...*" as a poetry fragment associated with this piece invites us to consider that the group is traveling in some capacity or another. Rouault's other pieces with refugees, children in the streets, and Christ in the streets invite us to consider Christ's presence in this journey. This seems to me to be an arrival after an unsure journey across water. This is not the solitary feel that many of the torso-filled pieces carry: this is that deep sigh after a long leg of a trip, when we are huddled on the shore, perhaps eating or drinking, glad to be this far at least. The horizon begs one to consider the landscape as a beautiful element, the sunset signaling the passing of time, the finding of safety after the insecurity of the water. The ellipses of this stanza connect it to the following poetic phrase, "...in the old neighborhood of long suffering."

The grouping of figures is perhaps the other beauty found along the way, the comradery, the community struggling together, surviving together. And perhaps if it is Christ with them, there is a presence of love, peace, of security within the insecurity.

Murmansk, Russia, 1993

The long polar night drug on into January outside of Murmansk, Russia. We last saw the sun on December 15th: it only tormented you a couple of hours around noon, hiding just under the horizon. Just enough light for some cross-country skiing helped make the days tolerable. By dinnertime, you were into the deep darkness of midnight in most places.

I slipped out the front doors in my boots good to -70F that my grandma sent me when she heard I was going to the Arctic Circle, and my second-hand heavy army coat with fur-edged hood and army issue furry mittens with liners on the inside. I needed some space for thought. There was a road that took me down to the river just under a hundred snow crunching steps. I checked the sky for northern lights and kept going out onto the ice-covered Tuloma River. Another couple of hundred steps put me right about in the middle of the river covered in at least a foot of solid ice topped with snow. There I put the entire earth behind me by lying down on my back.

At that time the temperature stayed around -40F, where Celsius and Fahrenheit intersect. There is no moisture in the air; it is solidified immediately. Under me the ice felt like a concrete floor. The shoreline was just a black silhouette of trees, the same for 360 degrees around, but none of this was in view as I lay there on my back. I could hear my breath, and any slight movement I made. When a truck came down the river road just beyond the trees, you would hear it for 10 minutes coming and another 10 going off into nothing.

Up was all I could see. And up was all stars, billions of stars. As my body relaxed, it seemed as if I might become weightless and fall into them. Weightlessly lifted up, off of earth, out into the abyss of stars like a spacewalking astronaut who loses his life wire and smoothly floats away into the distant suns. If I didn't look to my side, I could imagine Abram the patriarch next to me trying to count stars.

Then came the great bioluminescent colored curtains. Just imagine you are in a pitch-black theater, and all of a sudden a faint light from below illuminates just the bottom portion of the giant waving curtains. They look blown by a sudden concentrated breath and they move quickly at first and then gradually slow as the impact of the breath wears out. Some came in faint greens and reds and blues, but mostly they look like a milky glaze washing over the coal black sky. They fade and stretch out taffy until they look like a thin cloud. And you are aware again of the silence and the cold on your face, as you check the horizon to make sure you are still on earth.

As I was lying on the ice in the middle of the river, enjoying the silence and still fading curtains of northern lights a colossal thunder erupted. The movement of the current below the great plate of ice – like the earth's tectonic plates – shift and crack, shooting break lines across the river from shore to shore. I saw the lines in daylight, but never did I see any gap. In the silence you closed your eyes assuring yourself that the crack is downriver and would never swallow you. And after the thunder, the silence is absolute, and I float out into the stars awhile.

They said if your nose was red that was good, if it was white, "Sorry, too late." It was usually my cold nose that made me get up and scuffle back over the ice, into my room and mummy bag. There is a certain relief of getting off of the ice and out of the unsheltered dark.

The darkness of the polar night feels like forever, two months of feeling like you never fully open your eyes; but the stars, the northern lights really become the brightest objects in the landscape. Suddenly your place in the universe is apparent, tiny frail speck on a tiny frail speck of a planet. It is only in this immense darkness that one can perceive the northern lights.

Rouault seems to live in this kind of space during this period of his work, darkness of pigment—and suffering filling these images; but across the waters of suffering there is an even greater light than we were able to see before. The best bread you ever taste is the bread you have after a long journey and a growling stomach.

I recently got off the phone with a dear friend who had just undergone brain surgery. Before going, the doctors told him this might be it: "We don't know what we will find, but this doesn't look good." It wasn't cancer as they suspected, and now they expect a good recovery, but I remember walking outside after the conversation. Each blade of grass looked newly magical, radiant, sacred. Each step I made felt like a wondrous miracle. Buddhist mindfulness teachers lead meditations, mindfulness of death meditations, which evoke a similar awareness. This practice resonates with St. Sophrony's recommendation of the constant mindfulness of death.[28] The mindfulness of death is but the other side of the coin of gratitude and attunement to the beauty and vibrancy of life. Rouault in a similar spirit seems to take us to the edge, mindfulness of the dark so that we may wake up and see the flood of light all around.

GUIDED MEDITATION

Take a moment to find a place to be still and quiet. See if it feels ok to close your eyes and count 5 breaths. Check and see if you have emotional space to sit with this meditation.

Consider giving some room for awe. Where is the beautiful in the suffering of your journey? It doesn't justify the pain, but the beauty is there. Can you open yourself to wonder, surprise, to the small, beautiful moments in a hard journey?

Are there travelers or refugees, strangers you would like to open your heart to in a new way? Can you remember what it felt to be welcomed when you felt vulnerable and in a strange place?

When this inner reflection feels complete for you, take a few moments to return your attention to your breath and to the space around you. Perhaps spend some moments reflecting on the experience and take any notes on things you would like to explore further later or insights you want to hold onto.

To engage with the high intensity level audio version described in the introduction, scan the QR code or visit tinyurl.com/rouault-meditations.

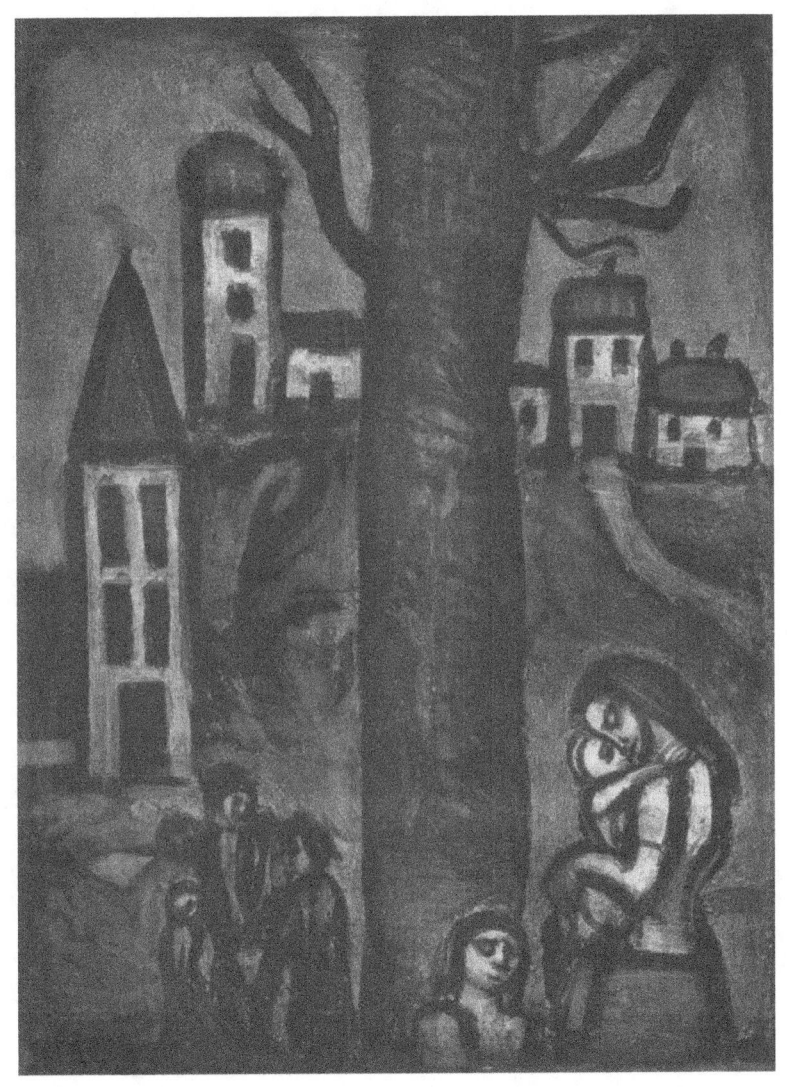

Plate 10

PLATE 10: THE OLD NEIGHBORHOOD

"...au vieux faubourg des Longues Peines"
"...in the Old Neighborhood of the Long Suffering"

Rouault's poetic line connected with the last print, "Sometimes the way is beautiful, in the old neighborhood of long suffering," is now completed. The viewer is placed in a neighborhood created with thick black lines, and scumbled grays pushing forward moments of dingy luminosity. There are two groupings of people and a large black tree that looks dead in the center. A couple of sets of buildings appear in the background that more or less fence off the figures in the image. Most prominent in the foreground right bottom, is a mother with a small child in her arms and another child with attention toward her.

The background structures have a lower single door, and windows above in a way that suggests faces or personalities in the structures. It is reminiscent of Mary Oliver in describing Edgar Allen Poe's *The Fall of the House of Usher*, "The gloomy mansion itself takes on the look of a face, with its 'vacant and eye-like windows'."[29] There is no perspective, or hard architectural diminishing perspective lines presented, just simple structures as in a child's drawing, flat with little if any depth. Despite simplified forms, one is not left with the sense that Rouault is depicting another world, rather a place with weight the grit of concrete spaces.

The buildings are almost the transgenerational spectators of local suffering over time. Likewise, the large tree in the center is like other city trees in impoverished areas of the world, where a tree belongs to no one, and has been abused to the point of being lifeless, limbless, perhaps even charred or burned, used to hoist up an animal for slaughter or an engine up out of a car. The tree, like the buildings, is the historian of the neighborhood, bearing the marks of longsuffering and abuse from generation to generation.

A group of children next to the tree are in shadow or just dirty, and appear to interact with one another. We can only suspect they bear the wounds of suffering, as does the tree next to them. The mother and two children in the foreground contrast with the rest of the print with highlights of the print falling on them that bring them forward even more.

Here is the second part of the associated poetic line, "Sometimes the way is beautiful, in the neighborhood of long suffering." We must connect back to this lightness and hopefulness in the beauty encountered in this place Rouault has created. As in the last print, these groupings of people, and especially the mother and children, become a focus for seeing this beauty of connection, much like the travelers together on a journey in the last plate. Or one may recall the mother and children huddled under threat of Nazis in Kathe Kollwitz. Here, the power mothers' love is highlighted in the face of suffering. Perhaps we can also connect this pair of images to "the joy of my salvation" words from the Miserere psalm.

It is perhaps not a stretch to see the Virgin with child in this image. The Eastern Orthodox church refers to her as the Theotokos, or the 'Mother of God." She is seen as the "first of among the saints." having embodied the love of Christ, heard the word, nurtured it, and given birth to the Kingdom of God through her love and responsiveness, becoming the pattern of the saints to follow. Rouault would have been attuned to the archetypal mother figure and the nurturing love of God demonstrated in this maternal love.

Here is the balm, the beauty within the neighborhood of the longsuffering. The mother can also be seen as the long-suffering one. Just as Mary suffered the passion of Christ as a mother, so archetypal parenthood is this longsuffering which endures hardship for the joy of love of children.

We are at plate 10 of the series and have been given a series of variations of common human experiences of suffering. Here with plate 9, and now plate 10, we get some hopeful food for the journey. Within the attentiveness to suffering is this filial love exemplified in this mother's love for her children: tender, intimate, personal, attuned and attentive, responsive and fitting. She sees her child and shows care. She stands with her face gently pressed to the face of her beloved child.

Beauty is the emissary of compassion. Beauty is the embodiment of love in the world of forms and meanings, sounds and syntax, science and phenomena. When I am graced to deeply experience the beautiful, it is a is face-touching sacred intimacy. Encountering the suffering of the poor, I found this love in the subtle beauty, the light, the extravagant complexity and yet unity in giving and receiving care.

Romania, 2005

Blue

Blue faded smooth secondhand scrubs
sky behind white clouds.
Start with white paint.
add a vial of alcohol thinned pure blue.
On some walls in five shades
painted each Easter fast.
Where the inner layers
have quit holding on

and paint pickers work off
a harvest of paint chips
counting the years
back to mud that holds all.

White lace curtains stretch
wall to wall over missing
panes of glass.
The afternoon illuminates
the netted white sheet
nearly an hour
until it disappears into
the neighbors house.
The wall sized filament
electrifies the blue
lifting the room
into thick golden air
and blue stained earth. (Journal 2005)

Romania, 2007

Utilitarian boxes that meet the basic structural need of shelter filled the cityscape. The Lonely Planet Guide suggested skipping Galati on your way to visiting the Danube delta. Winters took away the green foliage of the trees and exaggerated the dirty grey even more.

One Sunday morning we were crowded in our neighborhood church, no pews, some seats around the edges, just a mass of bodies in the nave. We staked out a spot like a picnic in a city part, to the right of the iconostasis and behind the chanters' stand. Our toddler and baby were seemingly in perpetual motion, making it feel like a constant wrestling match through the service. At one point, my kids made some noise during the service and an elderly lady gave me the stink eye. Couldn't she see how hard I was working? "Give me a break, Grandma," I thought.

Shortly after, a sweet old man – who had seen me struggling with the kids and knew my face from frequent attendance – came up behind me and just put a gentle hand on my shoulder. He said nothing as I turned to see who had touched me. There was a quick moment of recognition, a knowing smile. In the midst of my frustration, self-consciousness and even feelings of alienness in this foreign neighborhood, this gentle touch on my shoulder spoke what I was longing to hear, "I see you, you are doing fine, your kids are not a bother, in fact they are a delight, and I want you to know I am glad you are here right now."

Romania, 2008

Sometime later, six inches of snow made all the sidewalk cracks disappear, all the grey turned to white. The trees grew thick frost, turning black limbs to shimmering white. We wrestled the kids into their long underwear, snow pants, hats, coats, and gloves. My baby was hoisted onto my shoulders, and toddler pulled in the sled behind my wife and me. The black crows, black cats, and black dogs were like construction paper cutouts against the snow. As we walked together, I thought for a moment on the New Creation. Even as we are new creations in Christ, so the whole world, its raw materials, will all be transformed, be made new: in some ways the same trees, dogs, and forms, but transformed as the snow transforms the landscape, recognizable, yet totally new, clean, and pure. The cross on top of our church, usually black, was frost-clothed in white.

The mother Rouault depicts in the plate 10, "...in the old neighborhood of longsuffering" offers this gentle face-to-face touch, in the midst of images of scourging, reviling, and suffering images we have been taken through in the series so far. The neighborhood, like the tree in the center, has suffered long, but there is kindness and care that helps the weary traveler along the way. Here is the respite in the midst of the ascetic struggle through Rouault's visual Miserere Psalm. Here is a taste of verse 7, "Let me hear joy and gladness; let the bones that you have broken rejoice." It is perhaps a transformation of the suffering by the fact of communion. Poverty does not exist in the moments of sharing bread and drink, a good joke and a deep sense of togetherness. We may be in the trenches, the neighborhood of suffering, but being there together means our deepest needs for belonging are met.

GUIDED MEDITATION

Take a moment to find a place to be still and quiet. See if it feels ok to close your eyes and count 5 breaths. Check and see if you have emotional space to sit with this meditation.

What parts of you are in need of the nurturing love, the recognition that you are seen and heard, that you matter in the midst of all of the chaos of life?

Can parts of you identify with the children in the print, or with the tree in the center? How do you feel towards them as you see them? If your emotional intensity is at an acceptable level ask yourself what you would tell these children who suffer and have so little perspective and understanding? What can you say to them now out of your compassionate wisdom that time and perspective have given you? What did you come to believe about the world as a child that now you recognize is not the whole truth about who you are?

Can you go inside and tell your inner children what they are longing to hear? "You did the best you could, it wasn't because of you but because of what the adults in your life were going through, it was part of normal human development, etc."

Can you let these parts of you know they are wonderful, beautiful and worthy? If they cannot hear that just try to be curious about the resistance.

When this inner reflection feels complete for you, take a few moments to return your attention to your breath and to the space around you. Perhaps spend some moments reflecting on the experience and take any notes on things you would like to explore further later or insights you want to hold onto.

To engage with the high intensity level audio version described in the introduction, scan the QR code or visit tinyurl.com/rouault-meditations.

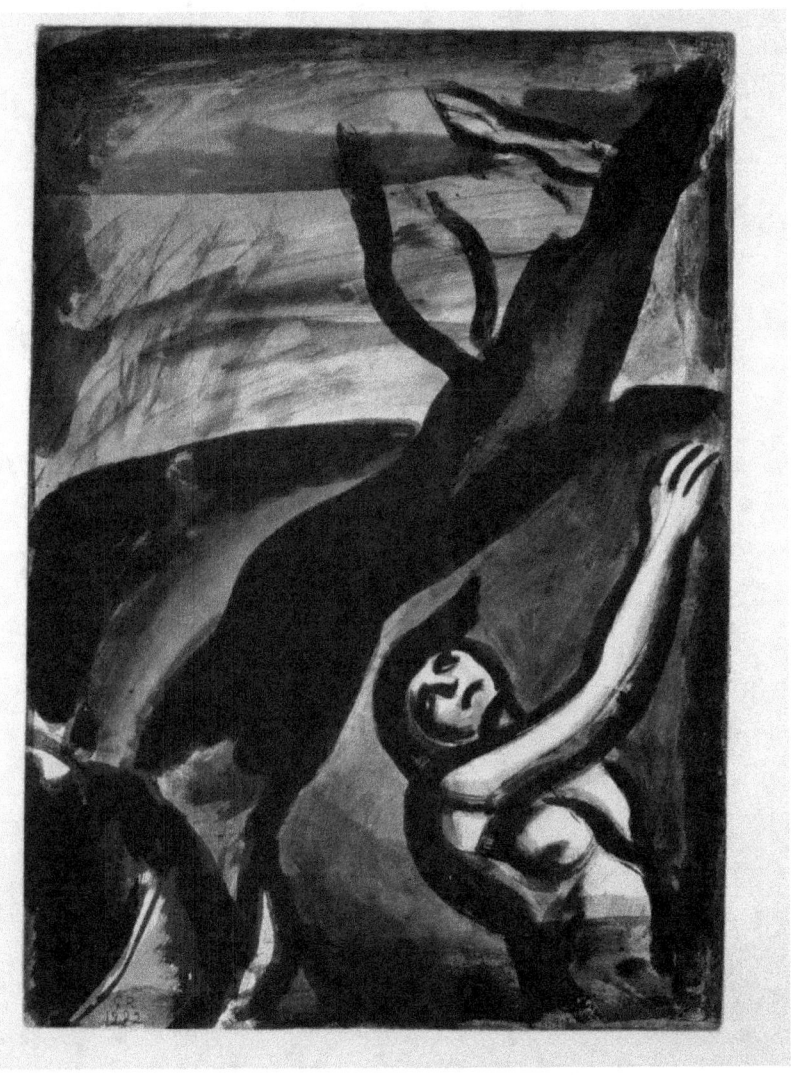

Plate 11

PLATE 11: CASTAWAY

"Demain sera beau, disait le naufragé"
"Tomorrow will be fair, said the castaway"

In Plate 11, connected with the poetic line, "Tomorrow will be fair, said the castaway," the viewer is given harsh angles as if the tree from Plate 10 is now being blown over. The horizon tilts in the opposite direction. The viewer is on a boat with the "castaway" trying to hold on to something for balance. As if they were seeing some movement of the skies, and some clearing dark clouds are moving off the left side of the atmosphere with some brightening sky taking over. The figure seems to balance on the deck of a ship with an angular pose. Perhaps the figure is adjusting sails or falling overboard we get the strong sense of being in the midst of peril. The figure has windblown hair, suggesting movement of the air or the body of the figure or both. This piece with its strong angles carries a transitory feel like chaff blowing in the wind, almost jarring in the context of all the other pieces which feel as stable as boulders in a field in comparison.

"Tomorrow will be fair" suggests some hopefulness along with the rising sun, clearing clouds. This is a hopefulness that anticipates the other side of a storm, the other side of despair and darkness when it is unsure. This is not easy hope. The poetic line associated with it is almost jarring in contrast with the unsettled feel of the image. It is the hope in the face of likely harm or death.

Galati, Romania Summer 2002 12:33 a.m.

A blast that seemed to shake the building startled me awake. My wife was not next to me in bed. I got up and hurried to the balcony of our 8th floor apartment overlooking the Danube and saw more blasts of fireworks. Looking hard at the flying colors helped to push out the feeling of being in a war. The night had too much blood and the nearness of death. The sickening powerlessness was oppressive in the room. Everything was shaking and I was an ant, a castaway.

My wife had had some bleeding earlier in the evening. We were at 4 months now and we lost the last baby at 3 months into the pregnancy. It seemed to be all over once again. The doctor did the entrance exam while smoking a cigarette. She suggested cleaning 'it' out and starting fresh. She was irritated that we weren't on board with her and so sat us down and held out her pinky finger and covered up all of it but the very tip. "This is how much chance you have that this baby will survive."

Without thinking a second, we said together, "Great, That is some chance. We will do whatever we can to try to help this kid make it." We were barely hoping to have a live baby in there, and now we had a fingertip of hope.

Fighting the blanket of grief from the first miscarriage as it slapped down over my head, slumping me in my chair, it felt impossible. This really sucks. Where is God? What happened to making things go good for those who love Him? The black gnarly smoker hair of the doctor and her wrinkly boney fingers pointed into that purest part of me that wanted to hope that life is really good somehow, and she jammed her gaudy red painted nail in there and bloodied it. It bleeds into the night and into my sleep, and to hear those explosions made me wonder if the whole world would soon fall apart.

Mariners Day was being celebrated out over the river, one of the summer feasts of Mary. Down below I could see the 500-year-old church named "the precious mother," referring to her care over humankind, as we are in Christ and He ever in her bosom.

The sailors blow off fireworks in her honor and many get a bit drunk, using her as an excuse. Mama is born – who can't celebrate that with some hard liquor? She suffers Christ's suffering as a powerless mother watching, who would gladly replace her son in suffering, only she can't. She is left with watching, in solidarity with her bloodied crucified son. I just feel like an impotent fool, banking on a God who doesn't seem to be backing me up.

He now lets me watch, like His own mother, my wife bleed and my son so tiny I can't even hold him. Doamne miluieste: Lord have mercy, that is all I got. No passionate cries through the ceiling, no courage to wail out to God. "God have mercy," it is so generic, it could be just for me, for my wife, or for the baby, if there is still hope. I am not sure I am interested in hoping, because it hurt too much the last time. It hurts to hope, and it hurts to not hope.

Getting back to the hospital in the morning, I found my wife in a corner room by herself. The tiny room had a bed for her, and a little bassinet, empty, made with thick wire and invincible metal welds and a small pad. We sat in fear, but also in hope, the tiny hope the length of the doctor's fingernail. We had been through this before and all the despair from the last miscarriage had returned heavy upon me. I tried to be strong for my wife as she was enduring four shots a day trying to keep her body from rejecting the baby still alive inside her.

After a couple of days, she began to tell me about Simeon the old man, the God receiver, the one who waited in faith his long lifetime to see Christ. The name Simeon means "he hears." It seemed that in this, God was saying that he hears us, we were not alone and it was going to be ok. As we shared this moment, I looked out the 6th story window of the hospital that overlooked the Danube River. Out the window was a majestic full rainbow, visible from end to end. It sure felt like another echo of, "He hears." "Tomorrow will be fair, said the castaway."

Where the "exile," "reviled," "scourged" from previous plates have the connotation of the break in human systems and structures leaving people desperate, here Rouault brings in the "castaway" with the connotation of the perils of nature, the sea rising up against human struggle. So Rouault offers some light, some hope, in the midst of the pain affected by natural phenomena. In natural disasters we speak of "an act of God."

And perhaps Rouault is referring to Psalm 51:11, "cast me not away from thy presence". The image has a drastic aloneness to it. As opposed to other images in which there are groups of people, here we have the fragile, on the brink, disoriented person fighting the winds and waves alone; however, there is light, and tomorrow promises to "be fair."

GUIDED MEDITATION

Take a moment to find a place to be still and quiet. See if it feels ok to close your eyes and count 5 breaths. Check and see if you have emotional space to sit with this meditation.

Do you have despairing parts that in the thick of it go to those existential places? If there is a god, why do you hate me?

Sometimes our suffering seems to have no human cause that we can blame or change, like health concerns, global shifts, wars, border changes, natural disasters.

Can you hold space for the parts of you that are burdened with the existential questions, the powerlessness of feeling tossed in an ocean alone in a raft? How do you feel towards the parts of you that can identify with this image, feeling castaway?

Can you let that part know you see it and understand it? Is there any of your compassionate wisdom you might offer to the part of you that feels knocked around by life? What have you learned in your experience that gives you perspective for the struggle when feeling in the midst of a storm? Can you sense that the hopelessness is a feeling held by just a part of you and not all of you?

When this inner reflection feels complete for you, take a few moments to return your attention to your breath and to the space around you. Perhaps spend some moments reflecting on the experience and take any notes on things you would like to explore further later or insights you want to hold onto.

To engage with the high intensity level audio version described in the introduction, scan the QR code or visit tinyurl.com/rouault-meditations.

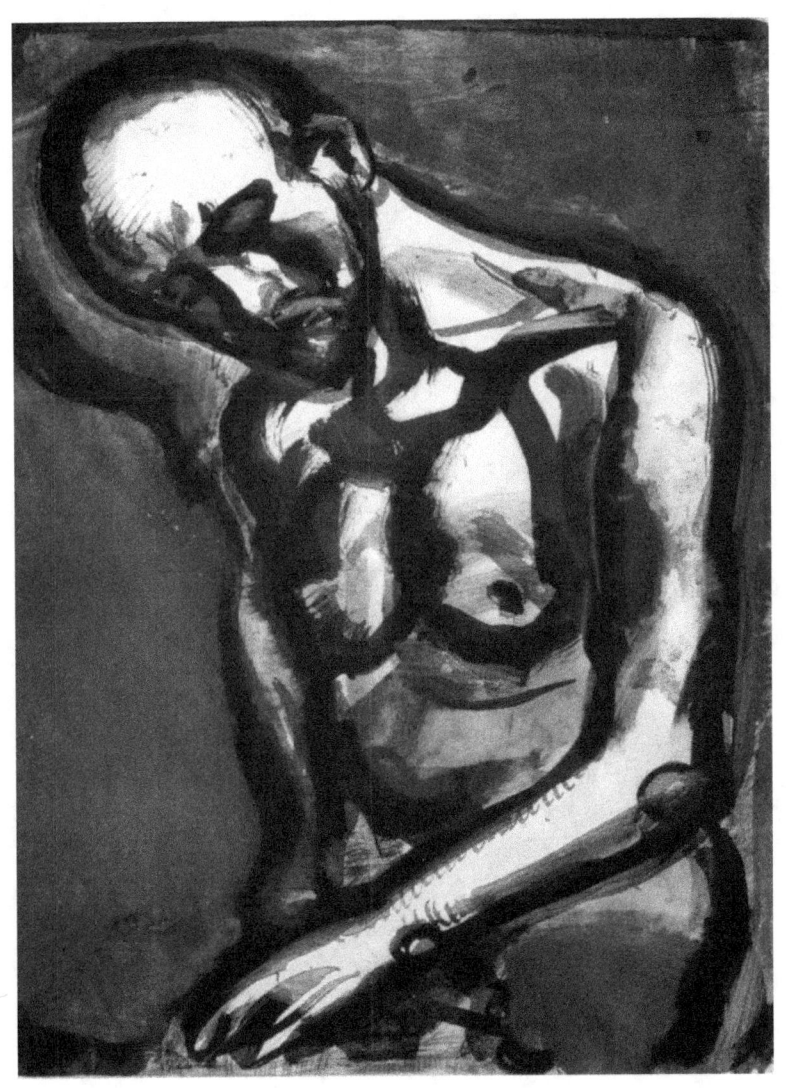

Plate 12

PLATE 12: HARD TO LIVE

"Le dur métier de vivre..."
"It is hard to live (= c'est dur à vivre)...(the hard work or job of living)"

This image is filled with a figure seated in a pose reminiscent of the Christ scourged composition, and it is another print connected by an ellipsis to the following print, Plate 13. He is downcast and serious, as if a weight were bearing down on his neck. There is a compact car feel to the composition, a figure pressed into the rectangle. The top of the frame is like a low ceiling constricting. Eyes are closed, increasing the sense of the internal aspect of suffering, and perhaps the shutting out of painful external stimuli.

It has some of the feel of communist portraits of the noble worker, the righteous laborer, the guts of society, the unsung hero who endures without appreciation for sustaining the system. And perhaps he is crushed by the same insensitive systems in which he is but a tool of muscle and skill. The viewer is brought in close so that they can almost smell the days' work and perhaps the smell of a beer at the end of the day. Or it reminds them of going to the bus stop early in the morning to find men looking like this, sitting on an outdoor bar stool on their way home from the night shift in the steel factory. "It is hard to live."

India 1998

Waking up from an afternoon nap in a puddle of sweat, we rose up from our now regular afternoon nap. Scheduled power outages meant a sweaty wakeup call at 3 p.m. every afternoon. Guests at an old vestige of colonialism, we stayed with the elderly widow in 'the big house' next to the orphanage. Between the brutal heat and the emotionally taxing work of spending time with the children, each with a different trauma history, we were more exhausted than normal.

Groggy-eyed in the midafternoon like an occupying Englishman in India, I looked over the neighborhood. There was construction going on a couple of buildings over and you could see the women construction workers – referred to as "coolies" – going up and down the building like ants. They moved with great attentiveness, intentionality, and grace as they carried a large, flattened bowl full of construction supplies like sand, cement, gravel, or larger rocks balanced on their heads. They accomplished this feat of endurance and balance while wearing a traditional Indian sari, a long flowing single piece of silk fabric. My wife was curious about trying to wear one and found instructions: "12 Simple Steps to Putting On a Sari." It is hard to imagine the wear and tear on the human body of this kind of physical labor over the course of a lifetime. "It is hard to live."

Romania, 2003

As we got to know some of the youth living on the streets in Romania, we often took time to get to know some of their families. There was no typical youth on the street. Some were literally orphaned, but many were from homes that had emotionally collapsed from the inside. One family in particular had four boys under eighteen that all spent different amounts of time on the street. A mix of destitution of their homes of origin, and the teenage desire to be where the action is, seemed to determine how many nights were spent on the street. Often home meant facing drunk parents, poor and oppressed themselves. Some were Roma suffering the racism in the aftermath of a couple of centuries of enslavement.

The dad in this particular case spent most of his time so full of alcohol you would be afraid to light a match around him, yet he still worked searching the city for any bit of scrap metal. He had a cart smaller than a child's wagon and a long metal handle welded onto it. Often it would be so full you couldn't see the cart below the sprawling metal pieces.

One day walking through the city, I looked to my right and noticed him. Head down, cart full, moving at a snail's pace with his own shit on the outside of his pants. He seemed barely conscious, but he still moved upright toward some destination. It was the closest thing I have seen to death in motion: trauma upon trauma, racial discrimination, generational abuse, domestic violence, poverty all dragging at this man, pulling him down. He is an image of a tragic warrior rising again after being torn apart by a colossal dragon. His motion was so slow that you had to stop to see whether he was actually moving.

This portrait also conjures the pose of the chronically depressed. The brutal inner struggle, the molasses brain state, struggling to get oneself to get up, to move, to care, to do anything. Rarely do the deepest depressions not include existential struggle: "does anything really matter," hopelessness that undercuts the will to fight the fire breathing monster. "It is hard to live..."

112

Rouault faces this common human suffering with a fierce bravery, as if he is not afraid in the least to go there. Human misery is not to be backed away from. Rouault does not shy away. He himself suffered his own grief, isolation and feelings of being misunderstood. He seemed to channel these feelings into empathy for humankind. Perhaps as he stood with his neck bent down in compassion, trying to empathize with the suffering, he channeled that common human struggle, marking his surfaces with the residue of our common fight to find meaning, purpose, belonging, safety and sustenance.

GUIDED MEDITATION

Take a moment to find a place to be still and quiet. See if it feels ok to close your eyes and count 5 breaths. Check and see if you have emotional space to sit with this meditation.

Can you connect with what it feels like in your body when you get to that "It is hard to live" place? Does that part connect with this image, the weary tired labor of life getting to be so much you're not sure you can go on?

Can you see this part and welcome it with warmth and care? Can you just be present to this part and let it know you see it, you hear it, and you are with it? If it feels right, let it know it does not have to be alone in the suffering, you are here.

Is there something you would like to offer from your compassionate wisdom or is a silent nonjudgmental presence what is needed? Go ahead and offer it to the part.

When this inner reflection feels complete for you, take a few moments to return your attention to your breath and to the space around you. Perhaps spend some moments reflecting on the experience and take any notes on things you would like to explore further later or insights you want to hold onto.

To engage with the high intensity level audio version described in the introduction, scan the QR code or visit tinyurl.com/rouault-meditations.

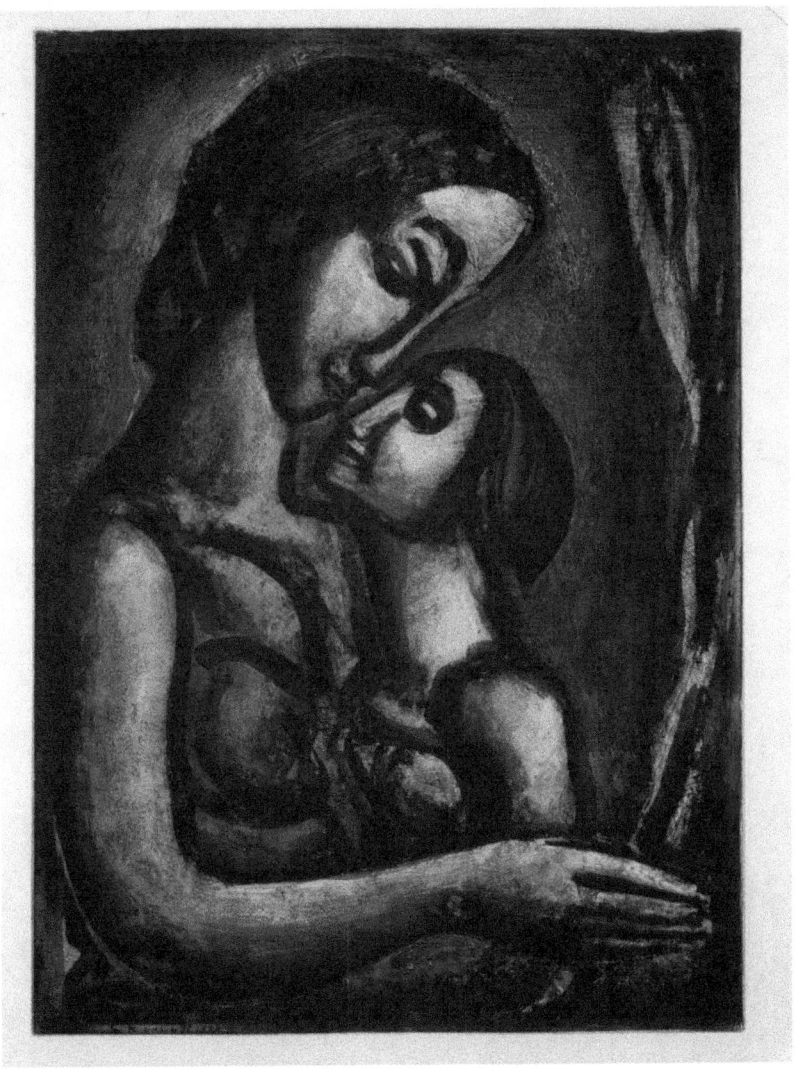

Plate 13

PLATE 13: SWEET TO LOVE

"Il serait si doux d'aimer"
"It would be so sweet to love"

The poetic line associated with the image completes the line started in the last piece, "It is hard to live…" with this phrase, "it would be so sweet to love." Taken separately, this piece could be accused of sentimentality, but Rouault comes to it through hardship, suffering and interior pain of the previous plate. Rouault offers us a mother and child for contemplation. There is a curious curtain being held by the mother. The curtain implicitly carries the idea of veiling or unveiling this intimate scene. There is a playfulness in the faces, not a suckling infant but a toddler, the interaction with mother, perhaps whispering, telling secrets, and playing a game of sorts. The arm and the curtain visually create a sort of protective border around the child, almost shielding it from outside. There are only bare essentials hinting at the archetypal nature of this image. This image holds the emotive power of the safety and belonging of mothers' love, "it would be so sweet to love." This image stands in stark contrast with many of the images leading up to us, full of misery and suffering, hopelessness, despair, human cruelty and insincerity. In full view is transparency, compassion and care, mutually held between mother and child.

Rouault seems to carry this theme throughout, that human care and presence mitigate suffering in the human condition, "…it would be so sweet to love" pushes the viewer to consider not an already arrived-at state, but rather a state of lovingkindness to come in contrast to the present. Almost as a proposition, a question, "wouldn't you rather…," dwell in the sweetness of love than in states of separation and loneliness? It is almost a challenge to the viewer to consider what are those barriers that keep you from this beautiful primal human expression.

Tania Singer in her work on the social neuroscience of compassion and Richard Schwartz's work on the Internal Family Systems model of psychotherapy both come to the same conclusion from very different entry points.[30] Compassion is not something we learn, but rather it is our natural state. In the work of Internal Family Systems, as the fear, anger, protective parts are peeled back, the remainder is an entity that is characterized by compassion. When fear is overcome and healed, what is left is love, care, filial kindness.

Developing out of the insights of compassion from the social neuroscience perspective, Singer teaches participants to unlock compassion through practices of mindfulness, attunement to self and others, gratitude and perspective-taking. What happens is that compassion is uncovered but not created, released but not taught. This primal parent-child care found in safety and in the absence of fear and trauma symptoms, is love, compassion, kindness, empathy, and understanding.

Figures like Evagrius of Pontikus, Gregory of Nyssa, and St Isaac the Syrian articulated a similar phenomenon. The result of dispassion or *apatheia* resulted not in nothingness, but *agape*. Evagrius stated, "The offspring of apatheia is agape."[31]

Ohio, Winter 1980

I can't sleep. My body is covered with red sores and they all itch. It is unnerving. When they get scratched, they itch more. The Benadryl seems like it helps for about as long as it takes to put on. I can't sleep and I am a miserable 5-year-old. Mom came to check on me, probably hearing me move around in my bed. She holds me in her arms, holds my hand in hers and gently caresses the back of my hand with one hand and slowly combs my hair with her other. I sink into her lap and it calms my nerves. Quietly, her lips move, and she whispers a foreign language I do not know. Its sound is comforting like her lap and her touch and her presence. The sounds bubble and roll gently like our little creek I have played in so much. Your bare feet sink into its warmth, and make you feel at home in her presence, in her prayer and in her song. These rhythmic linguistic sounds completed mom's embrace, and placed me in the nearest thing possible to her own womb. I knew I was going to be alright, that this would pass, and that mom was better relief than Benadryl.

Some say that loneliness is caused by the natural differentiation of child from mother we carry through our lives, the primal wound of losing our oneness with the one who gave us birth. Rouault's image here is interestingly a post-differentiation stage of development. Though I doubt Rouault was thinking in these terms, there is a different kind of love between parent and child when the child has a developing sense of self as separate. One can feel safe and a part of this bigger bonded unit, while at the same time growing into one's unique personality identity and preferences.

The loneliness wound is a beautiful homing beacon alerting us to both past oneness and future unity and belonging that I believe is our destiny. We are made for deep communion and intimacy in emotional safety. "To love would be so sweet."

Romania, 2001

One Sunday evening we visited the Catholic church on the other side of town, arriving just before the priest's message. As we were taking everything in, I noticed the sculpture of the scene known as the Pieta, off to my left. Mary is holding the dead body of Jesus, and she looks huge compared to the frail little body of Jesus. His body fits under the umbrella of her blue cloak. In that moment I felt the sweet presence of Christ, and began to understand the Pieta as a beautiful picture of solidarity, suffering, and compassion for the poor.

I saw Jesus as the one who became poor even unto the death, the heart of the kenotic hymn of Philippians 2:5-11. The sculpture has Mary compositionally covering the body of Christ. She has, in a pictorial way, taken the dead body, and in so doing, the death of Jesus into herself. His death is carried in her present life and allows her to fully rejoice in his resurrection later. It is a picture, not simply of the history of our Savior, but rather of the compassionate work of His bride, the church, in the present.

Mary is often associated with the church, at once understood as a real historical character as well as the example for all Christians, She is called "the first among the saints," because she hears the word, receives it into herself, nurtures it and gives birth to Christ or the Kingdom of God into the world.

Walter Brueggemann in *The Prophetic Imagination* writes, "But we do know from our own pain and hurt and loneliness that tears break barriers like no harshness or anger. Tears are a way of solidarity in pain when no other form of solidarity remains," and that "Suffering made audible and visible produces hope, articulated grief is the gate of newness, and the history of Jesus is the history of entering into pain and giving it a voice."[32] These words resound in the Sermon on the Mount as Jesus says, "Blessed are the poor in spirit for theirs is the kingdom of heaven, and blessed are those who mourn for they shall be comforted." These children on the street suffer from poverty and a kind of death in the world's eyes. They are cut off and marginalized, the poor and the outcast, and yet they are beautiful and worthy of the extravagant love of God. They are worthy of our tears, and worthy to have a voice restored to them in a world that would like to keep them silenced.

So Mary, the Theotokos, archetypal mother, becomes not the example just for women, but the prototype of spirituality, of being a vessel of divine love. The pieta is the only truly human response to suffering: attunement, compassion, solidarity, in short, compassion.

Perhaps Rouault reflects the sentiment of Plate 6 of the Miserere Psalm in this image, "But you delight in sincerity of heart, and in secret you teach me wisdom." The "sincerity of heart" in the simplicity of the mother/child interaction, and the curtain hinting at the wisdom taught "in secret." The compassionate gaze of Rouault mirrors the agape and apatheia of the early patristic writers. And that compassion resonates with both the social neuroscience of Tania Singer and of the Internal Family Systems model of therapy that understands a version of love which is not desperate to prove itself, but a love that is present and available, not concerned about its own image, but rather just as happy to act in secret, behind a curtain.

It is worth noting at this point that this image comes before four images in a row of portraits of individual women. I find it helpful that Rouault sets the stage of images portraying women in a more critical light with this image of powerful attuned compassion, which I believe to be not the meaning and purpose of only women but of all people. Marshall Rosenberg operationalized the core human need as "contributing to the wellbeing of others." This is perhaps the measuring stick of discerning whether our actions are meeting our most core human need, the expression of care for others.

The "pleasure woman", Plate 14, the woman with the "taste of bitterness" Plate 15, the lady with a "reserved seat in heaven", Plate 16, and the emancipated woman, Plate 17 all may be seen through this lens. The absence of fear is fullness of belonging, nurture and love as seen here in Plate 13 and the fullness of compassion for self and others.

GUIDED MEDITATION

Take a moment to find a place to be still and quiet. See if it feels ok to close your eyes and count 5 breaths. Check and see if you have emotional space to sit with this meditation.

What are moments in your experience when you were a recipient of compassion? Times when others demonstrated a care for you, seeing you, understanding you, being present to you without a need to fix you, but willing to help?

What does it feel like in your body when you recall those times of being cared for, nurtured, embraced as you are? You may have many of these experiences or a few, but just focus on the ones that felt authentic and sincere. Can you just sit with gratitude for that experience?

If you can, choose one of those people who seemed to always know what to say to you, or how to really make you feel you mattered to them. Now as you think about the current phase in your life you are in – the stresses, insecurities, worries, resentments and fears – just take a moment and ask yourself, "What would this person say to me right now that would help me hold perspective on myself, my situation or my worth?"

Take some time really noticing how even though they are not physically present with you, their love for you is with you and accessible even now.

When this inner reflection feels complete for you, take a few moments to return your attention to your breath and to the space around you. Perhaps spend some moments reflecting on the experience and take any notes on things you would like to explore further later or insights you want to hold onto.

To engage with the high intensity level audio version described in the introduction, scan the QR code or visit tinyurl.com/rouault-meditations.

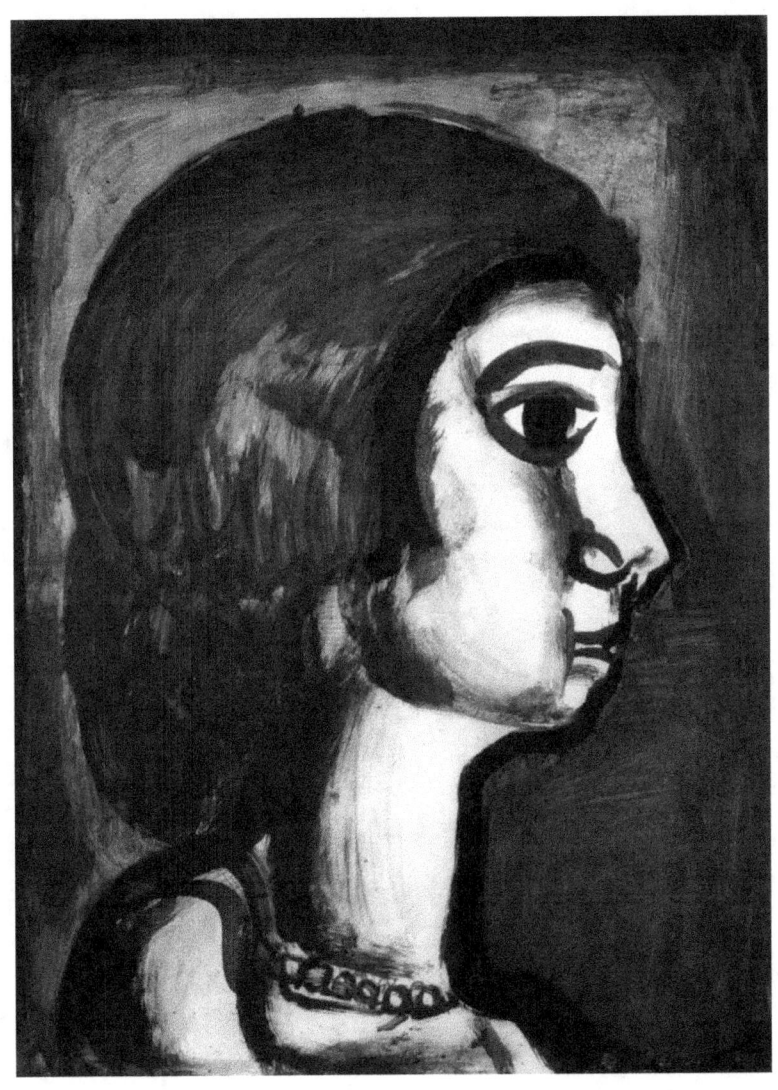

Plate 14

PLATE 14: PLEASURE

"Fille dite de joie"
"So-called pleasure girl"
(girl is used in pejorative sense and the play
on "fille de joie" implies someone in sex work)

With a simple profile – pearl necklace, dark hair, and one prominent eye – the image captures the feeling of a moment when this "pleasure girl" is at rest, maybe when she thinks no one is looking. Rouault captures the figure at a moment that betrays stereotype. Like his sad clown or sad wealthy woman, the internal contrasts with the outer expectation. At first glance the emotive quality of the profile is not of someone who seems to be having a good time. The associated poetic line bearing the phrase "so-called" inverts the meaning of "pleasure girl".

Rouault used contrasting dark gray in the background to push the lightness of the face, adding emphasis and balance to the composition. But also, the brightness of the faces for Rouault has a spiritual quality of imbuing dignity. This often adds a layer of meaning to the human subjects. While I would not rely too heavily on "light" as an interpretive lens for Rouault's work, it also seems to be an error to ignore it completely. Rouault saw divinity in Christ, connected to and interpenetrating the suffering of the poor, the convict, the refuge. It does not seem a far stretch that this element of light is a conveyor of the sense of divine presence in all human forms depicted by Rouault. The image of God penetrates from the rich to the poor, the judge and the condemned, the clown and the lawyer. All people carry this divine light, the divine image and interpenetration of humanity and divinity. One recalls Thomas Merton's vision in Louisville Kentucky at the corner of 4th and Walnut quoted in the first chapter, or any number of saints who discerned the face of God in their neighbors.[33]

Kentucky, 1996

Growing up the son of a house painter, I learned to cut a nice ceiling line with a 3-inch brush, paint a 9-pane window without leaving a trace of paint on glass, and how to leave a room immaculate without trace of a painter. My father was given a sweatshirt by his co-workers that read, "It doesn't get any better than this." Years later, I found that he was quoting a Milwaukee's best beer ad. His particular application of the phrase tended to be sitting around on five-gallon buckets at lunch in a garage, chatting with the crew about life, little league baseball, and daily life. His greatest asset was being able to connect with customers and make them happy with good work. Part of it was making sure you always show progress, even if you could do things faster by doing the work that wouldn't have looked like progress. He genuinely cared for his customers as people.

So now I was on a job and my dad's friendliness probably had rubbed off on me. Being captive in someone's home holding a paintbrush and painting all the trim in one room for several hours can sometimes be seen by a customer as a genuine openness to listen to all of their deepest problems. This was perhaps a precursor to becoming a therapist.

This particular job was an incredible home in rolling Kentucky hills; it had all the flow and feng shui characteristic of a designer's touch, low ceilings leading to high like Frank Lloyd Wright conceptualized. This woman was friendly and kind, offering water and appropriate hospitality you might offer a contractor. Her external life looked enviable to anyone passing by on the road. Multiple luxury cars, husband in a leading industry executive job; all the pieces seemed there. I brought into the home my silent thoughts of those friends in Russia in tiny concrete slab apartments, no dream of a car or a life without hard labor. I probably spent some energy holding back criticisms of the hoarding of wealth, the insulation from the poor and conspicuous spending.

Somehow in working in high end homes in Cleveland, Ohio for years, working for multi-millionaires, my father never seemed to lose sight of the basic humanity of his customers. Maybe some of this was in my awareness, some grace and compassion for the person's struggle and some suspension of judgement. After a couple of hours of this person talking to me while I quietly painted away, she shared her horror story, her secret spending, secret debts she had not revealed to her partner, and the fears of him finding out she had hundreds of thousands of dollars in credit card debts that she had been hiding. She talked of her despair that led her to obsessing over the possibility of suicide as a way out of the whole mess. She was not sure that her partner would stick around through another lie: apparently there had been other lies not quite this big. From all external aspects it looked like everything was going great for her. However, she was spending so much internal energy trying to maintain this wobbling tower of Jenga blocks, fearing the collapse. The outside betrayed the internal experience.

Romania, 2005

10 years old at the most, she grew up fending for herself. Mom drowned in poverty and failed attempts to find a way out of depression and hopelessness. The home was a couple of rooms with the pungent odor of alcohol and cigarettes. Ragina, the 10-year-old, was a movie star, rock star, and supermodel all at once. There was no convincing her otherwise. Her poverty did not bother her. She scraped together coins, traded what she could, scoured the secondhand stores to gather a wardrobe that could always reflect who she was. Other kids rolled their eyes and scoffed, but she just took it like a star getting bad press. "They are just jealous," she might say.

Regina carefully watched the stars on TV to learn with reverie every move: the tip of the head, the wink and nod, the runway stop and pose. She would learn their famous lines in English and get excited to use them on everyone. From her 10-year-old height she could briefly look down on anyone no matter how tall, before breaking into a smile and laugh. If there was a mirror anywhere in the vicinity, she already consulted it for any needed adjustment to her look.

Audacious fashion for this 10-year-old growing up in gut wrenching poverty was an act of defiance. Holding onto dignity, rather grabbing dignity with both hands when one might shrink back for invisibility. One side of it radiated a life-seeking force. The other side of the behavior was a fear of being overlooked, of being unseen and unheard, unnoticed, as if each ounce of glitter would increase her chance to be loved. She was always smiling, posing and ready to dance and have a good time, but in those brief moments when she was not in the spotlight, she looked something like Rouault's "pleasure girl", exposing the quiet sadness under the show.

Here in Plate 14 Rouault conjures a simple but nuanced profile. It may be interesting to consider Rouault's use of the profile versus the full-face portraits. Is it perhaps another layer of hiding, of the shame of a double life, perhaps of the betrayal of authenticity. In contrast with the face of Christ, full frontal portrait images where the eyes pierce the soul of the viewer, here the profile is almost a mask, a partial truth of the person depicted. As the poetic line suggests there is the surface appearance and then the internal experience, the "pleasure girl" is not shown experiencing much pleasure.

In the context of the Miserere Psalm, this piece then is not intended to point out the sinners in the world, the hypocrites out there, but rather to point inward to reveal dynamics of the human soul. As if Rouault says, "are you betraying your internal suffering with a facade?" And to bring back the litmus test of absence of fear and fullness of compassion for self and others, how do we stack up? Here is a person perhaps locked in the fear not being seen as valuable in some way, with good humor or being a good entertainer. These kinds of fears seem to cover over a deeper fear of not belonging, not being loved, the shame of never feeling good enough as you are. And surely there are the more primal fears of hunger and poverty.

In his earlier work he made many paintings of women in the sex trade. They were also neighbors earlier in his life and available models. On several occasions he depicts them looking in a mirror. It is as if he catches not just a model or sex worker, but by seeing them in a very mundane human moment of self-reflection. And through this Rouault invites us to go deeper and ask ourselves what we are so afraid of that we have to perform for the world around us, that we give our true selves away? What keeps us from seeing the dignity of divine light radiating already in ourselves, that given quality of being, and being beloved as the child by the mother in the previous plate?

GUIDED MEDITATION

Take a moment to find a place to be still and quiet. See if it feels ok to close your eyes and count 5 breaths. Check and see if you have emotional space to sit with this meditation.

Are there people of wealth and influence who activate dehumanizing parts of you? Have those parts been frustrated with the seeming disregard for the poor and needy?

Is it possible your judgements mask your own disconnection from the suffering and poverty of those around you? Guilt feelings around lack of responsiveness to suffering neighbors? See if there is a polarization in you, where one part holds guilt around the suffering of others and another part just wants to forget or redirect attention to those who might be more guilty? Is there a way to appreciate the guilt part that may want to motivate you to action as well as the redirecting part that may worry about giving away too much time or resources?

As you look at this image created by Rouault, do parts of you identify with this woman, creating a facade of having a good time while really betraying your more authentic feelings perhaps around meaning or connection or something else?

Can you give this part that hides behind a smile a little appreciation for trying to keep you accepted and loved?

Could you see if it is ok to focus on the part the smile hides and ask what it is needing? What is it worried about missing, what does it want for you? Can you at least acknowledge what it is longing for? And if it is possible can you find a way to address the concerns or make a plan to?

When this inner reflection feels complete for you, take a few moments to return your attention to your breath and to the space around you. Perhaps spend some moments reflecting on the experience and take any notes on things you would like to explore further later or insights you want to hold onto.

To engage with the high intensity level audio version described in the introduction, scan the QR code or visit tinyurl.com/rouault-meditations.

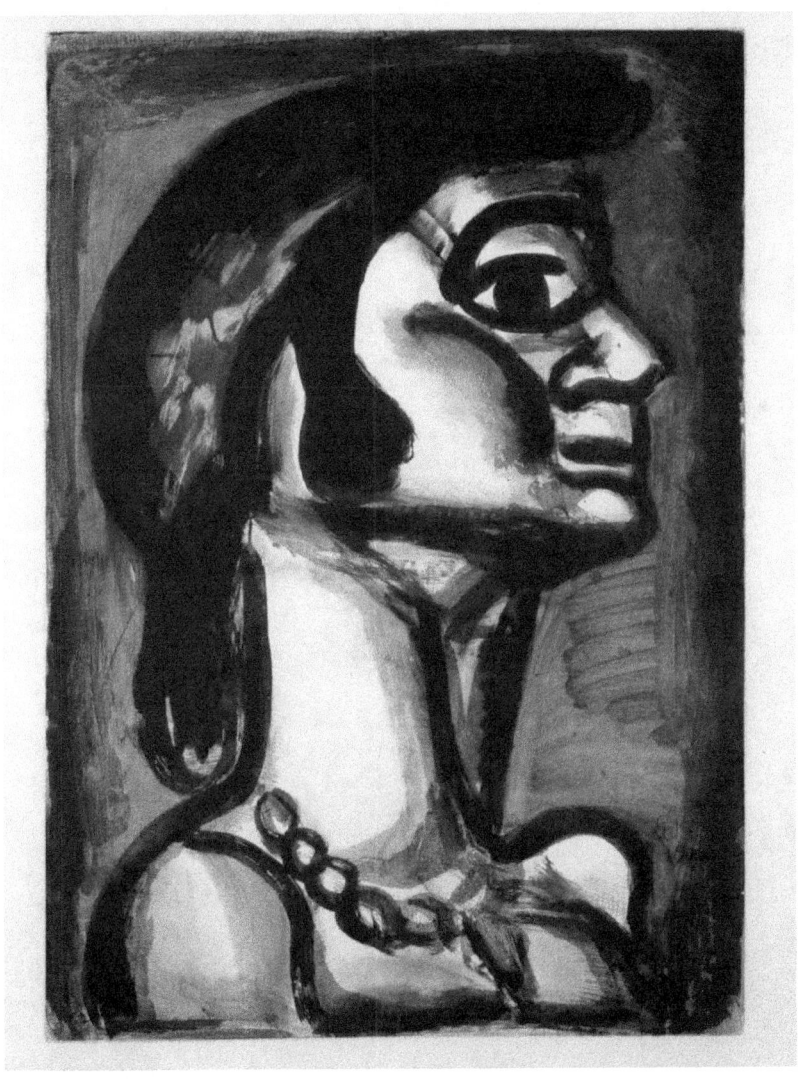

Plate 15

PLATE 15: FRESH TO BITTER

"En bouche qui fut fraîche, goût de fiel"
"In the mouth that was once fresh, the taste of bitterness"

As the *Miserere* moves, Rouault offers now a second profile in a row. From the subtle contrast of the "so-called pleasure girl," external happiness versus internal struggle, now we are given a more explicit contrast in the poetry of freshness to bitterness. A woman with a pearl necklace is depicted in black and white, like an x-ray image, eliminating all non-essential elements. The profile has an elongated neck and upturned chin. The neck is as long as the face, which is almost twice as long as it might be, naturally accentuating the experience of swallowing something bitter; making it feel as if it goes on forever. The eye, not following the usual foreshortening of an eye in profile, gives a worried side-looking glance. The eye is almost directly addressing the viewer as if it were looking straight ahead, unnaturally bracing. The upturned mouth and prominent cheek line add to the impression of bitterness in the mouth. Dark hair contrasts the light of the skin in the face, neck, and shoulders as well as the contrasting contour lines which are so characteristic of Rouault's greater body of work.

This profile is very large in the picture space, giving the sensation of being directly next to this person at a dinner party or some such occasion. It is a personal meeting in close proximity to the viewer.

Pearls in the period Rouault was making these pieces would have still been a significant status symbol, since manufactured pearls had not made popular or inexpensive while he was creating these images.[34] Natural pearls would have been for the elite, and a very portable wealth, especially useful during war time.

"In the mouth that was once fresh, the taste of bitterness" intones loss of innocence. What was once fresh and is no more? Was it the simplicity and freshness of beginnings, of naive and pure intention, or desire spoiled with harsh consequences, perhaps unintended, but still hard to face. We can see this image in the light of the systems that deliver pearls to one human and poverty to another. The lance around the person's neck is at once pearls of the elite as well as the chains of wealth. There is contrasting joy and guilt over wealth in the experience of many sensitive souls. Even more so in war time, the disparities between rich and poor go from feeling like an interesting peculiarity to being gross injustice.

Comfort and protection of the rich versus the trenches on the front lines for the poor suddenly can make anyone uneasy, maybe stealing some of the joys of comfort and position from those not too insulated to feel it. It is hard to enjoy yourself when someone is miserable in the next room. There is a mix of worry and sadness, of holding it together trying to let the bitterness pass. "Will it pass, will there be more, can I ever get back to the 'freshness,' the childlike innocence, or is it gone forever?"

Additionally, women were socially chained into tight roles regardless of class or wealth. Perhaps this is part of the loss of freshness of hope, possibly in the bitterness of the person portrayed here. Was Rouault sensitive to the relative freedom and bondage of woman at all levels of society? Maybe it is the bitterness of hoping for a social status in a profitable marriage turning into an arrangement that feels like suffering and loss of identity, loss of purpose and meaning. The promise of pearls can turn into the chains of custom, social limitations and the guilt of holding wealth while the poor suffer at the gate.

Ohio, 1991

Making some extra cash working with the painting company dad worked for, I found myself in an elite clubhouse at the bottom of a stairwell with a closed door next to it. I was scraping, sanding, and painting some water damaged risers at the bottom of the stairwell. Without any notice, the door next to me opened and there looming above me was the company boss and the millionaire that was overseeing work on the club. I awkwardly stood and was introduced by the boss to the man he was trying to impress. The boss mentioned to the man that I was headed to Czechoslovakia in a week. The man of wealth was delighted to acknowledge we were in a club of humans who travel for a moment. He was very friendly and kindly gave me a hearty handshake and honored my youthful adventure with a smile and a "have a great trip." I felt important and respectable.

I went about my business, and once the man left, the boss came and found me in the shop. He was irate with steam coming out of his ears. I was puzzled. He went at me. "Do you know what you did?!"

The volume increased. "Do you know what you did??"

I shook my head and said I had no idea. My mind was racing to figure out the mystery. A third time, "Do you know what you did?!"

"Wow, it must have been absolutely terrible," I thought to myself.

Finally, he said, "When you were talking back there, you said 'yeah' three times" (instead of a solid 'yes sir'). You sound like someone from the other side of the tracks."

All I could think of the rest of the afternoon was, "Yeah, I am from the other side of the tracks. Who are you trying to kid?"

The boss bent over backward to make his rich customers happy. Another time he offered to kick a tile guy off the job because he had long hair. I enjoyed overhearing the owner tell him that she trusted his tile arrangement judgement more because he was probably more artistic based on the length of his hair.

The existence of the class divide became painfully clear when I was expected to change myself, hide aspects of myself to fit in that environment. My pain lasted a few moments, but Rouault presents the bitterness of wealth in a subtle yet poignant way. I doubt his intention was for us to judge and criticize this woman, but rather to pity her. His friend Léon Bloy did not mince his words when it came to the rich. He said, "The rich have a horror of Poverty because they have a dim foreboding of the expiatory interchange implied by her presence."[35] And this is perhaps the meaning of Matthew 25, when Christ says, "I was hungry and you did not feed me..." Maybe we know intuitively and fear that in the end we must reconcile with those we have wronged. After all, we see that it was Christ, our beloved, who was neglected in those many disguises.

Romania, 2003

The fashion of Romanian women takes after French runways. All black is the standard: if not all black, mostly black. Against the backdrop of the black and white of Romanians are the Roma women wearing many bright patterns and colors all at once.

Roma roots go back to India and the fashion is a cousin to the bright colorful patterns of Indian dress. It was almost comical to see the boisterous bold sounds and colors, from music to dress, of Roma on the streets doing business alongside the communist quiet training of European Romanians and their austere Francophile fashion. Roma boldly held onto their dignity despite being enslaved for 200 years, being sent to their own concentration camps by the Nazis, who ordered all criminals to be executed – and by their definitions all Roma were criminals – and having villages burned down despite having been there for several hundred years. Their survival way of life felt like a middle finger to French fashion, to conformity to social standards, to the communist quiet, and to forgoing their authentic existence for some social custom. If they had gold or jewels, they wore it with pride as their birthright. They accepted no societal pearls that would only function as chains on their expression of independence. Even when in poverty they dress like royalty.

As Paul Farmer said, "If I am hungry, that is a material problem, if someone else is hungry that is a spiritual problem." Perhaps when our hunger is satiated, our basic needs met, that is when we experience the joy of freshness, of satisfaction, of feeling alive. Bitterness is the feeling of having gotten what I wanted and realizing I am alone. I have achieved it to the exclusion of others. I am a child who, having fought for his toy, now has no one to play with.

Generosity, however, may be extended from anyone regardless of socioeconomic status. To empathically welcome another as equal, to recognize a common humanity beyond what we wear and which clubs we enter or beg in front of... is this lack of empathic vision not the sin of Dives?[36] His failure to see the common humanity in Lazarus at his doorstep all those years? His failure to give him a handshake and a smile?

GUIDED MEDITATION

Take a moment to find a place to be still and quiet. See if it feels ok to close your eyes and count 5 breaths. Check and see if you have emotional space to sit with this meditation.

Return to plate 15 at the beginning of the chapter. What parts of you identify with this woman Rouault depicted? Is there a part of you that feels trapped in an image game? It may be a part that protects your image through striving for material things, but it may be a more subtle part that wishes to always be seen as intelligent, or funny, or always knowing what is going on. Does it sometimes get extreme or go overboard? What resonates for you? Try to focus on that part for a few moments.

If you have some openness and curiosity about this part, can you ask it why it is working so hard to keep up a kind of image? What is it worried about happening to you if it were to relax and let down the guard sometimes?

Were there times in your life when you got hurt that really energized this part to do what it does? If you are feeling compassion for this part let it know that. Are there other ways you can help this part that may be stuck in the past? Can you let it know you are ok now if that feels true? See if there are any other ways you can show some care for this part.

When this inner reflection feels complete for you, take a few moments to return your attention to your breath and to the space around you. Perhaps spend some moments reflecting on the experience and take any notes on things you would like to explore further later or insights you want to hold onto.

To engage with the high intensity level audio version described in the introduction, scan the QR code or visit tinyurl.com/rouault-meditations.

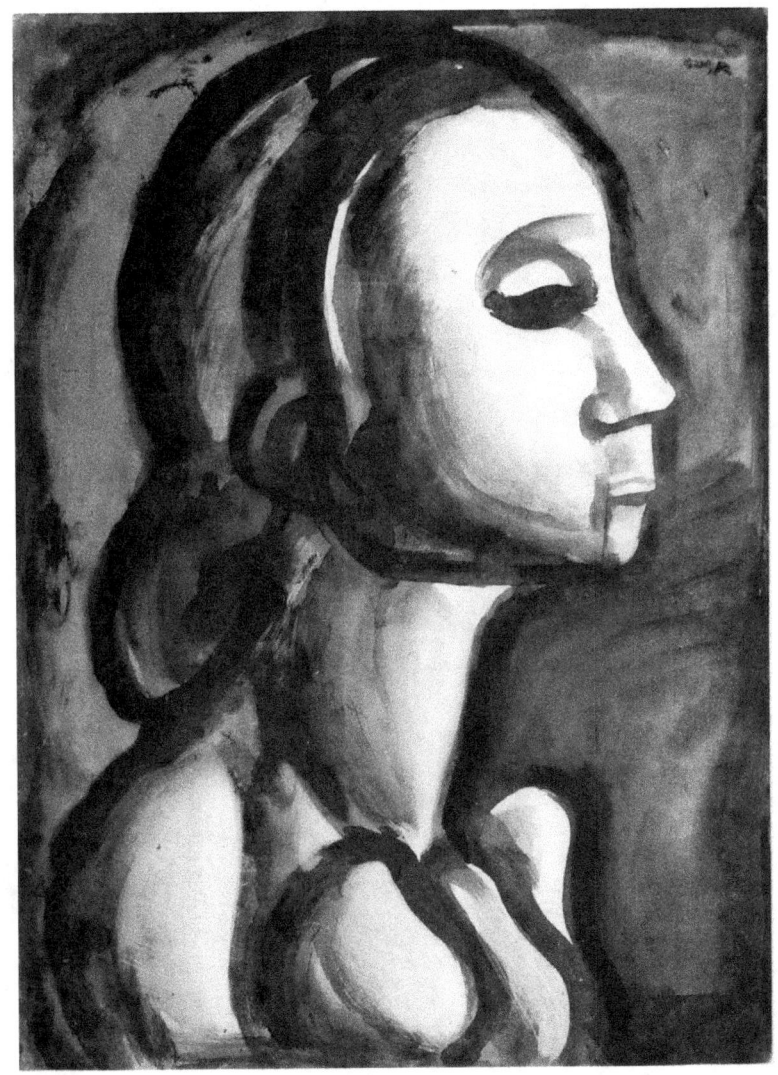

Plate 16

PLATE 16: RESERVED SEATS

"Dame du Haut-Quartier croit prendre pour le Ciel place réservée"
"The Society Lady fancies she has a reserved seat for Heaven"

The third of four female profiles, coming after the "so called good time girl" and the "freshness to bitterness," is this image which will be followed by the "Emancipated woman, at two o'clock, cries noon." Now identified in the associated poetic line as a "Society Lady," this profile is distinguished by her closed or mostly closed eyes, perhaps imagining her place in heaven. Here there are no pearls or ornamentation. With placid eyes and light simple hair, she appears as a young society lady preserving her purity in the eyes of society, never crossing a social boundary while holding her reputation like a treasure to preserve her future. A "society lady" would have been subjected to many family and social forces to constrain any behaviors that might damage a family's place in society. The struggle of self-righteousness is akin to the position of the older brother in the biblical prodigal son story, following conventions for the sake of securing a future which contrasts the fellowship of love with the father in the story.[37]

In some sense the closed eyes disconnect her from suffering. The "supposing" is a psychological disposition of imagining one's own place, while closing one's eyes to one's neighbor. Here, the irony is that one can be convinced of one's own rightness while betraying true goodness and compassion. In contrast, the apostle Paul and the saint stories from church history reveal a disposition of supposing they would be the first in hell, chief among sinners.[38] The young society lady is both waiting and preparing for a good match to secure her future, and then Rouault poetically shifts the level of reality from the social to the cosmic. The social mirrors the cosmic and psychological.

In the spirit of the Miserere Psalm, we can ask how we are – or better yet, how am I – closing my eyes to suffering humanity, and focusing my attention in my own self-righteousness. How am I following the right conventions or rules to place me securely in the good category, to avoid the shame of others seeing me as bad? Matthew 25 challenges the reader that there is no human who suffers in whom Christ is not suffering as well: the poor, the prisoner, the least. One cannot self-righteously close one's eyes to the poor without also closing one's eyes to the suffering of Christ, where he is reviled, scourged, or a refugee. We get a similar closing off to Christ on the lawyer in Plate 19, eyes closed with the suffering in the room.

Mumbai, India, 1998

Our flight was diverted from a direct flight from Zurich to Mumbai, scheduled and missed, to a flight from Zurich to Bangkok to Mumbai. Descending into Mumbai, the landing gear came down and the descent was normal until a surprise dust storm turned everything a luminescent brown. The pilot jerked the plane back up and out of the landing path. The abrupt changes got groans from the passengers, now feeling like we were on a carnival ride. The plane tried to land and pulled up several more times before landing, and after a try or two it became evident what each person's religion was: everyone was either throwing up or fervently praying to their higher power.

When we finally landed in Mumbai and the doors of the plane were thrown open, a distinct fragrance of Indian curry filled the airplane. "So this is India," I said to myself.

We spent some time with an Indian family who we had met in the United States. Their home had been flooded with dust from the storm. They graciously hosted us in their home. At one point they invited me to teach something about leading music in a church service. I had ideas I wanted to share from my experience, and I am sure my 22-year-old self was full of deep insights and world changing ideas. It seemed like a pleasant enough encounter with some of my host's church members.

Towards the end of the visit, we had some time together. Our host finally let out what he had been holding onto. He let us know we were full of self-righteous judgement. My talk was perceived as belittling to the intelligence of the Indian congregants, assuming they knew less than they did. My American superiority was reprehensible, and my ignorance of the actual difficulties and challenges of life in India was offensive.

I was floored. I thought I was doing everything right. Just trying to help, I got put in my place. My sense of rightness was based on eyes closed to the experience of my fellow humans, which made it clearly disconnected and wrong.

This sort of closed-eyes spirituality is in direct contrast with that of The Virgin Mary, the Theotokos, the mother of Christ. She is seen as the one ever attentive to the suffering of Christ. It is unthinkable to visualize one's place in heaven without the whole family there with you, the first being the poor, marginalized, suffering, the accused, the mocked. Mary's heaven is only through suffering with compassion and redemption.

Rouault challenges the viewer to consider repenting from self-absorbed religion, a calculus of one's own destiny without regard for others. And even in picturing the self-righteous, Rouault treats them with a gentleness and affinity, with compassion for the protective role and the even more essential divine light deeper than the surface self-righteousness.

GUIDED MEDITATION

Take a moment to find a place to be still and quiet. See if it feels ok to close your eyes and count 5 breaths. Check and see if you have emotional space to sit with this meditation.

Can you identify any self-righteous parts in yourself, the assurance that you are on God's side, "At least I am not a sinner like...?" Is there a part of you that gets you to think a lot about how bad your political, social or personal enemies are?

Is there another part that wants to be a peacemaker and not have enemies and feels bad about this self-righteous part? What is the peacemaker worried will happen, when the self-righteous part is leading?

If this is fitting for you, can you find some curiosity about the self-righteous self-assured part? What might this part be afraid would happen if it made room for not knowing, for mystery and subjectivity? Were there experiences in the past that made the part afraid to not stick to your guns and be sure you are on the right side? What seemed to be at stake then? Is it still at stake now? Is it protecting belonging, or a sense of security, or something else? Can you take a moment and just appreciate the positive intention of this self-righteous part?

Would this self-righteous part be willing to cooperate for more growth and wholeness if it knew your belonging and safety was taken care of? Is there a way you could honestly reassure this part of you that you are loved and safe even if you risk being open to others not like you?

When this inner reflection feels complete for you, take a few moments to return your attention to your breath and to the space around you. Perhaps spend some moments reflecting on the experience and take any notes on things you would like to explore further later or insights you want to hold onto.

To engage with the high intensity level audio version described in the introduction, scan the QR code or visit tinyurl.com/rouault-meditations.

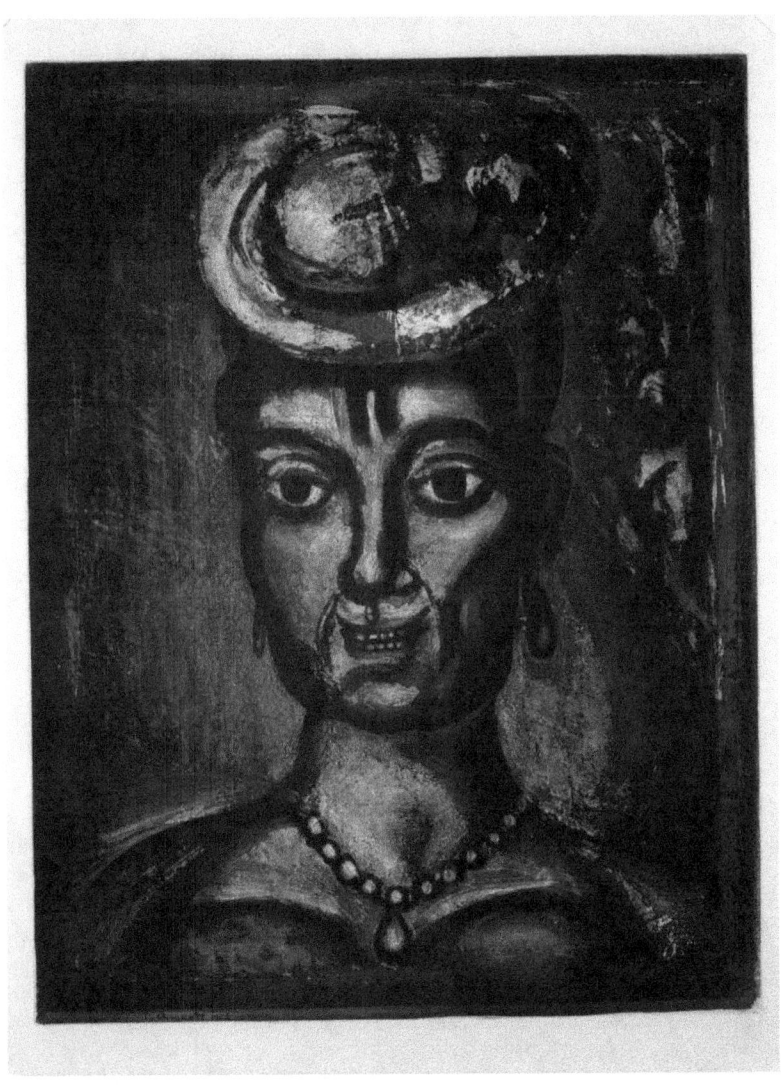

Plate 17

PLATE 17: EMANCIPATION

"Femme affranchie, à quatorze heures, chante midi"
"Emancipated woman, at two o'clock, cries noon"

Plate 17 puts forward another female portrait, this one associated with the stanza "Emancipated woman, at two o'clock, cries noon." Wide eyes engage the world. Her worldliness contrasts the "other worldliness" of the previous portrait of the woman contemplating her place in heaven with closed eyes. Rouault was conservative and in his writing anti-feminist sentiments are present.[39] This woman represents for Rouault a well-dressed society lady who is an activist for her cause. Perhaps Rouault pokes fun of the out of touch activist who has the privilege of not getting up early for a job. While the poetic line associated with this image suggests freedom and wealth, by the look of the woman's eyes one wonders about an underlying sadness, or a deeper-level dissatisfaction or hopelessness.

Rouault offers delicately textured surfaces as if pulled out of the dark. This woman has pearls in visual rhythm with her teeth, but also earrings and a hat. Tonally, it is one of the darker of the 4 portraits placed together for our contemplation. Her hair is up under her hat, and her hat rides high on her head. The hat catches light and rivals the face in its brilliance. The eyes are large, open and prominent. Whereas the previous portrait had closed eyes blinded to the surroundings, the wide-open eyes here feel to be the blank. One woman is driven to religious escapes and the other to contemporary activist pursuits.

Rouault had strong criticisms for the wealthy and especially those who were self-assured. The previous image is the self-assurance about heaven, and perhaps here is the self-assured political activist. Beyond the particular idea of feminist activism that Rouault probably bristled against, his useful insight here seems to be more about our self-assurance of rightness.[40] How can one be accurate of how things are or ought to be when one is insulated by wealth and social distance? The combination of disconnection and self-assurance is brought to light in Rouault's harsh contrast here.

Another layer present here is that of sleeping well into the day. To be unaware or disconnected is to be asleep to realities. One cannot be attuned and compassionately responding to the world when asleep. Of Edgar Allen Poe, Mary Oliver writes, "But it is sleep as Poe most sought and valued it –

not for the sake of rest, but for escape. Sleep, too, is a kind of swooning out of this world."[41] Rouault challenges our self-assured activism and begs us to consider what it would take to really attune and be present among those we claim to be helping.

Romania, 2001

Waking to the sun brutally entering my 5th-story windows, my bedroom felt like an interrogation. There it was again, that lump in the throat, the lead-balloon-in-the-gut feeling. The weight of our lost baby we named Lazarus, and the anniversary of his supposed-to-be due date; only the due date felt like a sledgehammer bringing it all back. I went to the bathroom and returned to our mattress on the floor, hoping to shut it out again, hoping to sleep again if I could overcome the bright sun outside.

I could feel the parquet floor with my fingers, the little 1x4 inch puzzle pieces that fit together in a back and forth, creating stepped patterns of squares across the floor. The edge of the mattress between my fingers, and the difference in texture between the material covering the corded seam and the bare mattress material under the sheet that had pulled over the edge reminded me of the journey through town bringing the mattress home.

We were trying to be as frugal as possible in respect of the poverty around us, so I opted for carrying the mattress home instead of hiring a truck. My coworker Dennis agreed to help. It was a sunny day, good weather, so after paying off the mattress we hoisted it up and began the 10-block journey across town.

There is no hiding when carrying a new queen-sized mattress. It is like trying to hide while carrying a billboard. It is an invitation, apparently: within 100 feet I began to get the questions, "How much did you pay for it?" "Where did you buy it?" "Oh, that's a good price." There was no culture barrier; I was a guy needing a mattress like everyone else, taking care of business. The simple questions felt like gestures of belonging to the human community. No question of citizenship, national origin, educational pedigree or occupation, I was just another human who sleeps. The lead weight of the grief pressed me into this mattress, as just another human who sleeps to forget.

When going out to meet the boys on the street at any hour of the day, some boys would be awake and others in their stairwell corners – lined with cardboard boxes and glue huffing bags – or in the underground infrastructure shafts they had found their way into. After ten minutes of first contact with the ones who were awake, you would see the groggy ones just woken up by their friends rubbing eyes, splashing water on their faces with a wry smile for having been caught midday, afternoon or evening asleep. They didn't want to miss a game of soccer on a handball court behind an elementary school, or the free sandwiches and fruit that would follow the game. Huffing and sleep tag-teamed to shove away the grief and pain for them.

I was feeling it now, the impulse to find a way to forget: "Oh sweet forgetfulness of sleep, take me out, take me away, let me swoon into another world."

While oversleeping has been demonized as a sign of laziness, self-indulgence, or even decadence, when we gently look at what it is doing, this part of us that seeks solace in sleep is acting like a pain killer. The pain seems to be too much, remembering feels like an existential threat, and for those who struggle with suicidality it certainly can be. Like any other distracting habit, it also works to take us out of our life and off the track of the deeper visions for life we seek.

It is a paradox that the part of us that seeks to deaden pain by oversleeping – and in so doing keep us going, because it can feel as if the pain would kill us – also makes it harder to live. We are half-asleep zombies coming out of the underground like kids living on the street. Sleep keeps us going but diminishes us too, as any overused distraction does.

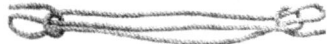

We can also ask on a more psychological or spiritual level, how are we asleep? I recently recounted to one of my kids some of my spiritual development. One came after a trip to India and beginning to read *Rich Christians in an Age of Hunger* by Ron Sider. I was confronted with an undeniable reality after the experiences in India, Russia, and Czechoslovakia at that point in my life.

The book has a section outlining the 500-some scriptures related to God's preference: His love for the poor, the orphan, the widow and the stranger. This was suddenly a different Bible than I was taught. How was it that I had read the Bible all these years and been asleep to something that looms so large? How could I have a Christian faith that was blinded to these 500 clear scriptures? We talked a lot about lots of aspects of scripture full of self-assurance of really getting it, but totally missed the poor in scripture. Perhaps Matthew 25:40 quoted already is one of the most poignant, "Truly, I say to you, as you did it to one of the least of these my brothers, you did it to me."

Rouault lived in the shadow of the friendship with Léon Bloy.[42] Bloy's harsh, incendiary critiques didn't end when he came over to dinner. He harshly criticized Rouault's "grotesque" images. Another object of his wrathful expressions of Christian truth as he saw it was his loathing for the rich, the class of people who had leisure in abundance, while the poor went hungry. Bloy's withering criticism of the wealthy resonates in this image of the rich self-assured activist.

One also wonders if this "emancipation" is not said ironically, for who in Rouault's point of view could be ethically freed from our common humanity, our bond with all people regardless of race, class or socio-economic status. The "emancipated" from empathy, compassion, fraternity perhaps, illuminate the very human struggle against the insulation of self-preservation that accompanies wealth. Religion in this context serves to blame the poor for their poverty and exonerate the "righteous" affluent from the need for guilt or compassion.

To point our fingers at those richer than ourselves is to spit out the medicine before it can do its work. In the journey of transformation Rouault invites us on, we are challenged to awaken at dawn, to see what is unpleasant to see, to see God in our neighbor and be moved to compassion breaking through our insulation of wealth, privilege or power. I would urge that we also be challenged to find a way to connect with your own exiled, poor, widowed and orphaned parts, and allow compassion to reach them as well.

GUIDED MEDITATION

Take a moment to find a place to be still and quiet. See if it feels ok to close your eyes and count 5 breaths. Check and see if you have emotional space to sit with this meditation.

Do you have a part that longs to escape, to party, to play? And the opposite, do you have pushing parts that reluctantly allow any break until you are ready to break down?

First, let us consider parts that advocate for comfort, rest, or escape. Can you set aside self-judgments about your need for comfort, rest and play? Are there parts of you that could relax and make more space for a balance of work and rest? What are you afraid of happening if you made space for play? Are there legitimate concerns that you could play forever and never get anything done? If you can address this fear and let the part know you will balance work and play could it relax?

If there is room to focus on the play advocate part ask it about why it gets more intense at times pushing you to play or distract? Is there a bit of desperate seeking of freedom to counteract the intensity of hard working parts?

Does the freedom seeking of one part feel like a betrayal of other parts? Is there a way to both attend to your needs for balanced rest and play while having enough room for your vocation, your unique way of engaging with the world in meaningful ways?

Can you hold with nonjudgmental awareness that both the play seeking part and the meaningful work part contribute in important ways to your overall wellbeing?

When this inner reflection feels complete for you, take a few moments to return your attention to your breath and to the space around you. Perhaps spend some moments reflecting on the experience and take any notes on things you would like to explore further later or insights you want to hold onto.

To engage with the high intensity level audio version described in the introduction, scan the QR code or visit tinyurl.com/rouault-meditations.

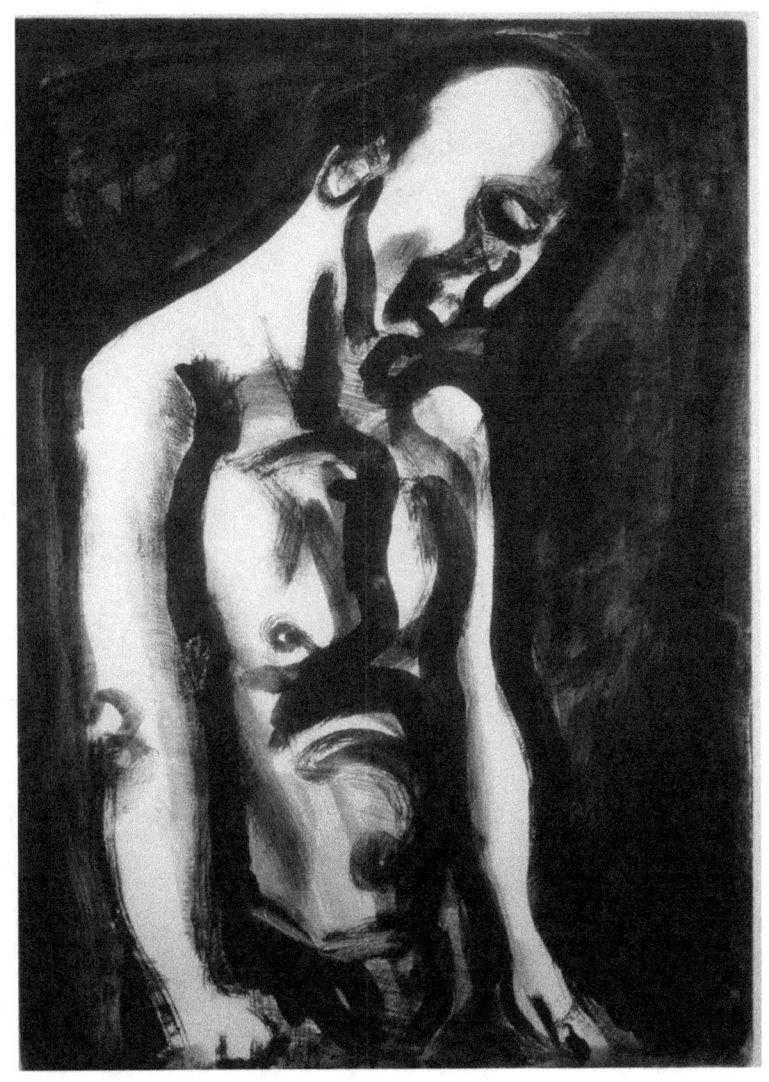

Plate 18

PLATE 18: THE CONDEMNED

"Le condamné s'en est allé..."
"The condemned went away..."

The whole phrase, of which this stanza represents the first portion, is, "The condemned went away... his lawyer, in hollow phrases, proclaims his complete indifference... beneath a forgotten crucifix." These poetic lines are lines from a single poem written by Rouault himself and appeared on separate pages from the prints themselves.

The condemned fills the page, head to hands. We are brought into an intimate space with the condemned, seeing only the upper body, naked torso, downcast, focused inward. The condemned man in light grey tones is on an ambiguous dark background. There is a tightness to the torso as if it holds back an oncoming attack of condemnation, lessening the blow of judgement to come.

The stanza conjures a courtroom scene, condemned on his stand, lawyer indifferently speaking with eyes closed to the condemned, and the image of the crucifix on the wall behind the judge. This was an allusion to the fact that in 1905 with separation of church and state laws crucifixes were removed from courtrooms and now in Rouault's time, "forgotten."[43] By depicting the forgotten cross back in the courtroom, the suffering Christ is on the wall again. The invisible reality for Rouault is that none suffer condemnation or affliction without the presence of Christ, who is present in all suffering. Inversely, there are none condemned who do not share in the unjust condemnation of Christ to death.

Kentucky 2011

As part of a year-long practicum experience in my counseling training program, I went weekly to the county jail. On my first visit, I led the group of 30 men in a session on parenting skills. First you meet an elevator, declare yourself to the controller through the video cameras, and descend several floors down to the level where all the inmates are kept. Then you wind through a maze of corridors, navigating with the signage towards your destination: block EE in our case. Once at the unit you call the intercom that rings the controller. They hit a button and the first set of doors open, letting you into a small room with large steel doors on either side.

The sliding steel doors seem like they would easily take off a limb if you didn't get through in time. Upon shutting and sealing you into the chamber, the inner doors then open under the controller's direction. There is an eerie feeling that these doors are completely outside of your control. No mere willpower could get those doors open if the invisible person in the control station does not want them open.

Here, you have given up all power of escaping by your own scruples. Sealed in, you have submitted to the power of another, willingly or unwillingly. Even as a volunteer, this becomes painfully clear as reverberating steel of the last set of solid doors thuds shut. You are now in a huge pie-shaped space with two floors of cells on either side, stairs leading up to the second floor cells, and a guard station in the middle of the room.

Me and my supervisor let the guard know what we were there for, and he made the announcement. Soon 30 men were gathering large plastic block chairs in a circle to begin our session on parenting skills. My supervisor suggested we start with demonstrating empathic listening. She meant to do it with 2-3 of the men. In my nervousness I understood to demonstrate it with each person in turn. So I asked the men to think about a time they remember, a pleasant moment with their fathers, or some other father figure if they did not have a father in their life.

"I remember the time when my dad took me on a trucking route. We sailed across the country together, talking and listening to music, and I learned about his love for Stevie Wonder."

"I remember a birthday where dad took me to a county fair, he let me play some of the games I had never been allowed to waste money on before."

"My dad used to wake up early and make grits. It was the only time it was just me and him until he left."

"I can't really think of any good stories with my dad he spent most of my life in jail, and he stopped writing when I turned 12 and got pissed off at him for not remembering my birthday."

"My dad showed me how to take apart an engine, got me a way to make money at 15-years-old fixing everybody's junkers."

"My dad didn't talk much, but we would take drives together with the windows down, sometimes go fishing. He couldn't fish for nothin' but it was nice to not have to talk for a change."

As each of the 30 told his story, I followed each by repeating it back in my own words, trying to pick up on the core feelings and what seemed to make it matter so much to them. With many there was brief eye contact, a recognition of a thread of connection, of having this guy from the outside name accurately, sit in it for a moment, validating the beauty of why the story mattered. There was a felt experience of feeling seen, feeling into our common humanity.

To most people on the outside this was just a room of "felons" ineligible to ever vote again and unlikely to ever get past a background check for most jobs with benefits; these men were condemned and tucked neatly three floors below ground level.

Walking with men and women trying to transition into life after prison, their lack of choices became painfully clear. They struggle to find a minimum wage job while friends and family demand immediate repayment for all the loans they offered while they were inside. They are maybe sleeping on mom and dad's couch – if they are still talking. Their kid asks for the latest video game console, and the guilt and remorse of all the time spent away from them catches up, and then they have a number on their phone. One call, and two hours later they could have the cash in hand to buy their kid that game console.

They feel the "vultures descending," the hopelessness of getting a living-wage job, the condescension of their family, and their vulnerability to go back to the one thing that reliably offers some peace and calm, and maybe feels like it is the only thing that would keep them from hurting someone.

The condemned's worst enemy is the internal shame, guilt and exiling of painful emotions. "Nobody wants to hear my excuses." "Just because I grew up watching mom get beat doesn't mean I get a pass." Rather than being led away, the stanza says, "the condemned went away". Rouault shows how in the end we often self-exile. We protect others by removing ourselves. "I must suffer the consequences and suffer silently because no one wants to hear it." Rouault captured all of this, with all its emotive power and depth, in this image a hundred years ago. Prisons may look different now, but the shame worn on the face of the condemned feels the same.

From a therapeutic perspective, the exiled pain, suffering, and shame become the nuclear reactor inside that all other parts fight tirelessly to keep away. This is the part that needs desperate healing if there is to be any chance of walking the tightrope and staying away from the behaviors that keep the pain at bay. There is the belief that if we do not punish – and punish severely – the "bad elements" among us, they will grow and destroy our culture and peace as we know it.

Likewise, the only path of healing is to go to our exiles, our felons, our condemned, and find paths of restoration, reintegration, and restorative justice. It would require empathy and compassion to listen deeply to the on-the-ground causes of "delinquency." Are we giving folks options if there are not living wage jobs available to "felons?" Do we not bear the shame and guilt of perpetuation of structural racism, the evolution of Jim Crow laws and mass incarceration?

Can we see the humanity and consider ways of erasing the debilitating and forever label of "felon?" Can we begin to see that they are us, they had fathers and mothers who had fathers and mothers who struggled with systems and structures, successes and failures, that we all bear the same image, seek after the same universal human needs? Rouault begs us to see ourselves in this image of the condemned.

And what of the parts of yourself that bear shame and the feelings of "forever badness" in your internal system? Rouault has a knack for illuminating our common human struggles with a directness that is often difficult to look at. A deflection to see others in these images helps exonerate us, but our own struggle with self-condemnation remains: "I am bad because I felt a certain way when things happened." An inability to break the cycle of self-condemnation makes it nearly impossible at times to stop the cycle of condemning our fellow humans. On the other hand, some of us find it easy to give everyone else a pass while we secretly live with the pain of harsh self-condemnation leading ourselves away into exile.

GUIDED MEDITATION

Take a moment to find a place to be still and quiet. See if it feels ok to close your eyes and count 5 breaths. Check and see if you have emotional space to sit with this meditation.

As you see this image of the condemned what do you notice wake up in you? Are there parts of you that have felt condemned by others? By the world? These are often very tender parts. Can you just spend a moment acknowledging them? If it feels helpful, place a hand on your chest or where that condemned part shows up. If it feels honest send a message to the part and let it know you see it and will work towards bringing healing to it. If you are feeling compassion for it see if you can extend some of that compassion that this part was longing for when it was being condemned. If it is connecting for you, take your time with it.

Check if there is space now to see if you can connect with any part of you that wants to condemn others? If you have some curiosity about this condemning part, as it why it tempts you to condemn others? What is it afraid of happening if it doesn't point the finger at others? See if you can hear the positive intention under this condemning part. Is there a history it carries that explains more about why it picked up the strategy of focusing on the wrongs of others? If you found the intention, can you thank the condemning part for its intention and see what it needs in order to shift strategies?

When this inner reflection feels complete for you, take a few moments to return your attention to your breath and to the space around you. Perhaps spend some moments reflecting on the experience and take any notes on things you would like to explore further later or insights you want to hold onto.

To engage with the high intensity level audio version described in the introduction, scan the QR code or visit tinyurl.com/rouault-meditations.

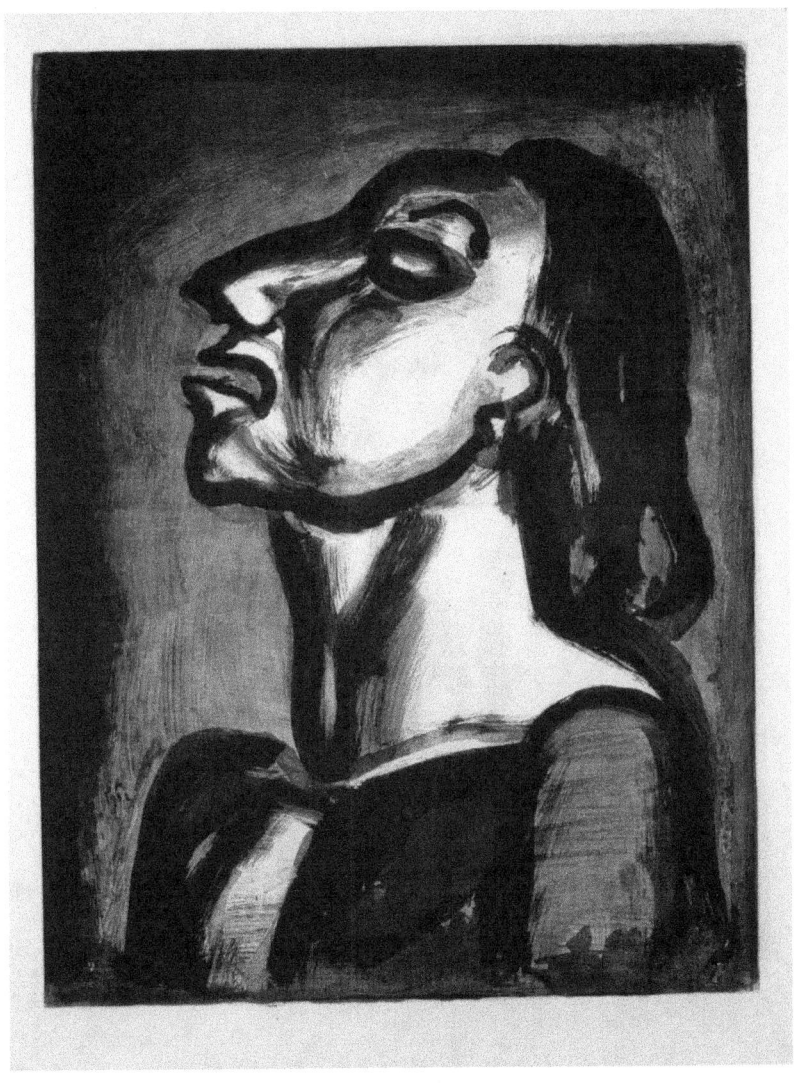

Plate 19

PLATE 19: HOLLOW PHRASES

"son avocat, en phrases creuses, clame sa totale inconscience..."
"his lawyer, in hollow phrases, proclaims his complete indifference..."

Eyes shut and chin up while speaking, the lawyer's bust fills the space. The attention focuses on the yawning, speaking mouth spilling phrases into the air. Open mouth, closed eyes, the lawyer's verbal faculties act without visual connection to the subject of his speech.

The whole phrase, of which this line represents the middle portion, is "The condemned went away... his lawyer, in hollow phrases, proclaims his complete indifference... beneath a crucifix forgotten there." Here we face the disconnect, the loss of attunement with the suffering. Closed eyes and an upward-turned face are the gestures containing the entire movement of condemnation, of othering, isolating, and specifically here, incarcerating. The "indifference" accentuates the emotional disconnect between the condemned and the lawyer.

At face value we can focus on the active brutality of indifference, though there seems to be pain in the face of this "indifferent lawyer." Here perhaps is the glimmer of compassion Rouault may have seen, even for this condemnable character. Perhaps, psychologically speaking, this is an example of how we exile our own inner indifference. The part of us that is indifferent may worry about what will happen to me if I open myself to your suffering. I will have to open to my own, and that is perhaps not admissible in my inner courtroom.

Romania 2006

This is a first person interpretation of a story told to me after the fact by some of the boys living on the street.

"The police are giving us an apartment! Are you coming or not?" The bunch of us hop into the police van, and see the grinning cops joking with us. They usually swear at us, but never are they happy to see us.

The city spins outside the van a few times and we pull up. "5th floor", we trapse up the stairs one after another. "Who can bust in the door?" We all jump up and start pounding on the door. There are no sounds inside, just echoes of beating on the door. John falls in on his side on top of the mangled door and there she is.

In the kitchen lies an old woman. She must have been dead for a while now.

The kitchen is moldy and smells like the bottom of a kitchen garbage can. On the woman's face is an old, spotted, bleached house shirt.

"The granddaughter was sent to the orphanage: there is no one left to carry her out boys. Here is a bag, let's get her down to the van, we'll talk about the apartment later." It is one of those houses where there are no corners, only worn edges and solidified gum in every corner, like stalactites growing in a cave. The corners fill in until the home rounds into its primal cave-like form. It is the malformation a home undergoes the world over when depression and poverty gang up and have been winning for a long time.

Dark, damp collections of carpets, clothes, shag strip in the bathroom; split toilet seat, scraps of wood, broken furniture characterize the apartment. We hear echoes in the walls, neighbors gurgling through the bathroom vent. We all find places around the body and carry her over the broken door, spiraling down together like the "Lord of the Cows" bug with each of us as a leg.

We carry the black bag down the five flights of stairs, and each of us knows what to do with death: laugh in its face. Except when we carried Mike out of the sewer last year after he got beat up. He drank himself till he choked on his own vomit. We all hated him anyway and you don't want him haunting you, just because you laughed.

So we tell jokes. We joke that the body would ride nicely on the top of the van, and we could aim and drop it down quite easily. The police are quiet for once. Those two hate us and love us at the same time. We all know it.

We scuffle out the back of the van, stopped at the morgue entrance at the back of the hospital. Placing the body on the hospital stretcher, for a moment I remembered my grandmother. Her smell; the way she always touched my ear and couldn't get me to eat enough. The way her bare feet looked in those jelly slippers in the summer, blackened toenails. I thought of my mother, and hell, the last time I saw my dad, my brother fishing, and more about my mother. I feel a nameless black blob coming up my chest and saying, "So do we get to use the apartment or not?"

"We'll see what the mayor's office works out, and we'll let you know. I am not sure it will do any good, you'll still be back at the corner smearing your dirty rags on car windows, pestering good people for change."

The police, as with the lawyer in the image utter hollow phrases, distance with blame and shame. They justify the dehumanization and exile to the sewers those homeless youth by utter hollow phrases that indicate that the case is hopeless: why help, why try, "They are going to do it anyway."

So in the world, and so in our internal experience, the hopelessness that we can change further exiles our own pain. For fear of the intensity overwhelming our inner system, we keep it at bay, keep our inner pain, holding young parts of ourselves in the psychological hidden sewers, only to have them embarrass us from time to time with unwanted appearances. By getting triggered and overwhelmed, becoming tearful out of the blue, we lose our playfulness, our joy, our spontaneity. Our exiled grief becomes the ticking time bomb we fear and vow to never let out.

So, to our intense emotional spillovers, our indifferent lawyer inside gives the old, "I'm fine, no big deal," hollow phrases and complete indifference, slamming down the sewer lid for a while longer.

GUIDED MEDITATION

Take a moment to find a place to be still and quiet. See if it feels ok to close your eyes and count 5 breaths. Check and see if you have emotional space to sit with this meditation.

Do you have any parts that tempt you towards indifference like this lawyer? Can you notice where the indifference shows up in your body? Rather than judging the indifferent part, can you find some curiosity about what makes it do what it does?

If you can be in a posture of curiosity or compassion, ask it what it is trying to protect you from by taking you to indifference at times? What is it afraid would happen if you were too understanding, too empathic? Can you appreciate the positive intention of the indifference? If you can, let it know you see what it is trying to do and appreciate the underlying goal.

Can you ask the indifferent part, if you could find a way to not get carried away with empathy would it allow more room for connecting with the pain of others? Is there a history of caring too much? Does getting close to the pain of others trigger your own pain that feels unbearable?

In some cases for the indifference to relax it needs to know you won't be overwhelmed by a pain-holding part or taken over by caregiving empathic parts that could give up your needs in the midst of the needs of others. Can you just take a moment and appreciate what you can of the way an indifferent part may be advocating for your needs not getting lost?

When this inner reflection feels complete for you, take a few moments to return your attention to your breath and to the space around you. Perhaps spend some moments reflecting on the experience and take any notes on things you would like to explore further later or insights you want to hold onto.

To engage with the high intensity level audio version described in the introduction, scan the QR code or visit tinyurl.com/rouault-meditations.

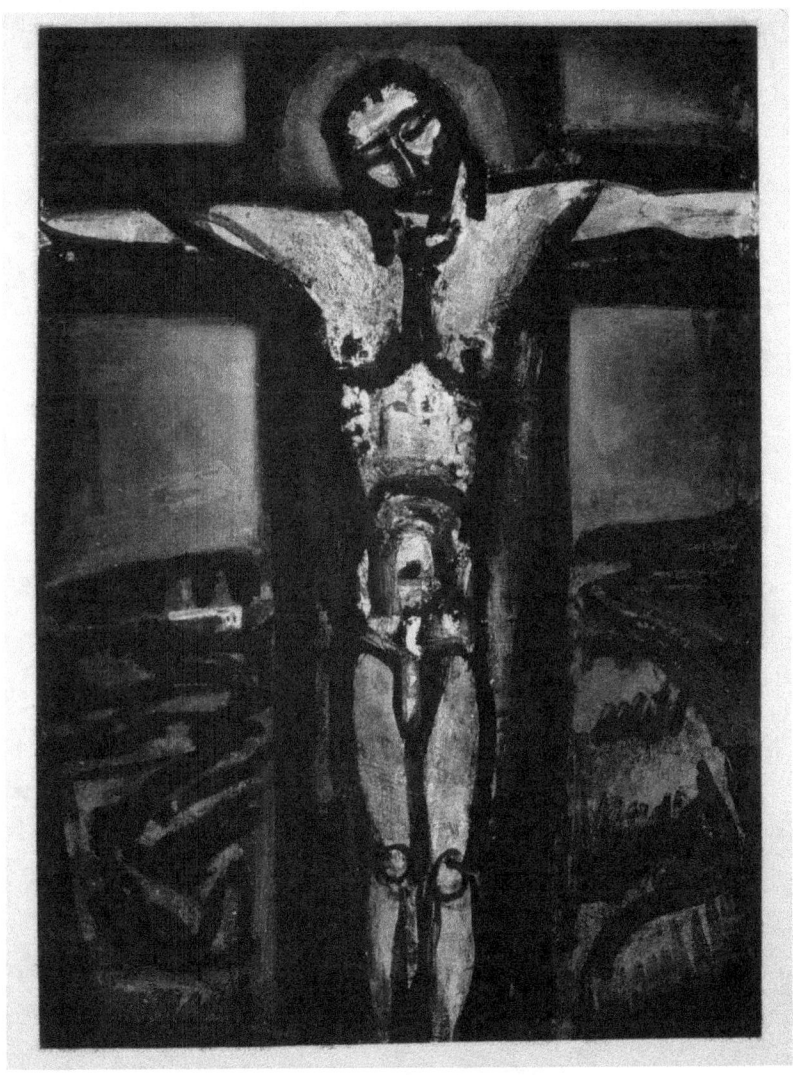

Plate 20

PLATE 20: FORGOTTEN

"sous un Jésus en croix oublié la"
"beneath a crucifix forgotten there"

The whole phrase of which this associated poetic line represents the last portion is, "The condemned is led away...his lawyer, in hollow phrases, proclaims his complete indifference... beneath a crucifix forgotten there."

In contrast with many of Rouault's more populated crucifixion scenes, this one shows Christ alone in an ambiguous landscape. Undistinguishable shapes, perhaps buildings, foliage, roads may be in the distance, but this is the forgotten crucifix. A crucifix would have stood above the judge in the courtroom before they were removed in 1905.[44] It is an up-close rendering of the courtroom crucifix that is now "forgotten there" in the courtroom by its removal.

Rouault gives the viewer a front seat to the tragedy of the cross: we see full torso and appendages without the hands and feet in the frame. Visually, the blackness of the wood of the cross pushes the flesh of Christ forward in the space, making it radiate light in contrast with the black around the body.

This image completes the scene if one reads the single sentence broken into three lines associated with these three pieces. First, the condemned went away; then, the lawyer seems to yawn through the process, disconnected, eyes closed, indifferent; and finally, this image carries the irony that this is all done in the absent presence of the image of the Christ, condemned and forgotten.

The halls of justice are shown to be indifferent to the suffering image of God. This indifference judges God in the disguise of the condemned. In Rouault's depiction, even in his condemnation and death, Christ radiates with the dignity of the image of God in human flesh.

Romania, 2001 - *Excerpt from letter to supporters*

Walking through town, I passed a dirt-stained little girl searching through a dumpster for any little treasure she could find. Later a Roma family sitting under a tree between the sidewalk and the busy street. Then closer to my house are several ladies, age and weather wrinkled, in the dignity of salvaged clothing and a little foil framed icon begging you to recognize the presence of Jesus in them and respond with some spare change.

There are the men who push their little two wheeled carts through the city searching for scraps of metal to trade for cash at recycling places around the city. They may be bold enough to push their clumsy little carts in the busy streets challenging glittering Alfa-Romeo's and ordinary Dacias alike for some smooth road. The downward, hopeless posture and dark complexion lifelessly pulling steel pieces looks like barbaric slavery. Apart from an annoyed honk or a choice word from some mocking children, these men are the invisible presence of Christ marching through the streets tied to their steel crosses.

Some of these men are the absent fathers of the children recovering from the night's fears by sleeping the morning away on the roofs of a restaurant, a toy store, a bookstore, and a flower shop. The Roma in the front of the building selling flowers give them some change for taking out their trash. The other kids on the park benches in the back share with them some laughs and fear and loneliness accompanied by getting high off of breathing in a little bag with a splash of silver metallic paint.

They each have a name and a story, their own scars and missing teeth, and a hidden beauty few ever wait to find. For most, these kids disappear behind a driver's side window shutting, among a row of Roma selling flowers, or under the ocean of materialism which keeps the world sophisticatedly drunk and blinded from acknowledging their humanity.

Maria is usually the last lady I pass on my way home. She is 78; lives with an 86-year-old in a 7th floor one room efficiency concrete apartment. Her pension doesn't quite cover her utility bills and leaves her to sit and beg at the foot of a mirror faced building at the end of a strip of clothing stores, travel agencies, cell phone dealers, and cash exchanges. It is painful for her to eat most food, as her teeth are giving up and no longer wanting to hold on. Though the pain in her gums and that of the loneliness and humiliation of begging each day are real and present to her, to most, she only represents the failure of the Romanian social system. She is but a political advertisement for the post-communist era, which fully embraces American consumerism and individualism leaving the poor and the elderly to fend for themselves.

A firm, confident knock gets me to my door. Through the peephole is the same woman who came a week ago with her baby asking for food. The other day, some moments after I opened the door to speak, my neighbor informed me that I need not open my door for "these kinds of people."

St. John Chrysostom said, "What plunges us into disaster is not so much our sins as our despair." In our despair and hopelessness we find ways of forgetting, of blinding ourselves to reality. We subscribe to the plentiful rationales cleverly disguising ways of forgetting the humanity of our neighbors and making us feel as though we have a valid Christ-like faith. The homeless are lazy alcoholics; street kids simply continue to choose to live on the streets; the Roma are thieves and unsociable; the elderly are a nuisance, and the poor are poor because of bad religion or personal choices absolving us of any moral responsibility. After all the reasons and popular wisdom rationalizing the poor and marginalized among us, they remain real human beings and the tangible presence of Jesus among us.

Despair teaches us to make the poor invisible. We hide them from our eyes behind bars, car windows, hide them under our overpasses, in the southern hemisphere, or south of our border. Despair teaches us to not feel guilty or take a second thought or look because they chose their fate or are simply not really fully human. Courage and faith call us to give our lives to the point of dying, suffering, and entering into the suffering and death experienced by the poor among us.

Romania, 2006

Dr. Daniel Hughes, a leading child attachment therapist, agreed to come to Romania to conduct sand tray therapy workshops for children's home workers in Constanza near the seaside. We were desperate to find new ways of helping the children we were working with and had recently come to understand the power of attachment styles on the children's well-being.

A group of 25 people huddled in a small room, focused on Dr. Hughes and his translator at the front of the room. He described the 4 basic attachment styles, foundations of his therapeutic work, the uses of sand tray therapy, and some examples in his development as a therapist.

Through the magic of the sand tray, little figures become the internal parts of the child, the victim, the protector, the perpetrators, the inner golden child, the rageful soldier, etc. There is no directing of the child to pick a certain figure: children naturally pick a figure that matches the internal circuit or part with how it would like to be represented.

In one particular case example, Dr. Hughes went through the history and background of a teen he had worked with, trauma upon trauma, loss of parents, abuse, shame, exile in the social system, exile from the family system and the exiling of his own dark emotion from his internal system. Vulnerability was too risky, so all vulnerable emotions were locked away deep inside.

Dr. Hughes detailed the therapeutic moves in the process, building trust with the adolescent, recognizing the fears of vulnerability, validation upon validation of internal and external struggle. Through the subconscious made concrete in the sand tray the inner drama was played out; the therapist descended into the hell of the teen's inner experience, down the ladder into the sewer, into the darkness, until he reached the inner exile sitting alone and hopeless, all but dead.

The young child in the darkness could hardly believe that someone had reached him; he was not alone anymore. And then the lost child was able to carefully share it all: the abuse, the shame, the pain suffered in silence over the years, the misunderstanding, the condemnation and contempt received from years of defensive anger and protective behaviors misunderstood as evil, badness, hopelessness, and irredeemability. The therapist sat with the boy in his darkest place, patiently, hopefully, allowing the young boy to be fully seen and heard, witnessed in a way that had never happened before.

Once the boy had unloaded everything he needed to, the two journeyed hand in hand out of the tomb, out of the sewer hiding, breaking through the street level into the light above.

I was shocked at the parallels between this hell-harrowing rescue of the inner wounded child of the teen, and the passion of Christ: the descent from distance and power, taking on of flesh, empathizing with our human state, the dramatic descent into hell, bringing out the lost captives, breaking the power of fear, shame and guilt, restoring the lost and exiled to their original dignity and purity, bringing souls out of separation and condemnation into new connection, new relationship, restored to the family, restored to themselves to new hope and new life.

One may go a step farther in interpreting Rouault's triptych here. Paul Hessert, in *Christ and the End of Meaning,* argues that because Christ was condemned and killed by the religious and political system of his day, he managed to strip bare the folly of those systems, showing their inability to produce righteousness. That system of external laws and rules actually managed to kill God. It is explained that Christ undid the religious systems, and completed all that was needed in order to restore humankind to relationship with God. This is echoed in the idea of "just believe," "no works necessary" to get to God.

Attunement to God, self and neighbor, and a focus on Universal Human Needs, becomes the restored tree of life, "the exiting from the game of right and wrong" which killed God. This may be what was understood as "life in the Spirit" replacing the law.[45] Psalm 51's version says,

"For thou desirest not sacrifice; else would I give it:
thou delightest not in burnt offering.
The sacrifices of God are a broken spirit:
a broken and a contrite heart, O God, thou wilt not despise."

Very quickly in the history of the Christian church, new sets of external rules and laws replaced the old – new rubrics for condemning our brother, sister, neighbor. So today, as in Rouault's day, there was a split between the Christ who identifies with all condemned people, the invisible people and parts of ourselves, and the popular religious Christ who is like the indifferent lawyer , judges with closed eyes, exiles and condemns to outer darkness.

Rouault's vision solidly stands on the version of Christ who is condemned with the condemned to the end of time. His Christ does not exile but only identifies, descends and rescues from darkness. This Christ makes visible the suffering of those who have become invisible to us, and eternally remembers all who seem to have been forgotten.

GUIDED MEDITATION

Take a moment to find a place to be still and quiet. See if it feels ok to close your eyes and count 5 breaths. Check and see if you have emotional space to sit with this meditation.

What is stirred in you as see Rouault's image of "Forgotten"? Try to just be present to what is awakened in your awareness. Do you have a part that hold feelings of feeling forgotten?

And are there protective parts that actively work to make sure you never feel forgotten again? Overlooked or ignored? If so notice how those protective parts show up for you. Recognize their effort and see if you can appreciate it.

See if there is openness and compassion to attend for a few moments to any part that has held those feelings of being forgotten, overlooked, or ignored. If it feels emotionally safe, try to connect with this part and ask it about what it experienced, what moments it holds onto around feeling forgotten? Try to just stay in a compassionate holding space with this part to hear whatever it brings up.

Ask the part what it was like to go through those rough times. Is there a way you can show that part you are not forgetting it now, not ignoring it, or overlooking it? See if there is anything you can do or say to the part that might help get what it needed so many years ago. Is there a way you can honestly assure that part you will return to it when it feels forgotten or needs your comfort?

After spending whatever time with your forgotten part, can you notice any more openness to the forgotten in your family, community, country or world? If not, just be curious about the parts that are still afraid of making that space for others.

When this inner reflection feels complete for you, take a few moments to return your attention to your breath and to the space around you. Perhaps spend some moments reflecting on the experience and take any notes on things you would like to explore further later or insights you want to hold onto.

To engage with the high intensity level audio version described in the introduction, scan the QR code or visit tinyurl.com/rouault-meditations.

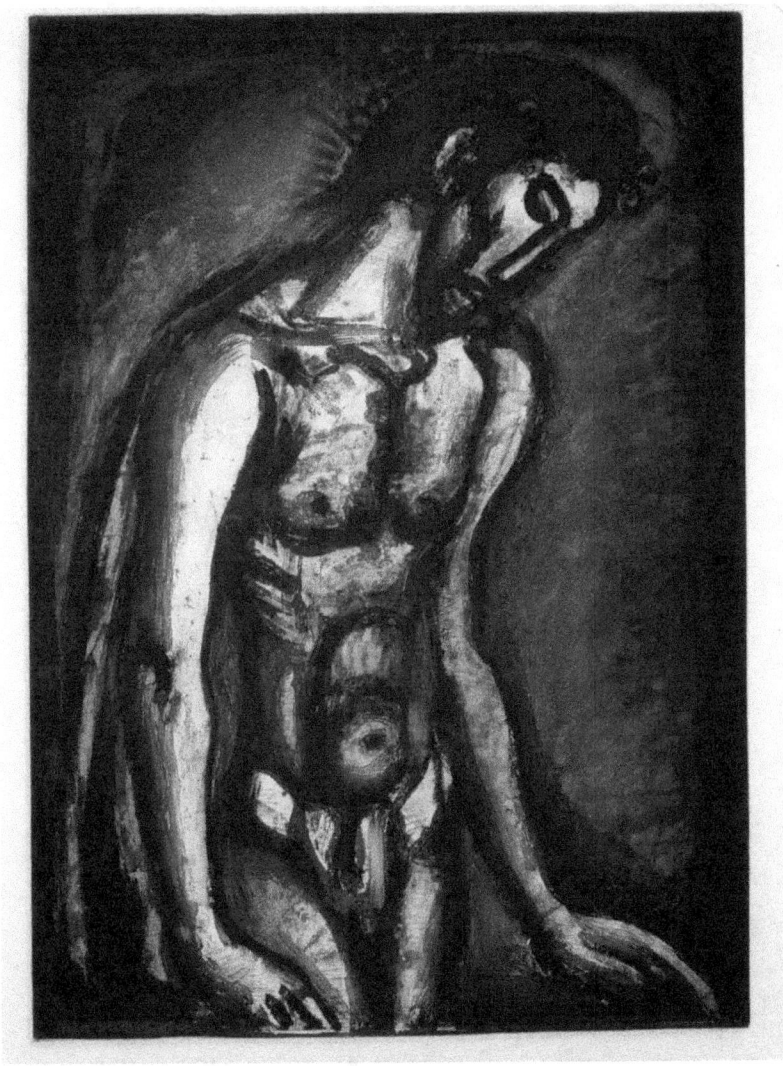

Plate 21

PLATE 21: OPPRESSED

"Il a été maltraité et opprimé et Il n'a pas ouvert la bouche."
"He was oppressed, and he was afflicted, yet he opened not his mouth."

The position and structure of this composition is almost identical to that of plate 18, the image of "the condemned." With a naked torso, the figure is bent over, prepared to receive more blows. Hands both curve downward, palms toward the ground to assure the viewer that this Christ has relinquished all, divested himself of all power and possession; he carries only shame and humiliation, oppression and affliction.

Here we are given a rough idea of the crown of thorns, mixed with some lines that seem to be Rouault's way of representing the halo, or radiating glory of his holy figure. This figure also has a subtle impression of the seamless robe worn almost like a cape, as a Roman soldier might wear it at the time. All of these elements point to the mocking and scourging of Christ, the crown of thorns mocking him as "King of the Jews." The cape mocks his priesthood perhaps, as the robe was seamless as would be that of a priest's liturgical garments. And then there is the nakedness, the humiliation and shame of standing in public unclothed. The curve of the body and the elongated nose bring some attention to the small mouth that is closed, as he "opened not his mouth." Shame and humiliation are met with silence.

There is a quiet meditative placidity to the suffering of Rouault's Christ. He seems to receive the suffering but connects on an interior level with suffering at large. Christ's suffering is an embodied empathic movement into the suffering of all those people who suffer in all times and places. With eyes closed, he perhaps even remains attentive to his own suffering without lashing out at his perpetrators, without protecting Himself against the pain, or exiling the anguish; but rather being present to it and in so doing becomes present to the pain of all human suffering.

The stanza of this piece comes from Isaiah 53:7, "He was oppressed and He was afflicted, Yet He opened not His mouth; He was led as a lamb to the slaughter, and as a sheep before its shearers is silent, so He opened not His mouth" (NKJV). The liturgical imagery includes the lamb sacrificed, the seamless garment of a priest, the all-powerful King who tears down the exiling distance reconciling the powerless. There is now no one who is afflicted or oppressed alone: Rouault's Christ suffers with all sufferers.

His silence becomes meaningful as well. When no words comfort, the silent suffering of Christ is present and speaks the only word necessary, "I am here, suffering with you, you are not alone."

Kentucky, 2000 - *Journal entry*

I saw a part of the 1992 Wuthering Heights movie based on the Emily Brontë novel, and it is the Roma, adopted brother Heathcliff, that is the wicked villain who the innocent girl falls for out of true friendship and a lot of unconscious pity. It carries the theme of Woman as failed savior, Roma as genetically flawed and unredeemable, and the system of decorum, family blood lines, and remnants of feudalism that damn the young lovers to eternal torment.

The love they have is real but impossible. They are killed by their love, trapped in the unjust social norms and economies. The horse-loving Roma turns into the psychotic devil who digs up the grave of his dead lover so he can lie beside her once again.

These long nights working in the hotel reception can conjure the feeling that you are stuck in the dark, or that awful idea of being buried alive, left powerless in the darkness, to borrow a little of Brontë's gothic style. It is that dream of being unable to rise when danger comes. It takes me back to another long night I thought would never end.

It started with a three-hour trip for a doctor's appointment that I didn't realize wasn't till the next day.

Last time we came to Bucharest was our last to stay at the Ionescu's little apartment. Last time in town, we had shown up at the tiny one room apartment, and the youngest daughter cracked the door, smiled and passed a note through, leaving the door chained. Her father had given me a package to take with me on my trip to the big city to deliver to his other daughter. When he delivered it, he saw I was taking Ion with me, and that Ion was Roma. We use Roma rather than "gypsy" now, as it is what they call themselves. Roma means 'man' in the Romani language, as opposed to 'slave' which is the meaning of the Romanian word used for Roma in Romanian and other eastern European languages. The word 'gypsy' comes from the mistake that somehow Roma came from Egypt, rather than India. Ian Hancock's ethnography, *We are the Romani People,* tells the story[46].

The note given upon arrival read, "You can stay tonight but please never come to stay again with "gypsies." I felt the sting of racism and the exhilaration of being in the middle of a real racist event. I am not just another white guy, or probably I am the white guy trying to save the black guy and being a racist in my own special way.

So today, or yesterday rather, we were scheduled for an MRI. Ion is an 18-year-old Roma kid, mostly raised by his grandfather, a hat wearing loan shark, street corner smoking, neighborhood king of sorts. In 1856 Roma were officially released from 500 years of slavery, and never given any reparations for the oppression, leaving them to fend for themselves in a highly racialized society. Most found trades from the skills they had gained while enslaved.

Ion had moved out – well, he was kicked out of grandpa's house for not producing, which meant not giving up enough begging money each night to pay his keep. He was surviving on the streets by his own devices. I had known of him for some years. Some would see him following people with a psychotic look in his eyes till they would give him money to go away.

He moved into the home we set up for kids wanting to come off the streets. His mother had run from the hospital when he was a newborn, stealing him away from the system before he received a birth certificate. We got him after a solid year of paperwork and waiting, trying to prove that he exists, and to prove that he is not a criminal trying to create a new identity.

I began taking him to a free clinic in Bucuresti, a 3.5-hour train ride from our town. The first appointment he sat on the table in his shorts, and the doctor pointed at every scar from head to toe one by one and Ion gave time, date and event details and persons involved for each one. I was traumatized just watching the wounds wind into beaten Roma kid stories.

He gave the data as if he were telling what he had for lunch. They were marks of invincibility, proof that he could not be killed, could not be conquered. No beating or 'accident' could tame his will. They were not to be mourned or complained. They were his trophies, his way to stick his middle finger out to the world and say, "Go for it, try to kill me, it will just make me feel more convinced you can't move me."

So now when we got to the hospital where the MRI was scheduled and waited in line. The appointment time came, and we waited another hour and a half, until we were told that we were on the schedule for the next day. So much for staying at Ionescu's apartment; now I had to try Sorin the New Testament professor. I couldn't stay in a hotel with a kid, it just doesn't look right. White male and Roma kid checking into a hotel always looks pretty shady, especially considering all the white male predators seen and caught in Bucuresti, trying to exploit the 1000-some homeless youth around central station.

I finally get a hold of Sorin. We can't stay with him; he lives with his mother in a one room apartment. He meets us at his office and sets us up in a conference room. We look at the icons, the leftover hors devours from an earlier meeting that day, and check e-mail on the computer while Sorin goes out trying to get us a place to stay the night.

Only now do I imagine that the fact that I was with a Roma kid was the problem that made his return take some three hours. I was wiped out and Ion was restless. Finally, Sorin came with keys. He had acquired some keys to an empty dorm room in the seminary. It was summer and most students had vacated the building. We would walk up dark quiet corridors, all concrete walls painted to shoulder level with glossy paint and to the ceiling with chalk.

The room was what a new student starting in a new room would see: hard wood floors, empty wardrobes, beds without linens, windows without treatments, empty walls. By this point I was just grateful for a resting place. I bought toothbrushes and Sorin gave us some toilet paper, but other than that I had my daypack and voice recorder for telling the time.

Ion quickly laid down on his bed, a vinyl mattress, and tried to sleep. His breathing got louder as he fell asleep, and I was left awake alone in the room, blinking with the fruit of 10 years of capitalism blinking through the windows in the form of apartment top flashing billboards. My head was pounding from the day of eating greasy fast food, Turkish sandwiches, and cheap coffee. I had nothing for my headache. I rolled on the sweaty vinyl, trapped between blinking neon, stinging mosquitoes, pounding heartbeats felt in my aching head, and the turning of Ion's against his vinyl mattress.

It was around 3a.m., August 7, 2004, in Bucuresti, Romania. I know I fell asleep because I woke up. Ion called out to me from across the room. He said calmly that his nose was bleeding. I got up and turned on the light to see that there was blood all over his mattress, all over the wood floor and spots were still dripping from his head. We unrolled toilet paper, and smeared blood around, I got him to lie down again after wiping up his mattress, I showed him how to pinch his nose and hold his feet up on the end of the bed. The shock of the sight of blood everywhere had my heart racing, and the pounding of my head pushed my eyes shut. I gave up on making the blood marks disappear on the floor, shut off the light and lay back down. "God help me get through this night."

The room was smoldering hot, and there was not even a shimmer of hospitality, of home. It was a desolate hole of concrete: hard, merciless, and radically unconcerned.

I tipped again on that waking-sleeping point, back and forth, that point where you fall into yourself and then into your stable sleep self that has no geography, but the place you sleep most often. I tipped into Ion's mind, into the account of every scar. I tipped into the room where we were received guests – but only guests that could be trusted with the concrete of a prison cell. I tipped into the coffin for a second, that feeling that you are completely helpless in your own skin, in your own dark damned Roma skin: determined by it to be an ass, to return the expectations of the world, because they will accept nothing else. I tipped into that moment 17 years ago when Ion told

188

himself, "To hell with the world. I am going to exist by my own force of will, if nobody else gives a damn."

Coca Cola flashed in reverse neon script, and I hate Coke. My head pounded and my stomach turned the Turkish sandwich over again. I can run from this kid, but he is me. If God forsakes him, I am damned too. If he is left living in a dark casket, so am I. Will this night ever end?

My mattress burped under me as I shifted again, laughing at my overly serious thoughts. We have a room to stay in and the night can't last forever.

"He was oppressed, and he was afflicted, yet he opened not his mouth." It may be important to note that though Rouault uses high contrast in many images, in this particular piece, this image of Christ lies in a pool of dark grays and blacks. This of course intensifies that luminosity of his flesh, the rough-patched, scumbled strokes which become the marks, scars and wounds. In his body dwells the stories of oppression.

It is no wonder this was the kind of Christ that enslaved peoples have found hope in, even when the messengers were their oppressors. They saw through the classist, sexist and racist readings of scripture, the Christ who is always suffering with, afflicted with, the oppressed.

It is impossible to oppress, to silence and disregard other humans without doing it to Christ himself. This is the mystery Rouault counts on: Christ in all and through all, the light that illuminates all things, the love that suffers all things, unifying the whole humanity in Himself.

GUIDED MEDITATION

Take a moment to find a place to be still and quiet. See if it feels ok to close your eyes and count 5 breaths. Check and see if you have emotional space to sit with this meditation.

Rather than being a world of oppressed and oppressors, consider that we are in a world in which the dialectic happens inside of us. Our internal conflict is mirrored externally. My inner oppression of dark parts of me, shadow parts, energize my political and social actions to exile those people and groups that represent my own shadows. For example, it is more fruitful to let go of the thought that you are unilaterally either racist or not racist, instead notice that you most likely have racist parts and nonracist empathic parts and work with each of those parts.

Who are those people, political groups, countries, or teams that get me most activated? Who makes you angry? Can you sit with this anger for a minute and ask, what it is about these enemies of yours that makes you so riled up? What is it inside of you that gets defensive, protective, or combative when you think of them? Why does it matter to you so much? What feels threatened?

Now, are there parts of yourself which they represent? Maybe parts that feel weakness, shame, insecurity, hopelessness, powerlessness? What has cut you off from your vulnerable parts, that makes it hard to offer compassion to them? What are you afraid will happen if your vulnerability is revealed? Have you come to believe perhaps that acknowledging suffering is weakness, and intolerable?

Can you hold space for your own parts that represent the things you loath in others? Can you ask the loathing to give you space to just care for these vulnerable places? Can you hear their story, be present to the pain they hold, knowing that you are strong enough to handle intense emotions?

Can you find a compassion posture to offer the part some care and understanding for the intention, knowing it isn't the whole picture? Can you see and hear your oppressed parts so that you can stop oppressing them and those people in the world that represent them to you?

What makes you afraid to be compassionate to your inner suppressed parts? To find understanding, a new connection with them, and perhaps new ways to honor the deeper needs without the obnoxious strategies on the surface.

See if you can find any softening towards your enemies inner and outer. You may need to take time later to return to some of the parts arising in this section. For now, just appreciate how many parts may be involved in our participation in both inner and outer oppression and how they are intimately linked.

When this inner reflection feels complete for you, take a few moments to return your attention to your breath and to the space around you. Perhaps spend some moments reflecting on the experience and take any notes on things you would like to explore further later or insights you want to hold onto.

To engage with the high intensity level audio version described in the introduction, scan the QR code or visit tinyurl.com/rouault-meditations.

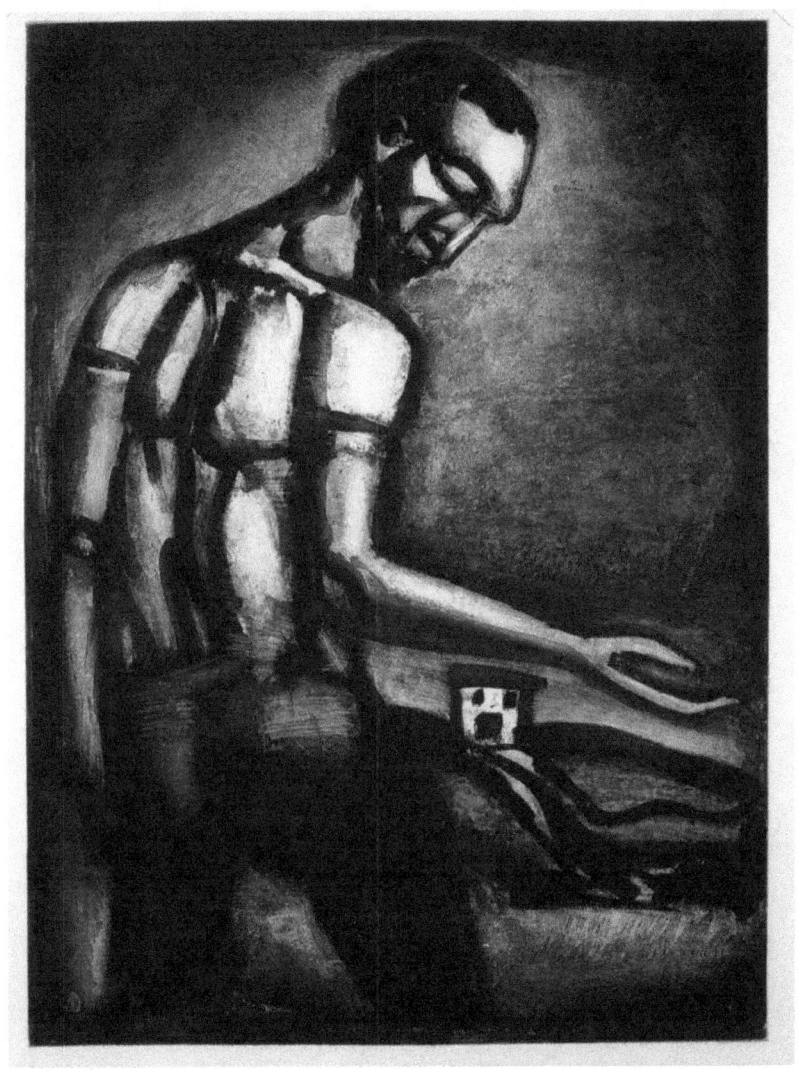

Plate 22

PLATE 22: SOWING

"En tant d'ordres divers, le beau métier d'ensemencer une terre hostile."
"In so many different orders, the noble vocation of sowing in hostile land."

The arm in a near right angle, the facial focus on the hand and the gentle curve of the body radiating from its center point from the hand, all draw the viewer to the action happening in the open hand. It is an open hand, offering its contents to fall to the ground, but carefully, with gentle guidance and care. Rouault takes us tenderly into the human dilemma of deciding to try when it seems there may be no hope, when there is no guarantee of return, when our cause seems hopeless.

Following the "He was oppressed" image of Christ suffering abuse, the composition of this piece is similar in the positioning of the body; but rather than seeing the front of the torso of Christ, here we see the back of a man turned to the side. Here the figure is clothed in a white, bright shirt. The brightness of his clothes perhaps recalls the Miserere Psalm, "Purify me with hyssop till I am clean, wash me till I am whiter than snow." Christ is purged in the last image, and now we have a simple farmer sowing seed. Christ's right hand is turned downward in the previous image, emptying himself to the end, grasping onto nothing. And now here is the gentle and careful sowing of seed, spreading it out with the ancient hand-sowing technique lost in most places today.

The stanza challenges the viewer to consider what is meant by, "in so many orders or levels of work," "hostile land," and the "nobility" of this vocation. Georges Rouault said, "It is not the worldly eclecticism of knowledge of many things that enriches, but perseverance in a favorable furrow and loving silent effort of a whole life." [47]

Rouault perhaps saw his own vocation as sowing in a hostile land, to create art that followed the vision he had of the world. In many ways he was an outsider, never fully embraced by the Catholic Church, though he remained a faithful Catholic. He was a devoutly religious person in a time of diminishing status and popularity of religious systems as faithful guides for modern people. And the form of his art, while related to modern art of his time, did not fit neatly into categories of art movements. He seemed to sow his art in a hostile land with no guarantee of return.

Living in France through two world wars, he must have contemplated the act of sowing in a time of great upheaval and may have drawn the image from real life scenes of French farmers working in the time of war. Sowing seed is a concrete act of hope, counting on stability over time, hoping at least that if the sower does not reap the fruit, someone along the way will. Perhaps this is part of what makes "sowing in a hostile land" a noble vocation. It defies what seems to be futility, acts on faith and hope, seeing a possible good outcome when it seems an unlikely bet.

The artist's hope is that somebody, somewhere will find the fruit of their work, understand it in some meaningful way, and commune with them across time and space. I am aware that as I write this it has been over a hundred years now since the *Miserere* series was sown in faith and hope by Rouault.

In seeing the sower in the context of the previous Christ image, John 12:24 is recalled, "...unless a grain of wheat falls into the ground and dies, it remains alone; but if it dies, it produces much grain." The Romanian Orthodox tradition of offering sweet wheat grains to the poor on behalf of the departed comes from this passage. As any child who plants a seed will ask, "Will it ever come up?"

Finally, there is a house and a road in the image. The house has the simple door and two windows that create an open mouth and eyes, as if the house itself is afraid, contrasting with the hopeful act of sowing seed. Rouault creates atmosphere and contrast with his textured sky that sets off the black edges of the figure, creating almost a halo of light around this "noble vocation" in action.

This moment is the time of decision: to hold onto the seed for a better year, better soil, less risky land not under the threat of war. Or to sow now what you have, where you are, and to believe it is good enough.

Romania, 2002

Two weeks ago, together as a community, we celebrated Romanian Labor day with a picnic across the Danube. As Galati has grown into a big steel town over the years, the river continues to serve to contain the city's swarming activity and growth within its banks. It carries raw iron ore up to the steel mill and floats back down refined steel products. It serves as a park and a respite for weary city folk, a cheap romantic walk along the shore, free food for patient fishermen, and a bath for those daring to go in. Though it serves the life of the city, the river claims a number of lives every year: drowning victims, macho guys thinking they could make it across, or drunken careless men lost in grief.

We met at the ferry early in the morning. This floating flatbed transports trucks, cars, shopping-bag-carrying foot passengers, and on Labor day sunglass-wearing cool guys taking their girls out for the day, charcoal bags, fresh vegetables, water jugs, and our mixed-bag community: developmentally delayed kids, street kids, Americans, modestly dressed overworked Romanian caregivers, a Welsh kid with a big smile, small kids with their moms out for the day with us, and a few kids that looked familiar to me but I didn't remember their names. The ferry isn't a magical little winged thing, but a magical big smoke-spewing, gas-guzzling work whale which transports dreamers out of the city into a dreamy primitive world on the other side of the river. It works its magic on-the-hour every hour, whether you realize it or not. A deep boat horn blew and we were off.

With a heave and some screeching metal and rubber the ferry heaves into its secure dock for the unloading of semis, tourist cars, Roma sunflower seed sellers, and sun seekers. Due to the fact that there are no bridges across the Danube for miles around, there is a stark contrast of the city on one side and fields and distant hills on the other side. With the river crossing you are immediately in a totally different place, country roads, sparse country one-story homes, farmland, grazing animals and grasslands. Our crew marched together a half a mile or so down river to a spot along the river with grassy molehills and some shade trees, and a place to play soccer and a little volleyball.

After setting up the net, our kids piled onto the newly charted volleyball court, which was set up in the same direction as the river to avoid losing the ball downstream. Nine and ten on a side, everyone ready to serve and no one really understanding the rotation, my Romanian skills were stretched as far as my patience, to keep a game together.

Two little boys who had been playing together kicked their flat soccer ball onto the court. Their eyes got big, being sure that they were now in the game. They were quickly moved off to allow the rest of us to continue our big kid's game. Florin and Daniel continued on their way playing their toddler version of soccer in another area. Florin is the oldest son of our godchildren. Daniel was his cousin and best friend.

A couple of months later I got a call saying Daniel had been killed at an intersection where he was with his cousins, begging. His older cousin forgot about him; he stepped into the street at the wrong time and now he is dead.

My friend and godson Alex, one of Daniel's uncles, asked if I would come with my camera to the funeral and take pictures for the family. We arrived at eleven in the morning at the mother's house. The open casket had already been carried out of the house to begin its procession to the church. The body had been with the family in the house since his death a few days prior. They requested assistance from the state to bury the boy, but the mayor said he couldn't give any response till Wednesday. It was only Monday and the body had already started to decompose in new summer heat. The family decided they couldn't wait any longer to bury Daniel, and today – Tuesday

– was now the day. Alex hadn't slept for two days straight and had already lit another cigarette.

I found Alex to give him something, and he was mumbling about the priest giving them a hard time and wanting money or something. The pallbearers started moving following a deacon carrying a cross and a leafless branch decorated with different treats Daniel would have liked.

There is nothing like the horror of seeing a dead child. His poor eyes were bulging and puffy. His chin was covered to hide some unbearable deformation probably from the accident or the decomposing of the body. The mother followed directly behind the casket weeping, howling, and calling out to her boy to come back to her. "Come home with me my boy, don't go away. I'll play with you whatever you want, just come back to mamma, don't leave your mamma, our house is a desert without you, you are my little flower, come back home with me…" She hobbled along, half carried by her sisters. She wore all black except for the cheap, rubber, blue plaid foam slippers.

The casket was set on the funeral table built to hold an adult corpse. Thick black plastic protected the table from dripping candle wax. A candle holder placed at his head contained the handful of 1,000 lei candles. On the body was placed an icon of the mother of God, with a soft wax candle spiraling down onto the perpendicular surface of the icon, to hold itself upright. His baseball hat and matchbox cars lay by his head. Candles were lit and placed at each corner of the casket. The mother continued to cry out loud while the priests sang, "Christ is risen from the dead, with death conquering death, and giving life to those in the grave," and. "Holy God, holy mighty, holy immortal, have mercy on us…"

The gospel from John 6:27-33 was read over Daniel's body:

"Do not labor for the food which perishes, but for the food which endures to everlasting life, which the Son of Man will give you, because God the Father has set His seal on Him." Then they said to Him, "What shall we do, that we may work the works of God?" Jesus answered and said to them, "This is the work of God, that you believe in Him whom He sent." Therefore they said to Him, "What sign will You perform then, that we may see it and believe You? What work will You do? Our fathers ate the manna in the desert; as it is written, 'He gave them bread from heaven to eat.'" Then Jesus said to them, "Most assuredly, I say to you, Moses did not give you the bread from heaven, but My Father gives you the true bread from heaven. For the bread of God is He who comes down from heaven and gives life to the world" (NKJV).

I was directed to take some pictures of the body from the foot of the casket. There was just enough light to be able to shoot without a flash. The church had large windows, and the group of twenty mourners was crying, making the sign of the cross, fixing falling or burning-out candles, arranging the body, watching the priest and the cantor, and swatting flies away from little Daniel's face. The snaps of my camera seemed profane in the moment, but no one seemed shocked by the noise of the shutter. Another guy directed me to exit ahead of the procession out of the church, so I could get a shot of the casket as it came down the stairs. "Lord have mercy, Lord have mercy, Lord have mercy, in the name of the father and the Son and the Holy Spirit. Amen..." I fumbled with the camera but got the shot off as the moaning group slid down the stairs for the march to the gravesite.

The casket was put into the back of a one-ton flatbed with wood sides. The family and all the kids piled in, and I was asked to ride too, so I could get some shots as soon as we got to the cemetery. Four kids held two ribbons in an 'X' over the body as we drove through the city. Little Florin found my lap. He pointed and giggled at the live chicken in the corner of the truck bed and then made pecking sounds and threatened to peck at my face. He would reach out to balance himself by grabbing the corner of his best friend's casket. He noticed his shoes, the purple gauze covering his jeans, the hands that lay limp over a handkerchief, and he noticed the matchbox cars, turned and smiled and said, "cars...I have one too..."

The mother found her place at the head of her son and continued to howl out to Daniel at ambulance-siren volume to come back to her. To my right were four more kids. A little brother sat in his sister's arms. Another little girl sat by herself under the cross and the tree branch, bearing cookies and pop. An uncle yelled out to the driver and the priests the way to go past their house to mourn there for a moment. As we passed the intersection where Daniel stepped into traffic, they asked me to stand up and take a photo of the intersection. Stop lights, cars, the courthouse, shops and venders, concrete, street signs, ads, white lines and faded grey lines came into the viewfinder. I sat back down and Florin found his place again on my lap.

We stopped in front of every church on the way for the priest and cantor to pray.

The cemetery was gray under the presence of the steel factory, which is the horizon, the whole horizon. It is panoramic, as the cemetery below is wide. Smokestacks and girders, cranes and blank square buildings, with the sea of crosses from the cemetery below. These were the shots. A dead little boy, waling mother, uncles ruffled about the insensitivity of the priest, and kids, Daniel's buddies all around with big blank eyes trying to make some sense of the spectacle they walk through. We passed the grave of children who died of AIDS when their medications ran out, we passed the grave of Annamaria and of Lazarus, our son miscarried at three months.

There were other snapshots my mind took involuntarily: the priest hurrying the mother away so they could close the casket, passing out cigarettes, solidarity of the street boys at the grave, a last shot of the closed casket, the invite to a meal at the mother's home, Elena asking why his eyes were swollen, Valerica's "Let it be a lesson to you kids," the lady at the church cursing "those drivers," the blame on the cousin who was supposed to watch him, and the aunt who had custody and the mother at work when it all happened.

I spent a lot of time trying to lock out some of these excruciating memories. After I developed the film and printed a set of photos, I handed the negatives and photos to the family, hoping to never see these images again. The death haunted me. It piled onto that part of me that held onto the grief over our miscarried first pregnancy, Lazarus, the death of a 10-year-old I knew in high school, and of my grandmother when I was only a few years old. It just felt like a large ball of gack, tar threatening to catch me forever, debilitating me from being able to do my life. It felt dangerous to get too close to this hopelessness.

Sometime later I went to confession at the hospital chapel, confessing my hopelessness and frustration. What is the point of all of this work, if it shows so little results? The kids still die, still huff glue, still get beaten by drunk dads, still get exploited?"

The priest responded gently, "it is not our business to worry about results, but to love, show compassion, and do what we can to honor the image of God in those He sends our way."

My complaint about results probably said more about my privilege, the privilege of "effectiveness" and the avoidance of hopeless situations. Those with less power, the poor, the marginalized, and widows have little choice. Rouault's piece captures, not only wartime fears of futility, but the standard state of affairs for those without voice and power: they must sow with no guarantee of return.

They are the peasant heroes of all times and places who endure, fight for their children, and persist through oppression, injustice, and being demonization. They are the ones who embody "the noble vocation of sowing in hostile land."

The Miserere Psalm says, "Sacrifice to God is a broken spirit, a broken, contrite heart you never scorn." I do not believe that God enjoys people feeling terrible. A broken spirit and contrite heart is one in which the walls have been torn down. The point is not the breaking, but the uniting of hearts that is enabled by the breaking. Breaking paves the way for restoring the presence of the divine in the temple of the human heart.

I believe another layer of this corresponds to the Internal Family Systems Therapy model's understanding of exiles. Inner exiles hold the pain and brokenness, shame and guilt of our inner systems. Protectors are walls, those parts that shield the exiles from receiving more pain. Pride, anger, gluttony, lust, avarice. etc., protect the exiles from further suffering while typically increasing the chances of more pain.

One could read the above verse as "God will never scorn your exiled parts; in fact, that is exactly the place He would like access to, so He can heal you and know you and be known to you in the depths of your suffering parts." The scripture here focuses on the reconciliation between God in the holy place of the human heart, but this seems just as true on the level of our own relationship to our exiled parts.

Rouault is always asking his viewer to consider themselves. Here he asks if we will choose the noble vocation, to sow or not sow, love or withhold love, open ourselves to compassion or freeze up in hopelessness? "In so many different orders, the noble vocation of sowing in hostile land."

GUIDED MEDITATION

Take a moment to find a place to be still and quiet. See if it feels ok to close your eyes and count 5 breaths. Check and see if you have emotional space to sit with this meditation.

Can you recognize a part in you that wants to sow, to hope, to push ahead? Is there also a part in you that is afraid to sow, afraid to hope because of the potential disappointment, the pain of unrealized hopes? And maybe see if there is a part that just holds hopelessness in your system, that when it gets out it seems to shut everything down? Sometimes the way to living in more genuine hope is siting with and understanding the hopeless parts better rather than avoiding them. If this makes sense to you, see if there is some openness to engaging with the part of you that holds hopeless feelings in your system.

If you feel comfortable enough, see if you can just see how you might notice the hopeless part show up in your body, or any images or sensations connected to it. Once you do that see how you feel towards this hopeless part. If you start to feel the intensity of the part ask it to give you some space so you can help it.

If you are feeling a lot of anxiety of anger towards the part, just stop here and consider returning to it with a therapist at another time. Just take a moment to acknowledge that the hopeless part is there and you will work to get to it when the time is right.

If you feel compassion, curiosity and openness to this hopeless part, see if you can just ask it to share with you in a way that is not overwhelming, some of the moments and memories that made it feel things were hopeless. You first task is just to help the part feel heard and understood. After that you can see if you have some wisdom and perspective that might speak to address the reasons this part began to feel hopeless.

Help this part as you might a small child that has been stuck in a way of seeing things that isn't quite accurate. Sometimes presence, understanding, and connection is the answer to hopelessness. If that resonates for you just sit with the part and give it some sense of your attention and compassionate presence.

When this inner reflection feels complete for you, take a few moments to return your attention to your breath and to the space around you. Perhaps spend some moments reflecting on the experience and take any notes on things you would like to explore further later or insights you want to hold onto.

To engage with the high intensity level audio version described in the introduction, scan the QR code or visit tinyurl.com/rouault-meditations.

Plate 23

PLATE 23: LONELY

"Rue des Solitaires"
"Street of the Lonely"

Rue des Solitaires presents us with a quintessential European side street. The blacks, grays, and lights produce a shadowy overcast atmosphere in which the scene lives. The structure of the composition depends on the hard diagonals created by the roof lines and street lines, much like the school art class perspective exercise of creating a one-point perspective drawing. High contrast in the image draws one's attention to the building that occupies the center of the print. In this image in particular, as seems to happen with architecture in his other works, the buildings have a very living, personal feel to them: the dark holes for doors and windows take on a certain personality of watching ghosts or skulls with hollowed-out eye sockets. They are not the warm, hospitable homes full of light and warmth in a dark damp landscape: these buildings give off the feeling of cave entrances. Working through World War I, they could perhaps be abandoned, windowless structures.

When one looks carefully down the street, there seem to be two indistinct figures on the street. They mostly blend into the streetscape, but for their round heads with small sparks of light atop amorphous body forms. In light of the accompanying stanza, it would make sense that these figures are almost invisible, blending into the dark barrenness of the scene. The proportions of the buildings to the figures emphasizes their smallness, their seeming insignificance. This is in stark contrast with Rouault's many figures that fill the space with imposing torsos, leaving the viewer little else to see but the person up close. Here we are left squinting to try to make out these distant figures. This distance gives the viewer an increased sense of separation, of aloneness.

There seem to be a couple of trees in the distant background that are reminiscent of Plate 10, "In the neighborhood of suffering," the broken, dismembered tree that stands in contrast to the nurturing of life of the mother in that image. Here, it seems we are left with the desolation, emptiness, barrenness without the nurturing, without the maternal presence holding the child, but rather these two ambiguous figures in an abandoned street or alley.

As Christ said, the rocks would cry out if the people were silent; here is the feeling that the loneliness of creatures is too much even for these animated-inanimate buildings.[48] In Rouault's streetscapes, the structures carry a humanity, even a compassion, where human nurturing is absent. It is as if God sees the lonely in the form of these silent structures. Regardless of whether Rouault saw it exactly this way, as anyone who has walked down a lonely street like this has experienced, there is always an eerie feeling of being watched through the many windows and doorways, as if there is a presence even where none is seen.

And perhaps the second figure is like the 4th man in the furnace in the Old Testament story of the three youths in the fire, an angel, a divine presence within the painful fire of loneliness. The composition and subject parallels his painting, *Christ in the Suburbs, 1920–24.* Where the presence of Christ is explicitly with those in the street.

Romania, 2004

The Hotel Buchegi was our go-to cheap place to stay when we had to go to pick up visitors from the airport in Bucharest. We got off the train and crossed the couple of streets and got a room. Having gotten rid of our extra overnight bags, we left to find some dinner. I remember it being cold with no snow or ice. The asphalt turned white from cold and leftover salt from the previous snow. As we walked on a crowded sidewalk, I noticed to my right in the street a manhole cover lifting up and sliding of its own accord to one side. Glancing down the hole, one could see three sets of eyes catching light from above and shimmering like candles. There was a stunned stillness for a brief moment, a recognition of common humanity, but also the meeting of very alien existences. How does one come to find the underground tunnels a solution to cold and homelessness? And just as alien, the youth looking up perhaps ask themselves, "How do people live when not constantly concerned about safety, warmth and basic sustenance?" What would that even be like?

And so it goes with our internal exiled parts. Things get suddenly uncomfortable when they break out of their locked-away places, of their underground prisons, and show their faces in the form of an emotional breakdown, internally freezing at strange times or noticing emotional intensity at a movie that is a little beyond the movie's plot. There is a part that wants to keep that manhole cover shut, and keep those uncomfortable pain, shame, and suffering-holding parts away and hidden.

In my work as a therapist, I have a working hunch that our loneliness is the feeling of distance from our exiled parts, as mentioned in the reflection on Plate 5. In fact, we can actually be very much physically alone and yet experience a sense of communion and togetherness with other people. Few have never had the experience of being in a group of people and feeling quite alone. Somehow loneliness may have less to do with the numbers of people around us as it has to do with our own inner exiles being isolated and lost on the lonely streets of our internal world, without a nurturing home. In relationship, we may filter or exile important parts of ourselves, leaving our encounters with others on surface level, and our vitality locked under a steel manhole cover.

Romania, 2003

"Can we go visit the grave site?" That was all it took to slide the manhole cover off of my grief. I was a wreck. I was trying so hard to avoid this black gunk in my heart that had been weighing me down. Our little miscarried child was dead. What was there to do about it now? What would going to the grave site do now but make me face it? The weight of that black gunk just felt so heavy and it seemed to threaten my very existence. It carried with it so many questions and doubts, my illusions that the world was always good and safe, that if I held up my side and was perfect, then God would make everything go well for me. But this was even more than a challenged belief system, this was hard, unrelenting, heavy sadness. I have often found a solid steel cover for this pain by intellectualizing my way out of hard feelings.

Ohio, 1985

In the grove of trees was nothing to harm. Parents were talking or doing whatever adults do in the American Legion Hall, while my brother and I were in the gravel parking lot enjoying the innocent fun of throwing stones into the wooded grove, carelessly trying to hit a tree trunk or hear the stone split through leaves. We were a little restless after having been at the hall all day, and just in a place of finding something interesting to occupy ourselves.

This bubble of innocent play was shattered when one of my stones hit the side view mirror of my grandfather's car. I remember a pit in my stomach and the fear of having to tell. This is not what I was trying to do. I went and told my parents what happened, and they made me tell my grandfather. Upon telling him, there was a shearing disapproval, like a fiery blade cutting right through me. "You stupid kid, careless shenanigans," the "no" to my core being, slammed down like a sledgehammer. "You are not good." The pain was intolerable. "Never again," said a voice deep inside of me, "Whatever it takes, never again." The searing pain of this I feel even today as I sit in it, and the internal motor which guards me day and night, "never go there again, never get caught by that sledgehammer again."

I was caught a few years later as an early teenager. My grandfather had been a hobby sailor and a golfer and held himself as a classy guy throughout his life, despite financial struggles. When he lost everything in bankruptcy, he moved in and we turned our dining room into a bedroom for him, with curtains to divide off the room.

In the midst of this, he was trying to sell his outboard motor, the last vestige of his sailing career, by placing an ad in the newspaper. I was playfully trying to connect with him and joke around as we had done some in the past, and I made a comment about the poor sucker who thinks he is getting a decent motor. Instead of lighthearted banter, his wrath was unleashed on my teenage self. "How dare you question my integrity. You idiot kid, you don't know anything about anything." The fiery blade cut right through me again, banishing me once again from the garden, and from access to the tree of life. Shame reigned down again, and I said deep in myself, "Never again. This banishment is too painful, too hard, I will never be stupid, never incompetent, and people will love me and stay connected to me, I will belong. I will be classy, I will be good, I will be purposeful and not let playfulness possibly bring me this much pain again."

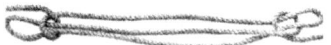

Mother Theresa, on her visit to the United States, declared our nursing homes to be the greatest places of poverty, the poverty of loneliness. Inner states mirror outer states. Perhaps our difficulty with the elderly is really our difficulty facing our own exiled weakness, our own powerlessness in the face of aging and death. We feel lonely because we are disconnected from our own selves, from those parts of us that hold the pain and hopelessness, the childhood shame. We have made vows to ourselves, "Never again." These vows become the sealed barriers to our exiled, vulnerable, terrified parts. They also become barriers between us and anyone else who triggers our exiled parts, be it a homeless person, the elderly, or a family member showing weakness and vulnerability.

Rouault had a way of imaging the inner and outer world at once in the same image as his friend Jacques Maritain describes in *Creative Intuition in Art and Poetry*.[49] Rouault has the courage to look down the lonely street, look in the underground tunnel and be present there without comment. It is as if Rouault can just sit down in this street on a stoop of a doorway and be present there. Even in the darkness of the eerie street he sees light in the stones; when none is there to cry out for the exiles, the buildings and streets themselves show light.

GUIDED MEDITATION

Take a moment to find a place to be still and quiet. See if it feels ok to close your eyes and count 5 breaths. Check and see if you have emotional space to sit with this meditation.

Do you have a rationalizing part, and the intellectual part that likes to explain away difficult emotions? A part that would much rather theorize about why things happen than grieve the reality of your experience? See if you can get to know your rationalizing part, not to get rid of it but to appreciate its intention. If you have some curiosity around your rationalizing notice where it shows up in your body. Don't be surprised if you feel it in your head.

See if you can ask the rationalizing part what it is afraid would happen if it allowed you to feel some of the difficult emotions? Where there times in the past when you felt so overwhelmed with difficult emotions that your life seemed like it could shut down? Just see what the rationalizing part is worried about if it were to open more space for feeling deeply. See if you can find the good intention, honor it and even offer appreciation for doing what it does.

Are there ways you would like to update the part? Are things differently now? Do you have more support now and perhaps security and ways of getting through grief without it overwhelming your life? If so, let the part know those things. Maybe it would agree to certain times or places when it would feel comfortable relaxing and letting you connect with parts holding strong emotion.

If it feels right for you ask the rationalizing part if it would give you a few minutes to just acknowledge those grieving and pain-holding parts it has been keeping you away from. If so, just send a message to the parts it has been protecting you from, let them know you see them and will work to get to them in a way that feels ok to the whole system. Notice any shifts in your body as you do this.

When this inner reflection feels complete for you, take a few moments to return your attention to your breath and to the space around you. Perhaps spend some moments reflecting on the experience and take any notes on things you would like to explore further later or insights you want to hold onto.

To engage with the high intensity level audio version described in the introduction, scan the QR code or visit tinyurl.com/rouault-meditations.

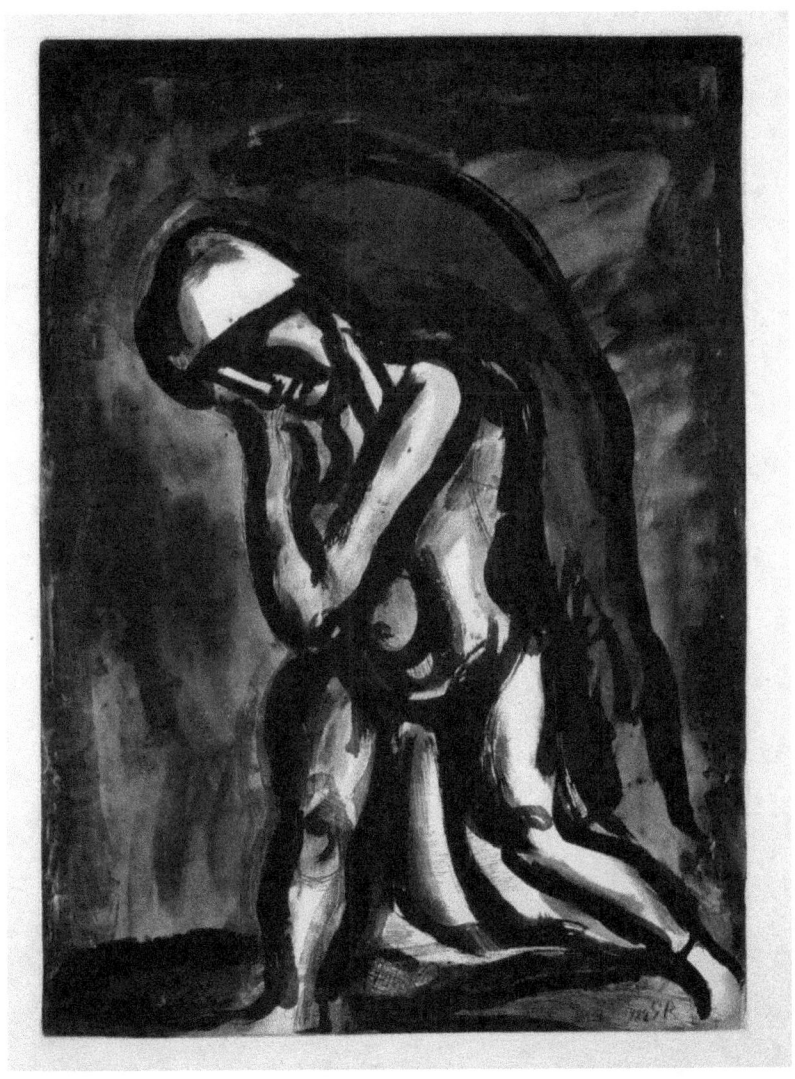

Plate 24

PLATE 24: WINTER

"Hiver lèpre de la terre."

"Winter, Leper of the Earth." Also translated, "Winter, Scourge of the Earth."

Trudging through a barren landscape, a figure with a dark ghostly shape covers it from above, hovering like a dark cloud or cloak. Visually, the dark form pushes the figure forward in space, contrasting the lightness of the body. The figure wears what appears to be a kind of helmet, like a simple soldier's helmet that holds the brightest spot in the composition and therefore emphasizes the head. The position of the arm tucked under the head gives it a very unnatural gait for a walker. One wonders if the figure is injured and holding an injury to the shoulder or face. Or possibly the person is heartbroken and resting its head on its hands.

Some translate the stanza as *leper* or *scourge*. By limiting the contextual clues given to the viewer, Rouault broadens the application of the image beyond mere journalistic accounting of the facts of a harsh war year winter. The figure seems to be a poetic personification of winter, trudging about as perhaps a leper of earlier centuries. One cannot help but remember the context of the Great War, of the "Turnip Winter" in Germany, the harsh brutality of war on the soil and farmland, siphoning off resources that would normally go to food production to be used as tools of war. Winter is hard enough, but winter during a world war is too much, like walking naked in the winter with only an army helmet for protection. One wonders if the figure is not in a starvation daze. Crops and food sources destroyed along with the earth means not just a cold winter, but a winter of starvation and death.

As I sit with this image as a whole, the connection between the visual forms and the poetic line associated with the image seems to be one of numbness. One aspect of leprosy is that it affects nerves and keeps one from feeling the pain of injury. Even so, winter brings snow in France, cold and ice numbing the landscape, covering trenches, excavated mounds of earth, holes left from explosives and landmines. Rouault's figure above in this light is perhaps a shell-shocked soldier or disoriented civilian, mentally disconnected from the overwhelming devastation, and even from their own nakedness, starvation and vulnerability, because it is too much to take in. Mental numbing-out of those traumatized by war mirrors the winter's numbing-out of the wounds of the earth: dissociation, disconnection, disembodiment and numbing-out become the protective state that permits one to keep trudging forward in the barren leprous landscape.

Murmansk, Russia the night of November 15-January 15th, 1993-1994

Waiting for the bus with some friends, the time was dark as always in the polar night. We stood in fur hats, some 12-18 inches tall. Women wore perfectly cared for multicolored fur hats that seemed to reach cartoon proportions in height. Men wore more simple black fur hats, ear flaps down. To my left in a group of twenty people standing in the 10 degrees below zero weather, was a man with his dog. He had the dog on a leash and was antagonizing the animal, getting him to growl and bark. The man, perhaps feeling powerful in control of such a powerful and potentially dangerous pet, just kept riling up the dog. I remember thinking, "I sure hope that dog doesn't get free, or it seems like it would take someone down with its rage." That was about the time it did slip out of the collar and back away from the man. The dog was quickly returned to the collar without incident but proved a nice distraction from the cold and the waiting.

On the curb in front of us was a miraculous pool of water in the midst of the 10 below zero temperatures. It must have been warm from being underground sewer water of some sort that was replenishing its heat and moving fast to keep it from icing over. I just remember being astonished at how large this puddle of water was in such cold weather.

The bus stop where we all stood was at the bottom of a gradual hill. The street ascended the hill, flanked by communist-era apartment buildings, bread stores, and a community bath house. At this time in the evening the town was mostly shut down, though you needed a watch to tell that it was evening. Several hundred feet up the road, we could all see clearly from the bus stop a figure coming down the street like a ball in a pinball machine: in slow motion, bounding off of the cars, trucks, and curbs – and sometimes all the way to the buildings – before being redirected down the hill towards us. As he got closer you could see his coat open, a teen perhaps 16 years old or so, blond hair exposed to the elements, bumbling down the hill, tripping along the way, getting up and ricocheting again off of whatever would redirect him to the middle of the trafficless street.

By the time he got near our group at the bus stop and now quiet dog, he seemed to be even unable to keep his eyes open fully. As if he was a circus act clown pretending to be drunk, he stumbled, spun around and landed face first, full body, in the puddle in front of us all. The group as one body took an instinctive step back to avoid the splash. The young man got up slightly more conscious, but oblivious to how cold it actually was, and how terrible it would be to be actually soaked with water in that kind of cold. He was numb from the alcohol, his leprosy shielding him from feeling winter.

What seemed like moments later the bus arrived, a young man got off the bus, grabbed the soaking teen and guided him onto the bus and apparently home.

Romania, Winter 2006

We had been investing heavily in our day center programs, meeting youth there instead of primarily on the street. From time to time, we tried to go to where the youth were still hanging out on the street to check on them, find new kids, and just be present with them. In winter it was often more difficult to find warmth and shelter. The underground system that delivered pipes of hot water for the centralized heating systems often became the warm refuge in the winter. Building fires in the underground pipe-filled tunnels often meant lots of smoke exposure, and when the boys would come up, they would have blackened faces from all the black smoke in the tunnels.

This time they had found their way into an abandoned store off the main street that had a wall knocked down but was boarded back up. Snow had drifted up all around for insulation and there was plywood wired shut for an access door. When we found the boys, we were let in after some time and entered their makeshift living room. They were quite proud of the luxurious fire: above ground, smoke went up instead of in your face.

There is a part of me that was revolted by the smell of boys that have not showered in a month, probably literally, and by the blackened walls, the cold barren space. Though not underground, it was still grizzly in its poverty, piles of bedding made up of old mattresses, old clothes and then the ever-present smell of the paint and glue huffed by the boys. I tried to focus on the humanity and the beauty under blackened faces.

"We brought some cheese pastries," we offered, and they brought out some packs of prepackaged crackers to share. One of the boys started singing a song we had sung together before, and everyone joined in. We were humans together who talked, sang and ate. Nothing else mattered for a moment.

In that moment, all of my revulsion is placed to the side for the sake of just being together. As noble as this may sound, it is also part of my own history of numbing-out. When things got chaotic in my childhood home, I went numb, when people were angry and hostile, I went numb, when there was a death and others were distraught, I went numb, and when others were emotionally devastated about anything, I went numb and started scrambling to help them with their difficulty. And as I turned this helper role into a profession as a therapist, clients got dysregulated and I went numb.

I had an exiled part in me that held the horror of all the chaos and death, the putrid reality of kids living underground, and the death of children. This part of me wanders the winter streets, shell shocked, vulnerable and exposed. For me the exiled horror only pops out a month or so after the smoke has cleared, when everybody else seems OK: when things are quiet and still, then this exiled part shows up.

The weird, sad, "for no reason" funk that comes on and the numbness becomes a weight-on-my-chest kind of sadness. The numb wears of, and I feel some of the sadness, before it gets rushed away, like the kids on the street would get shooed away, back out of sight, as if they never existed, so my own overwhelming feelings got exiled. I wonder if the Miserere Psalm doesn't echo the cry of our own exiled parts, "Do not thrust me away from your presence" (v11). So perhaps we fear that God will exile us as we have exiled our vulnerable, shell shocked, leprous parts? The psalmist says out of his own hope, "...a broken heart you will not despise" (v17).

GUIDED MEDITATION

Take a moment to find a place to be still and quiet. See if it feels ok to close your eyes and count 5 breaths. Check and see if you have emotional space to sit with this meditation.

Did you recognize numbing parts in yourself as you read this? When you feel the numbing out part take over, where does it show up in your body? Is it an all over feeling or concentrated in a certain area?

Do you have a sense for how old you were when this numbing part showed up to help you get through hard times? I wonder if you can notice this numbing part in some other way, perhaps another image or sensation. What might it look like?

Can you find some genuine gratitude for the work this numbing part has been trying to do for you even if it has kept you from feeling sometimes? If so, would you express that gratitude to the numbing part?

Does it feel ok to ask it what it is afraid will happen if it doesn't numb you out as much as it does? Can you ask the numbing part what experiences made it feel that you could not handle strong emotion, or wouldn't survive if it let you keep feeling?

Take some time to offer it any wisdom, perspective, or compassion around the times it is holding onto. Let it know you survived up until now, let it know how old you are, the safety you have achieved in your life. Reassure it honestly of any of the ways that its fears are now unfounded in light of your current life situation.

When this inner reflection feels complete for you, take a few moments to return your attention to your breath and to the space around you. Perhaps spend some moments reflecting on the experience and take any notes on things you would like to explore further later or insights you want to hold onto.

To engage with the high intensity level audio version described in the introduction, scan the QR code or visit tinyurl.com/rouault-meditations.

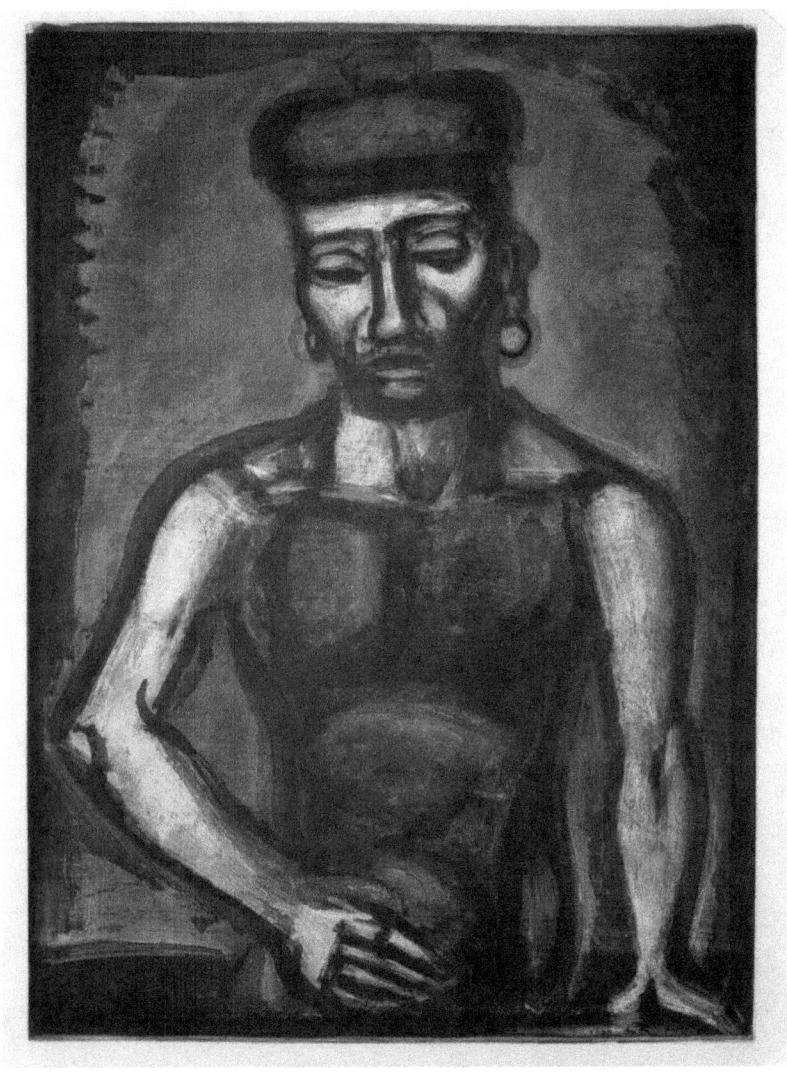

Plate 25

PLATE 25: THE SAILOR

"Jean-François jamais ne chante alleluia . . ."
"Jean-Francois never sings alleluia . . ."

Doering, in referring to Rouault's inspiration for one of his paintings says, "...at the sight of a poor butcher at work in his butcher shop on wheels as it passed down the street sent Rouault back to his studio to paint."[50] Rouault's careful observation inspired these forms that resonate with the inner experiences common to all people. And later Doering says, "Although this image of a common sailor is posed to suggest a man of sorrows, Rouault intends us to understand by way of the associated poetic line that religion did not often reach the laboring proletariat."[51] Here an image of a sailor as evident by the hat and earing connects it to the following plate as well.

Many of Rouault's stanzas, including this one connects poetically one print to the next, are from his own poems; "Jean-Francois never sings alleluia...in the land of thirst and terror."

Doering, in his essay "Lacrimae Rerum – Tears at the Heart of Things: Jacques Maritain and Georges Rouault," writes:

> "Maritain wrote of Rouault: 'What he sees and knows with a strange pity, and what he makes us see, is the miserable affliction and the lamentable meanness of our times, not just the affliction of the body, but the affliction of the soul, the bestiality and the self-satisfied vainglory of the rich and the worldly, the crushing weariness of the poor, the frailty of us all.'"[52]

Rouault was not satisfied with a distant, abstract idea of human suffering. He puts us in an intimate front row seat.

And "If we love that living human thing which we call the people...we will want first and foremost to exist with them, to suffer with them and remain in communion with them. Before "doing good" to them and working for their benefit, before practicing the politics of one group or other...we must first choose to exist with them, and to suffer with them, to make their pain and destiny our own."[53]

Rouault's world, his faith and outlook on his fellow humanity, is a radical and fresh voice even a century later. "To make their pain and destiny our own" is not the sentiment of polarization and self-righteousness we are finding on both sides of every debate. This empathic value of solidarity with the whole humanity is echoed again in Martin Luther King Jr in his famous words, "no one is free until we are all free."

Here is yet another instance of Rouault's empathic process worked out in shade, lights and darks and grappling with forms. With a dark framing around the edges of the image, and a thin horizon line at the bottom, a sailor stands presenting from the waist up as if holding a hand on a table. We are offered the hunk of flesh of the poor laboring person, arms and face exposed to the elements, face framed in by a straight brim of the French sailor's hat, hoop earrings evidencing travel and a dark shadow under the chin.

Our figure's eyes focus attentively on the task in hand through heavy eyelids. He, "never sings alleluia." Where would he get the time or energy or predictability to devote to a spiritual life?

Romania, 2008

For a time, we lived on a street that came to a "T" at the cemetery. From our gate you could look to the right and see an 8-foot concrete wall with a white cross of raised concrete in each section of wall. Each time a funeral procession entered the cemetery gates, family members would pay to have the bells rung on behalf of the dead. This deep peeling of the one huge funerary bell was part of our normal auditory landscape for those years, as it reached our home and beyond for a mile.

Our main bus stop was the cemetery bus stop, which meant 2 to 25 minutes at a time standing next to the gates and the bell. Next to those gates was a row of flower sellers and their carts. Usually, they were already there in the morning for the early bird graveside visitors, but in the evenings, you might catch one on the move. Typically, there was an incomprehensible amount of gear: unsold flowers in tall black plastic flower vessels, wooden stool, water buckets, extra clothing from the early morning cold, a large thermos, the umbrella all on two wheels at one end and a driving handle at the other. They would carefully navigate the curb, dodge through the busy traffic across Steelworkers Street, and then the curb on the other side to wherever they were headed off the main street to their dwelling place out of sight.

Their faces would be leathered, dark and worn, from being exposed to the elements year-round following the seasonless pattern of death anniversaries that brought people from all over the city, always needing some flowers. They became round in the winter with layer after layer of coats and handmade wool sweaters, with hot tea always ready in thermoses on their carts. Some spent slow times knitting through fingerless handmade gloves. It was hard to understand how the economics of it worked, buying fresh flowers in the capital city, maybe growing some in their own courtyard to sell alongside the bulk market flowers that came year-round.

Waiting for the bus, our small children would inevitably wander over to the flower carts, checking out the variety of colors and shapes, the papers and premade arrangements. There was a threadbare weariness of daily struggle in their faces, toiling almost directly under the funeral bells and year-round sun. But in the exchange of smiles with the kids and knowing smiles with me as a parent, they begged me to appreciate these quickly fleeting years, these moments like the first snowdrop flowers blooming in the spring that quickly pass.

Romania, May 1, 2001 "Slain Lamb Easter" - *Letter to Supporters*

As I write this letter, we have been in the midst of our Passion Week and Resurrection celebrations. As Romania is 86% Romanian Orthodox, we have experienced a little of their unique ways of celebrating this most holy week. The first sign of Easter for me this year was the appearance of millions of bright white buds on the trees in our neighborhood. They seem to call us to prepare.

Then we began to hear an increase in the beating of rugs throughout the city. There are big steel bars near every apartment building made to hold your living room rug and any other carpet while you beat out all the winter dust. The effect is impressive as you hear the deep resonating thuds like a call to worship and repentance. After the dust is beat out the carpets are washed with soap and dried in the sun. Romanians are spring-cleaning, painting, and rearranging their homes preparing for the coming of the Lamb.

My wife and I were in the outdoor market the other day and saw someone walk by with a "lamb that was slain" for the Easter meal. This doglike corpse, with no wool, mostly grossed us out with its bloodstains on its white clean-shaven skin.

Last night we met some of the kids who lived in the street to go to a midnight service which concluded around 12.30 am. Hundreds throughout the city carried candles through the streets and to their freshly cleaned homes well prepared for the resurrection.

As we met the kids in a dark little park behind some storefront shops where many of them sleep, I was once again shocked by the vulnerability of children in the dark with only each other for protection and warmth. Cardboard to insulate from the harsh cold concrete. Some smelled of the paint they had been breathing in to escape with for a while. One kid I knew approached me and offered me some cookies he had hidden in his coat and begged me to eat some with him.

Today I met another kid after church and he greeted me with the Easter greeting, "Christ is Risen" and I responded in kind, "He is Risen indeed." I invited him to come to the Easter dinner we were preparing for many of the kids and some parents. He just smiled and waved as he crossed the street letting me know he had some odd job he was doing for someone and couldn't join us.

In this context the resurrection celebration is a test of my faith and a challenge to my lifestyle. Simply put, I struggle with seeing these older kids continue to sleep on the streets, to be considered difficult if not impossible to be integrated into children's homes, who have no marketable skills, and spend much of their time simply avoiding the reality of their pain through breathing paint fumes. What does the resurrection of Jesus mean for these marginalized kids, those who don't fit into the systems of the world, and are considered a nuisance? And how can I see resurrection in their midst?

My lifestyle is challenged as I read, "Love your neighbor as yourself" and see Jesus at the house of the leper, associating with sinners, the outcasts of his society, and dying the death of a criminal. Christ lays for us a path of powerlessness and vulnerability, which greatly contrasts our patterns of calculated risks, love without risk, and guaranteed returns. Jesus' challenge to us is to a radical discipleship, which is to spend ourselves on behalf of the marginalized and poor, the orphan and widow. He asks us to call the poor our neighbor and visit them as a friend and consider eating around their table and treating them as brothers and sisters.

Let us continue to consider more than our personal salvations, but also what it means to follow in the way Jesus laid out for us. To see the cross as a call to repentance from the ways of power, prestige, and control to the way of obedience, of loving our neighbor, of losing power, control and security for the sake of finding fellowship around the table of the poor and marginalized.

The trees throughout the city gave the first signs of spring with their white buds. These buds clothed the gnarled skeletons that signified death throughout the winter. As I walked home after the Easter dinner with the kids, I noticed that most of these trees are now green. The spectacular resurrection whites are now a vibrant green. And somehow I know in a quiet place in my heart that the resurrected life of Jesus is still present in the world to bring new life and hope to our friends and brothers, the poor among us.

As Maritain is quoted above, speaking of his close friend Rouault, "...the crushing weariness of the poor, the frailty of us all," illuminated Rouault's approach to suffering in the world.[54] Suffering and affliction are never just "out there," an abstract intellectual reckoning, or somehow fuel for an ideology. It is seen, it is "existing with them," an experience like his encounter with the people in the street that inspired his paintings about the poor. But Rouault doesn't just use his experience as fodder to inspire pity or raise awareness of a social issue – though that probably happened – but rather goes inside himself with the revelation of the humanity of the other, to "the frailty of us all."[55] For Rouault, there is an "us" that is more real than any categories, and here Rouault crosses into profound depths of modern psychological understanding and ancient wisdom. There is a parallel between our treatment of the poor outside of ourselves and our treatment of the vulnerable weary parts within ourselves.

There are parts of each person that are worn to the bone, faithfully working, laboring, duty bound, afraid to play, that feel the hounds of death and destitution at their heels. These parts of us are praised and encouraged because their faithful service provides a lot of stability and care, and yet they are often driven by fear and dread. It is not joyful service, but "guilt and obligation" driven work. Often when this dynamic is unearthed in therapy, the question arises, "If I wasn't motivated by fear of approval, fear of not being enough, fear of being seen as bad, etc., would I just stop doing anything?"

Fear is a pervasive motivator, and most of us have been habituated to reward and punishment frameworks that are unaware that life could be lived for the sake of growth, development, celebration, gratitude and compassion.

Joyful and grateful service might evoke the thought, "Thank you for the opportunity you have given me to care for you." In this case, Rouault gives us the image of the one who cannot see any celebratory "alleluia" in their work. This is work as curse and fear, it is dehumanizing and disconnected from the beauty of the creative, growing, celebrating life-giving nature of human thriving.

GUIDED MEDITATION

Take a moment to find a place to be still and quiet. See if it feels ok to close your eyes and count 5 breaths. Check and see if you have emotional space to sit with this meditation.

Do you have a work-you-to-the-bone part in you that is motivated by guilt, fear, or obligation? Bent over, weary, stuck in the business of the task at hand, distracting you from looking up and seeing beyond the drudgery? If so, where does it show up in your body when it gets intense for you?

Can you picture your weary worker part? What does yours look like? How do you feel towards it now? Do you have any strong reactions to it, positive or negative? Can you ask those parts that step aside to give you space to just be present to this weary worker part of you? Can you notice some curiosity or compassion towards this weary worker part?

If it feels ok, ask this weary worker part what it has been trying to do for you? And what is it afraid of happening if it were not to drive you so hard? Are there memories it is stuck on when things went bad, that it is afraid of happening again? Can you offer any gratitude to the part for trying so hard to keep these kinds of things from happening ever again, or the fears from coming true? Can you address any of its concerns out of your curious compassionate place?

Are there pieces to the parts story that you wish this part knew when all of this happened? How is your life different now, and what is unrealistic about its fears in light of your current situation and wisdom? What insight does this weary working part really need to hear? Offer it what help you can.

When this inner reflection feels complete for you, take a few moments to return your attention to your breath and to the space around you. Perhaps spend some moments reflecting on the experience and take any notes on things you would like to explore further later or insights you want to hold onto.

To engage with the high intensity level audio version described in the introduction, scan the QR code or visit tinyurl.com/rouault-meditations.

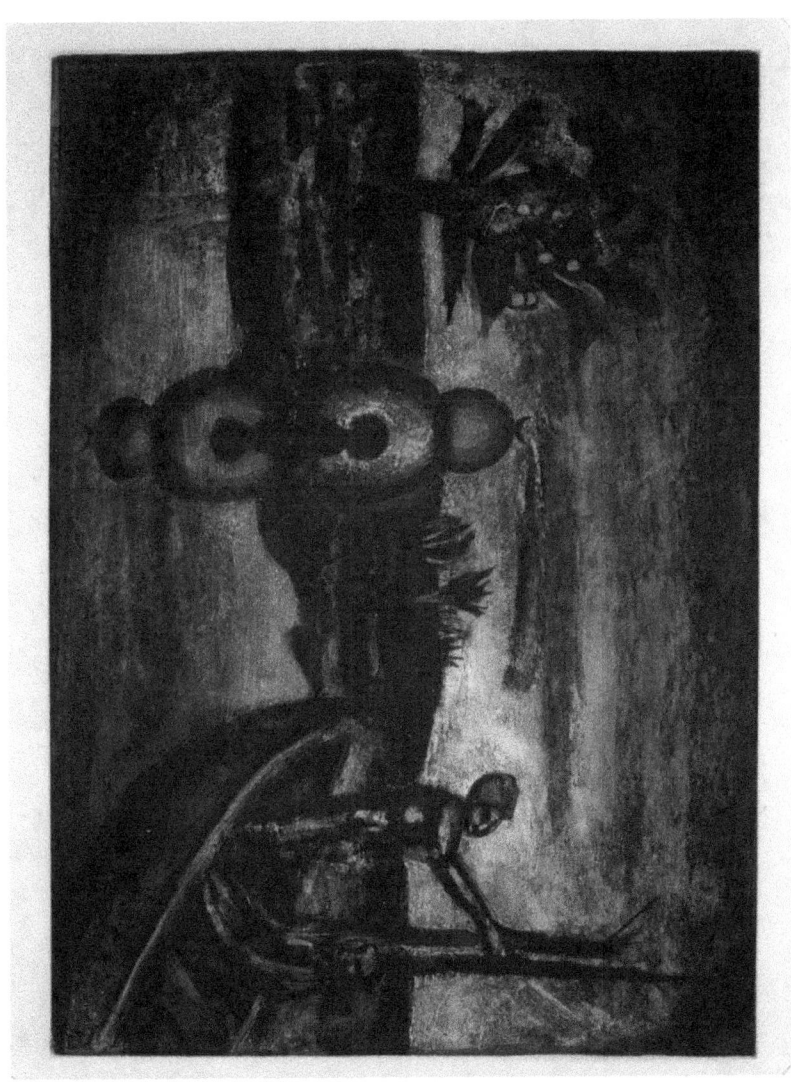

Plate 26

PLATE 26: TERROR

"Au pays de la soif et de la peur"
"In the land of thirst and terror"

"A dream world of faintly ominous character, this print was evidently strongly influenced by the famous painting, *The Poor Fisherman*, by France's great symbolist painter Puvis de Chavannes."[56] I can remember spending time with *The Poor Fisherman* date painting in the Musée d'Orsay, in Paris some years ago, making a sketch of a portion of the painting. It is a bleak landscape, silent browns and dirty greens giving the feeling of midday summer, with the haunting terror of hunger focused on the still waters hiding the fishing nets. The children playing on the shore only accentuate the fearful hope of pulling life out of this dead water.

The composition bears some similarities to Rouault's image here, Rouault's boat is oriented on the opposite diagonal. He puts the accompanying figure in the boat with the fisherman and adds a tree that seems to have fruit of some kind in it, and a dwelling that is reminiscent of an African round mud hut, perhaps seen in postcards from French West Africa. Similar to the *Poor Fisherman* painting, we have that same feeling of fishing in the still inland backwaters away from the bounty – and perhaps chaos – of the ocean. Both artists have a fisherman standing in a small boat, which adds to the sense of the deadness of the water. The sun may be rising or setting, leaving the figures mostly in shadow. The standing figure seems to wear a helmet, possibly conjuring a depiction of the French military presence in west Africa, pointing off to the right of the page to some unknown thing in the distance. The standing figure seems to be looking in that direction as well. The other figure seated in the boat appears skeletal-like, with deep-set eyes in shadow, as if death sits in the boat with the fisherman. The seated figure seems to be completely disassociated from whatever the standing character is doing, seeking, or pointing out. She seems to be almost observing the viewer of the picture, or looking back to the dwelling-hut, giving a hint of Gauguin's Tahitian figures (*see The Spirit of Death Watches, 1892*). Was she removed from there? Was she leaving voluntarily? Is she related to the standing figure, or being kidnapped?

Lastly, there is a hint of French colonialism in west Africa at the time, the African round mud hut almost fully reflected in the still water that fills the foreground of the picture. This device almost makes the dwelling hut a central figure in the composition, standing on the third of the page horizontally. From hut down to the bottom of the reflection covers more than half of the vertical span of the page.   The ominous dark landscape and the stanza cuing the ideas of thirst and terror create a river Stix atmosphere, an almost smoky, desolate river.   The characters do not appear to be fishing in any obvious way.

This mythic landscape scene takes us starkly out of an iconographic encounter with faces and torsos. Here we are shoved into a dark underworld where we are in a psychological space that echoes Rouault's teacher Moreau who specialized in conjuring symbolic mythic spaces. Rouault also carries some of the symbolist instincts of his teacher while avoiding the intellectualization of abstract symbols. Here Rouault seems to lead the viewer into a gritty space that resists condensation into one-to-one representations: this stands for that.   Rouault's working paradigm journeys into himself and wrestles with everything he paints: there is no "out there" for Rouault, he emphatically embodies and experiences whatever he depicts. By doing so, Rouault gives the viewer an experience of thirst and terror, rather than merely receding to it.

Kentucky, 2011

Upon arriving for work each morning at Eastern State Psychiatric hospital, I would wind up the back steps and use my key to get through a couple of locked steel doors. It gave me the shortest path into the room where we would do the shift change morning report: who was new, who was currently psychotic, who was still resisting medication, who was fighting, were there any incidents of abuse between patients, how much staff did we have on the unit that day, and most importantly to me, would there be an excess of males on my regular unit and would I get bumped to the crisis unit upstairs, the "low sensory unit." Today was one of those days I would be spending my shift upstairs.

Some time before, I had responded to a code, which meant all available extra personnel would run as quickly as possible to wherever there was a code happening. Usually this meant someone was getting violent in some way. You would hustle through back stairways and corridors to find your way. Part of you didn't want to get there first to decrease the risk of personal injury. This particular time, when I got to the crisis unit, there was already a swarm of light blue nursing scrubs hovered around the low sensory unit door. A man in the unit had taken his heavy steel bed frame from his room and was attempting to open the huge steel door by ramming the bed frame into the door. The problem was that we had most of the personnel outside the door. This screaming, tall, rage-powered man with a steel bed frame stuck in my mind. I'll just call him Bob here.

Another day I was "on close" with Bob. This meant that I was supposed to be 10 feet from him at all times. He was on the low sensory unit because he would get too associated with the behaviors of other patients and get violent, so the idea was that less people, less noise, less stimulation could be helpful to keep him calm. I was sitting just inside the door to his room, and he was sleeping away, or pretending to sleep. After sitting there for the better part of 2 hours with no change, he quickly sat up in bed and started screaming at me, incoherent things about the closet just behind me, as if I were letting a fire-breathing dragon into his room. After a moment he lay back down and made no move or sound for the next hour or so before I was moved somewhere else.

So today I was back, and he was in his bed. I was just inside the door, sitting in a chair with a clipboard that tracked my watch of Bob, and held my sudoku puzzles. Another rule of being "on close" with a patient was that even if there was another crisis happening, you had to remain with your patient. On this particular day there was a new nurse in charge behind the plexiglass nurses' station, sealed off with a locked door. The tiny room accommodated a couple of file cabinets, a desk, a phone, and little else. You could fit two chairs in the space, but only with some careful maneuvering. The little plexiglass office had a crisis button; this was the way to call a code if something was happening that needed assistance, getting every available person running in your direction. There were also a couple of remote buttons that you could carry with you around the sensory unit, in case you were away from the desk when something erupted. So I sat there with my clipboard and my little button.

This day we had a female on the unit that was notorious for her violent temper; she had spent many weeks in the sensory unit. I'll call her Lucy. She liked to color, and would often threaten physical violence if the nursing staff wouldn't find the specific crayon colors she needed for a particular picture she was working on. Lucy was around 5 feet tall, and a ball of muscle. From where I sat with Bob that day, I was only about 10 feet away from the plexiglass nurses' station, so I could hear, "I need pink and I can't find my pink anywhere, someone has taken my pink from me, get me a pink or I am going to lose it."

The poor nurse was young, fresh out of nursing school maybe, at her first nursing job, and now at 20-something, facing a very nuanced negotiation that could turn south very quickly. The nurse began pointing out the reality of not having any pink crayons on the unit or in the office, but didn't know about calling the activities director, empathizing more with the patient—at least feigning—not ever giving up on the effort of the search for a pink crayon. Instead, the poor nurse gave the patient a solid, "Sorry Lucy,

I can't help with that." All of Lucy's abuse history was triggered: the feelings of powerlessness, rage and injustice, all symbolized in this young white nurse's refusal to continue the effort to find a damn pink crayon.

All the rage then started focusing on the nurse, starting with screaming, "I'll get you, you…" The nurse was inside her protective plexiglass bubble, but to Lucy that bubble could be popped. She began throwing her body into the plexiglass door. That is when I hit the button. Again, I am watching this from 10 feet away, unable to stop guarding my patient in the room behind me. That is when time seemed to slow. I knew help should be on the way, but it seemed to take forever. Lucy methodically rammed all of her muscle-bound body into that door, until finally the plexiglass bent in far enough to come out of its frame, She went at the nurse and was on top of her in this tiny room before the unit was filled with blue nursing scrubs. Lucy was restrained, strapped to a bed, and given medication to knock her out. The young nurse did not seem to have any physical injuries, though understandably she was a nervous wreck.

My heart felt torn in half. Should I have broken the rules and intervened somehow? But I always had the image of Bob with a steel bed frame trying to escape, and his terrifying screaming at ghosts. If I had done something, what could I have done on my own? The depths of Lucy's pain and trauma all came out over a pink crayon; but really, it was about feeling unsafe and powerless, which seemed intolerable, "never again." I felt powerless and hopeless. I felt their terror made real for me through Bob and Lucy's behaviors. Sitting in their "land of thirst and terror," was a nightmare. Lucy was so starved for empathy she never got during her episodes of abuse as a little girl, she could not tolerate any sign of disregarding her needs. It took her to her most painful places. This is a hard place for me to even remember, and I was only there witnessing acted out trauma, and not the actual abuse these precious souls endured through their lives.

Rouault takes us, "…in the land of thirst and terror," to the place of powerlessness, the dark place where there seems to be no hope. Unlike the playing children in "The Poor Fisherman" by Chavannes (1881), Rouault's image has less of a feeling of a possible future. There may be some allusions to French occupation of west Africa, with the soldier's helmet on the man in the boat, but as with many of Rouault's images, he strips them down as if to challenge the viewer to focus on more universal archetypal experiences rather than the time-bound depictions.

Richard Schwartz, in his Internal Family Systems Model, discusses kinds of inner parts that operate in different ways.[57] This model has some kinship with Jungian analysis, with some differences in theory and practice.

One might see in this image a protector (the soldier) and the exiled part (the seated woman). Protectors operate to keep more suffering from piling on the exiled part. The anger of Lucy, a protective part, hides her vulnerable exiled parts that hold the suffering from her trauma history. Unfortunately, many of our protectors' strategies end up increasing the likelihood of more painful situations occurring, but their intention is to prevent further suffering to the exiled parts, the parts that hold the horror, pain or shame. Often protector parts keep exiles locked away far from the rest of civilization, the outer reaches of the empire, or in this case perhaps out of our conscious awareness.

In this image Rouault creates a space for me to notice my inner exiles, out in a dead tributary in an unknown mythical place, but a place we actually know and have experienced – though typically only in the nights where our mind is undistracted, or we are reminded of the hopelessness by some other life event, a death or loss.

This stanza completes the poetic line from the last image, "Jean-Francois never sings alleluia..." It is interesting to note that many have vibrant religious or spiritual aspects of themselves, can quote creeds full of hope and confidence, and can convince others of certain versions of truth. However, these inner mindfulness gurus, or missionary pastors or other kinds of spiritual emissaries, often have never reached these exiled parts that dwell in the outer reaches, the inner tributaries. Suddenly one goes from assured truth holder to totally insecure hopeless lost soul. Even the most spiritual among us often have exiled parts that have never been enlightened to the bigger picture; the hope, the possibility of healing, or even the ways other parts of ourselves have found healing, safety, and peace. The inner exile never sings alleluia, as they are often still so far upstream – and perhaps even seem threatening to our dogmatic systems to have lingering doubting parts. It is like the social program that has been enacted and made available, but the information has not reached the marginalized who could use it if they only knew what to do. The common person often is left without an "alleluia," without the comfort and safety of a healing spirituality that embraces all of them and brings them up to date in a reality in which safety has been reached. One might pick up a note from the Miserere Psalm here, "Do not thrust me away from your presence." The Jean-Francoises, the exile, those lost in the fear of thirst and terror, feel cast away from all hope of comfort, trust or safety.

Kentucky, 2012

Some time later I completed my Marriage and Family Therapy degree and started looking for counseling jobs while still working at the psychiatric hospital. I took a couple of hours off one day to go in for an interview at a community mental health center. Before I made it back to the hospital to begin my shift. I got the call that I was being offered the job. I found myself on my regular unit and sitting in the hallway in a chair stationed at the door of a patient who was being monitored closely due to his current risk status. In the hallway a patient was standing talking to one of my fellow mental health assistants. The patient was a very large male and he was getting uncomfortably close and making the female staff person very uncomfortable. Sitting there, I asked him to just give her a little space. He walked down the hallway upset that I had intervened but seemed to be going away to calm down. A few minutes later he calmly walked back to the area where I was sitting and stood to my right while I was still sitting in the chair. I noticed him moving out of the corner of my eye and as if in slow motion watched his fist pull back and then punch me in the right cheekbone. He quickly walked away and went somewhere by himself, and I stood there in shock wondering what you do after getting punched in the face. In some ways it felt better to have been punched than to be anxious about getting hurt by someone. Maybe this is why some people provoke others to violence, to just be done with the anticipation of it. While wondering if I would have a bruise on my face, I was still just in the glow of having been offered a job as a therapist. I may have been just punched but I was getting out of here.

A few hours later I was asked to shave the same man who had punched me earlier for interfering with his "moves on a girl" as he saw it. Patients in the hospital were not allowed to have a razor or use a razor on their own, due to suicidal and self-harm risk and liability for the hospital. That meant that staff had to shave the patients who wanted a smooth chin. There was an awkward moment at first as he was asking me if I would shave him. He offered an apology, for "earlier, you know..."

As I shaved his face, it was mostly silent. Not a hostile silence, just a human silence. He and I in a space, cleaning his face of whiskers, restoring a little dignity in a place where it is often difficult to feel any. As the stubble came off, it was as if the little boy was still there just under the surface, the kid who just wanted to be seen and heard, recognized, seen as valuable and beautiful. I could see that innocent boy under there hidden in the thick weeds of fear. His eyes were that of a 6-year-old framed in the wrinkled eyelids of a 60-year-old. And my own inner 6-year-old could silently say along with this man, "Please see me."

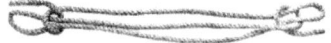

It is as if Rouault gives us in this image the foggy landscape behind the eyes of our human suffering, the loneliness and terror we feel at times. Some more intensely than others perhaps, each has his/her own moments of terror. Rouault invites us to enter here and connect with those parts of us that are lost in these inner landscapes of thirst and terror.

GUIDED MEDITATION

Take a moment to find a place to be still and quiet. See if it feels ok to close your eyes and count 5 breaths. Check and see if you have emotional space to sit with this meditation.

Often if our inner system is afraid of going to places it is terrified of, parts of us will work against accessing them. It is protective on the one hand but also blocks healing and conquering the unfounded terror. There is no shame in getting trained help to navigate through these dark waters of your psyche. If you feel ok working around the edges of the terror continue on...

If you can at least acknowledge your exiled parts that connect with "thirst and terror," let them know you see them. And if you can honestly, assure them that you will do the work to bring them healing. This alone can bring some comfort.

Do you have space to try to care for your parts locked in thirst and terror now? If so, can you try to see them in some way? Maybe the characters in Rouault's image work for you, or maybe you can imagine them in another way.

Where do you find them in your body? How do you feel towards them? Is there some curiosity or compassion present towards them? If not, you may need to wait until some of your other protectors are willing to give you room.

If you are feeling some compassion, can you sit patiently with your hopeless parts? With your parts that hold the unanswered existential questions? The parts that "never sing alleluia," because they have felt alone in their suffering. Can you just be present to the part, letting it know you are here for it and it does not have to be alone anymore?

If you feel comfortable enough, can you ask the part to share with you some of the pain it has been holding on its own from past experiences? Just listen as an attentive, curious, compassionate mother or father figure. Let it know you hear it, and invite it to tell you everything that it has been holding onto alone.

Can you let it know something about how your life has turned out since some of those memories it was stuck in? Can you let it know that the thirst and terror is past if it really is for you now? See if it would be willing to come to the present with you, and can you show it around your current life? How can you nurture and comfort this part and give it what it was longing for during the times of thirst and terror? What do you wish adults would have done for you then? Go ahead and try to offer that to the part.

When this inner reflection feels complete for you, take a few moments to return your attention to your breath and to the space around you. Perhaps spend some moments reflecting on the experience and take any notes on things you would like to explore further later or insights you want to hold onto.

To engage with the high intensity level audio version described in the introduction, scan the QR code or visit tinyurl.com/rouault-meditations.

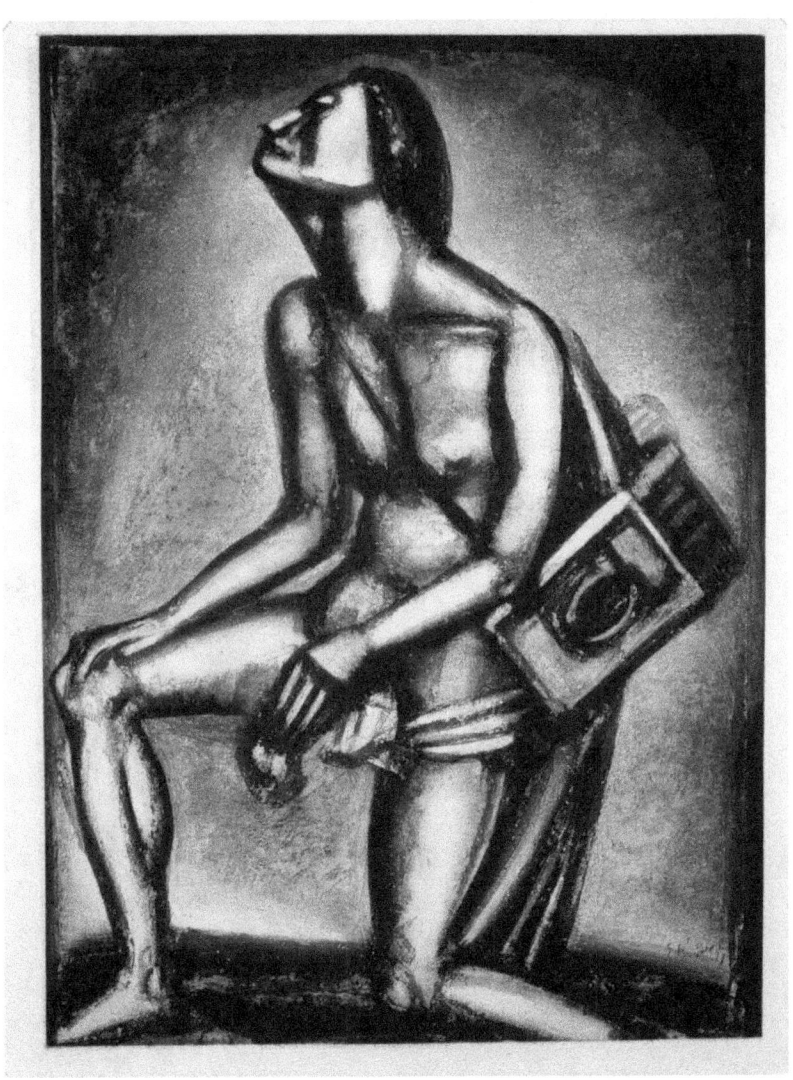

Plate 27

PLATE 27: FAILURE

"Sunt lacrymae rerum..."
"In all things, tears..."

Next, in Plate 27, Rouault confronts his viewer with the human experience of failure.

This poetic line is completed in the next image, "...He that believeth in me, though he were dead, yet shall he live." The stanza here is understood to be a reference to the words of Orpheus.[58] Traditionally, Orpheus is depicted in simple Greek dress and carrying a lyre, his musical instrument and primary tool, his art form that becomes his means to pass into the underworld and to enact the resurrection of his love, Eurydice, from Hades. The tale of Orpheus has meant different things to different ages, each placing importance on differing aspects of the story.[59] It is hard to be sure how Rouault would have wanted his image to be understood in connection with Orpheus.

Within the context of these *Miserere* pieces, there are perhaps general connections to the struggle of the artist, seeker of beauty, of art as a means of transcending death and the seeming futility of human endeavors. In the light of the next image, Plate 28, one would be inclined to see Christian theological interpretations of the themes of resurrection from hades in the Orpheus story.

In Rouault's image, the lyre is replaced by what looks like a World War I portable camera. This also draws on the front lines in the great war and the underworld of Orpheus, the artist who uses his craft as a way of engaging with the horrors of war and bringing back the memories of it home. The photographer is the noncombatant whose role is to carry information and memory from the front lines. In some ways this is the work of Rouault more generally in this project; beyond war, but including the horrors of war: the refugee, the poor, the displaced and the condemned, to name a few of the characters already treated in this *Miserere* series.

With Rouault's offering of a litany of suffering beings here in the *Miserere* series, perhaps he now includes the artist. The struggle to see beauty, capture its elusive appearances and to suffer and work with little reassurance that the work will matter in the end. Will all the singing for Hades and his cohorts amount to anything? Will love and joy ever be restored? Will a vision of the essences of things be enough to conquer darkness, fear, thirst, and terror? Or Dostoyevsky's question, can beauty really save the world or is it an artist's delusion?

The Orpheus story' image of death and resurrection, of entering hell and bringing out the beloved, has been interpreted by Christian theologians in light of the passion narrative. There is the breaking apart of the body of Orpheus as food or seed for future artists and beauty seekers, the remains which offer the artist's artifact beyond their own life in the world. This idea connected with the offering up of the body of Christ in the eucharistic life of the church.

Lastly, the story of Orpheus is also about the tragedy of doubt, holding the hope that his love is just behind him, gaining life from the dead. He breaks the contract with Hades by doubting and turning around losing Eurydice forever.

In Plate 32, after a depiction of the crucifixion, in the context of the risen Christ, Rouault gives us an image of Christ entertaining the doubts of Thomas. Who is more entitled to doubt hope and resurrection than the war photographer who has documented up close the death and destruction, fields of blood and barbed wire, trenches, and dismemberment? The human wrestling with doubt told through Orpheus connects it with not just Rouault's historical context, but also common human struggle through the ages. And perhaps the story of Orpheus and the artistic pursuit is a story of human failure and limitation.

Considering possible connections between this image and the Miserere Psalm, one may consider the role of the artist in a world of misery and terror. The very context of the Miserere Psalm is the event of Nathan the prophet telling a story to King David that awakens David's anger at the perpetrator in the story (2 Samuel 12). He is the recipient of an art form detaching him from his context, into an alternative reality – i.e., the story – and then bringing him back to a more accurate and profound self-knowledge.[60]

One of the functions of art – certainly in Rouault's case – is a deep seeing of reality, disconnection into a world of forms, characters, emotions, and states of being which illuminate our shared human disaster and make way for a resurrection from the dead; psychological detachment which creates space for illumination of the nature of things.

In this body of 58 prints Rouault seems to be creating a path of repentance, of self-discovery and growth, of facing the darkest parts of our inner worlds. He takes us into a dark, black, gray, and white world where the black is not avoided, but rather becomes the clay out of which something beautiful is drawn out.

The very context of the Miserere Psalm, according to tradition, is that David had the husband of Bathsheba sent to the front lines of battle, to his very likely death. This is echoed in the psalm, "Deliver me from blood-guiltiness, oh God" (KJV). David, feeling his complicity in murdering a man through the mechanisms of his power, recognizes himself as guilty of the highest offense, the shedding of blood, the destruction of one bearing the image of God. David in this psalm dares to ask God for deliverance from the just punishment for his action, expecting and hoping that God may take him up on the idea. David fails to love and protect his people, and instead is the perpetrator of injustice and violence. He is slammed in the face with his human failure and offers that honestly in the psalm.

This revelation of his guilt comes through a form of art. That art of storytelling delivers David from his delusion within his power and entitlement, on a journey into the narrative of the prophet Nathan's story. David finds himself enraged at the injustice in the story, demands justice be done until he is reconnected to his own context, "you are that man" (2 Samuel 12:7). The detachment and reattachment process that happens in art is a journey into the inner world of each person, where they are offered an opportunity to be reconciled with previously disowned parts of themselves. Art offers that possibility of increased wholeness, integrity, and peace through this process. as does religious liturgical and narrative life at its best.

Romania, 2005

For nearly two hours we talked, I on the couch and Bob on the chair. I don't remember much of what we said, but after a week in our community home for boys wanting to come off the street, he was done. The sense of my failure rolled in the back door of my mind like ashes when the chimney gets cleaned. He was saying gently, "I can't." And now I realize that he was hanging out and talking, not considering actually staying, but only trying to let us know that it wasn't because of us; he just saw that he couldn't live without sex, without control, without being the boss, without drugs, and more freedom. In other words, it did not seem safe to trust.

He agreed to stay and have pancakes before leaving, and by then we were laughing and joking. I was pouring and frying pancakes on the old blue frying pan when a column of fire appeared – something like the old Bible story book pictures of the pillar of fire – straight up from the 14-inch pan, in a perfect vertical shoot, as if a fountain of fire was unbottled from the pan, pouring into the ceiling. It was a perfect cylinder of fire 14 inches around from bottom to top. It would have seemed beautiful if it weren't so terrifying.

Pulling the pan away from the stove, the column of flames disappeared as suddenly as they had come. Then we laughed and awed at our possible fate, a burned-down house, or singed eyelashes. It was a phantom beyond our powers to fix. A little later Bob walked out as he said he must.

I was confronted with my human frailty and impotence at once. I was feeling powerless to help this young man, his experience of the awful hopelessness of life on the streets, trapped in drug habits and dangerous coping. But then this strange perspective came into that moment, this fire, out of control for the moment, the reminder that we were all alive and we were together in this thing even if Bob didn't work our program. Maybe my perceived human failure isn't such a big deal.

I was reminded of Mother Theresa and the sisters of charity, and how their measure of success is to honor the dignity of each person that they come across. Though certainly we should work to help all those that we can, success is recognizing and honoring the divine image in one another.

Part of me dreamed that if only I could fix Bob, I would not have to face the hopelessness in myself. I could ride on, healing others, and prove to myself that all is not lost. Why does failure matter? It may be that it is our hope that if I succeed people will love me, want me, and want to be part of my life. If only I have some amazing success stories, people will have to see me, hear me, and care about what I say – and I will feel that I matter. What this strategy misses is that nothing you can succeed or fail at will make you matter any more or less than you do already.

In that moment of life and death around a column of fire, we were stripped bare, to our naked humanity, beings that exist together. All of the building, renovating, saving street kids strategies could have gone up in flames in an hour. What remains after our failure is what was always there to begin with, the meeting of persons bearing the fire of the divine image.

With "In all things, tears…" Rouault seems to be systematically unmasking all of the societal and personal strategies for success, power, attainment, and self-righteousness. We are laid bare in the repentance process Rouault takes us through. Like King David the psalmist's brokenness, we have nothing left to show for our work. We may go to hell and back and in the end, doubt, fail, find ourselves hollow and cheated by the promises of projects that were supposed to guarantee our importance. Our strategies that we thought would guarantee relationships or eternal favor from a god who is ever so grateful to us for our efforts born of guilt and obligation. It is as if Rouault, with King David, sees that we really bring nothing to God: there is no power to coerce divine favor. The only thing to bring is a "broken and contrite heart" (Miserere Psalm v.17).

Failure, human failure, is ok.

In fact, it is perhaps the most acceptable part of us. Failure functions to strip away the false messiahs of control, regularity, power, competence, continual intensity, hypervigilance, and any other human project to guarantee our importance. Failure illuminates our essential worth, our unchangeable value, the light of the divine image that illuminates all of Rouault's figures.

GUIDED MEDITATION

Take a moment to find a place to be still and quiet. See if it feels ok to close your eyes and count 5 breaths. Check and see if you have emotional space to sit with this meditation.

When you hear the word "failure," do you notice any place in your body react? Where do you hold your past failures? Perhaps you feel it in the pain of feeling incompetent, inferior, powerless and unable to do something? What feelings show up as you even consider connecting with your part that holds the pain of failure? Can you see if those parts will give you space to connect with the fear-of-failure part? If not, can you ask those parts what they are afraid of happening if they were to give you access?

Notice again where the fear-of-failure part shows up in your body. See if you have some openness and curiosity to understand this part better now? If so, can you ask what this fear of failure is especially afraid of? Failure in relationships, career, certain kinds of performance? Were there moments in your life that really made this part active to protect you from the pain of failure?

What do the part fear would happen if you failed again? Are there moments they are holding onto that they said, "never again?" or "that will never happen to me". Have the part made a vow to never let you risk failure again in certain areas of your life? Can you let the part know you are understanding it and offer any appreciation you feel.

Perhaps with more understanding of what is driving the intensity of the part, can you offer wisdom, perspective, and compassion for those fears of failure? What would realistically happen if you failed again? Would you survive? Have you found other sources of love and security that would buffer you not if you failed somehow?

When this inner reflection feels complete for you, take a few moments to return your attention to your breath and to the space around you. Perhaps spend some moments reflecting on the experience and take any notes on things you would like to explore further later or insights you want to hold onto.

To engage with the high intensity level audio version described in the introduction, scan the QR code or visit tinyurl.com/rouault-meditations.

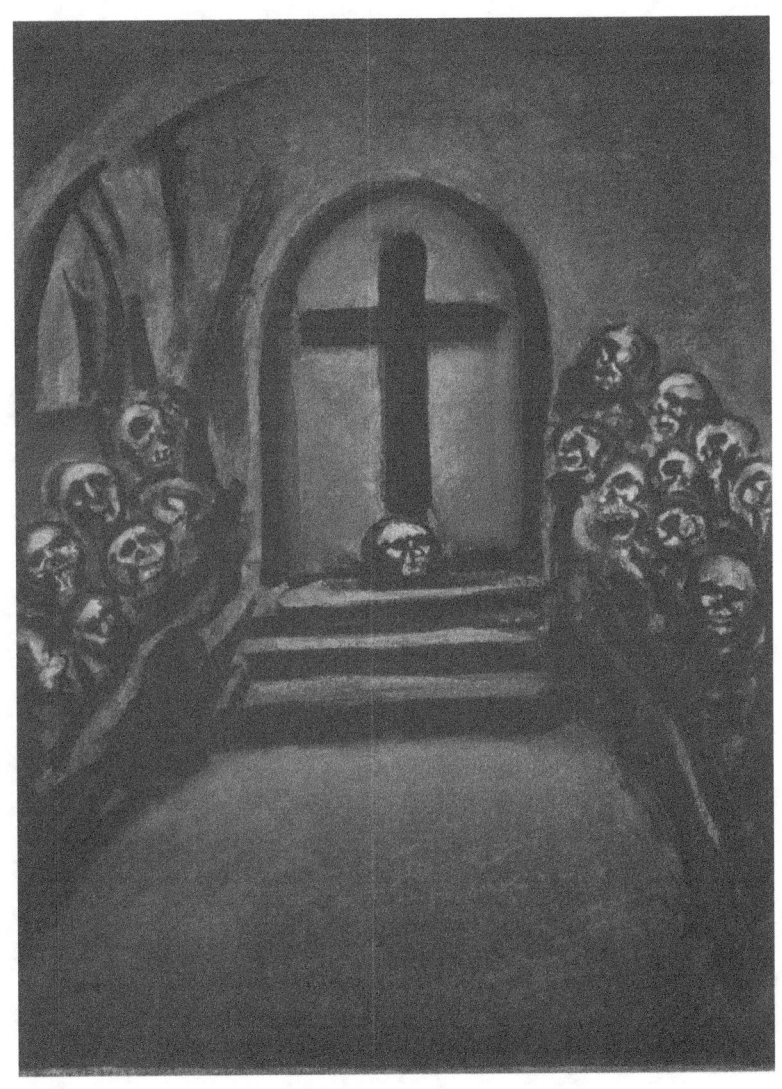

Plate 28

PLATE 28: BELIEVE

"Celui qui croit en moi, fût-il mort, vivra"
"He that believeth in me, though he were dead, yet shall he live"

This stanza completes the poetic line from the previous plate, "In all things, tears," "He that believeth in me, though he were dead, yet shall he live." The image is of a charnel house or ossuary.

I can't remember which Romanian monastery we were visiting, but I remember it was after seeing the church and sharing a liturgy with some friendly monks. One monk led us through a break in the tree line down a dirt path, taking us to an outbuilding. I may or may not have understood the Romanian word for the place he was showing us, but the place, as a thing that might exist, had never dawned on my Western mind. Stepping into the charnel house of the monastery, a room much like the one in this image on Plate 28, one is immediately arrested by a density of experience, like that of tasting a cooked reduction, a concentration of cooked down flavors; or like the "chutnification" process described by Salman Rushdie in *Midnight's Children*.

Low ceiling and arched windows. The room had tables and ledges around the walls of the room, and a long wide table in the middle, leaving enough room for the pilgrim to safely walk around the room without bumping into the skulls and bones filling all of the surfaces. The charnel house I visited had all of the skeletal remains in neat separate piles, with names of their retired inhabitants written in black ink on the skulls. Even with some preparation, it is an unsettling experience. Each skull is a remnant of a whole life of love, beauty, suffering and joy. Birth and death.

Being in close proximity with a human skull with no mediating structure is perhaps part of the point for the monastic life. One can find many artist renditions of the theme of *memento mori,* a contemplative with a skull on the desk next to an ink well.[61]

Much could be said about the theology of the dead, of incorruptible bodies, sacraments around death, and burial or prayers for the dead. St Silouan the Athonite said, "Keep your mind in hell and do not despair."[62] Morbid as this seems on the surface, one can think of the mindfulness of death – a spiritual practice found in many religions – as but the other side of the coin from gratitude, the mindfulness of the beauty of life. Both function to get to the marrow of what matters.

In modern times many medical dramas capitalize on this same dynamic, the life and death setting of the hospital creates the catalyst for speaking about things that are most meaningful. At the birth of a baby and the death of a loved one our values become clearer.

Rouault's ossuary house image is set up as if it is a theatre of the dead, set in rows waiting on the cross on the stage. The cross is backlit, creating a hard contrast between the lightest and darkest tones in the image, focusing the viewer on this rough cross in the center. The skull beneath the cross in iconography typically refers to the skull of Adam, which was said to be buried under the place where Christ was crucified. The first Adam and second Adam meet on Golgotha, the place of the skull, specifically Adam's skull. Rouault's image, with the skull of Adam under the cross, carries a universal application: God's compassion on all of humankind for all time, from Adam to you.

Though the cross holds lights and darks, so do the skulls. Rouault's skulls are reflecting light. Not to make too much significance out of this, but one might suppose that he sees light and life, and hope, here even in the dried bones. Much like some of the images of rising bones further in the *Miserere* series, these are bones on their way to resurrection, not annihilation into dust.

These skulls have the living, moving feel of a crowd waiting for a courtroom verdict, worriedly murmuring to one another almost. This would reflect the poetic line, suggesting, "though dead...yet shall they live." Even the charnel house contains light. In some sense one might see many of the plates up till now in the series as charnel houses, dark places that seem hopeless and yet are illuminated with a radiating image of indwelling divine light. John 12:24 says, "*...except a grain of wheat falls to the ground and die, it abideth alone: but if it die, it bringeth forth much fruit,*" reframing death in terms of anticipation.

The skull under the cross almost seems to be preaching to the congregation of skulls in the galleries. There is no sign of life in the image. We were taken through the "land of thirst and terror," then Orpheus and his journey to Hades; and now we are in the waiting room, waiting to be dust or Ezekiel's dry bones reconstituted, resurrected.

It almost feels merciless, the way Rouault dredges the depths of despair and suffering. One can only imagine the horrors of war, the social and personal suffering Rouault lived through. It is as if he goes through methodically collecting all the dark corners of human hopelessness, and invites the viewer to hope, not around, but through the depths of suffering. Anything less for him is religion as a fear-filled opiate addiction.

In the Eastern church Holy Friday services start late Thursday night, a virtual funeral service for the burial of Christ. I can remember entering our neighborhood church before the service began, and in the front center was set up a table with the embroidered icon of the deposition of Christ, the table overflowing with flowers from neighborhood flower gardens decorating the icon.

Penitents would make their venerations, kissing the icon of the Christ taken down from the cross, and then proceed to crawl under the table and back around to venerate a second and third time. It is one of the ways the eastern church has found to experientially "enter into" the death of Christ.

Then Holy Saturday follows. Holy Saturday is the celebration of Christ's harrowing of Hell. The journey is much like that of Orpheus, rescuing his love from death, conquering death by the beauty of His own self-giving love; yet in this story Christ has conquered death and Hell. Many eastern preachers say the resurrection began the moment Christ died and began the harrowing of Hell, the journey to free all those locked in hell, to break the doors of hell forever.

Easter liturgy is celebrated at midnight, the moment Easter or Pascha day begins. The faithful begin a liturgy around midnight after the Pascal prayers. Parishioners finishing in the wee hours of the morning and being at their own neighborhood church will typically walk home, resurrection-light candles in each hand. Many people with departed loved ones will make a stop on their way home to the cemetery, to leave a candle of the resurrection light on the grave of their departed. Some of the gravesites of the well-to-do are more like screened in porches, with a door and steps down into well-lit tiny space, with room for the cement-encased casket, room for a place to sit, and a tiny table big enough for a piece of bread and a strong drink. The resurrection light is carried to the graves and used to light a funerary candle designed to withstand some wind and stand guard for half a day.

Seeing a place like a charnel house in Rouault's time would not have been nearly as unusual as it may be now. In the Catholic cultures, where saints are also venerated and the bodies of the faithful are watched for miraculous signs, we find similar places. In the bowels of the Lima Metropolitan Cathedral in Peru, we visited the skeletal remains of the faithful carefully stacked in neat circular rows, skull after skull.

Living through the war years would have made Rouault acquainted with many departed souls, narrowing the space between the living and the dead.

In this place of death Rouault gives this stanza, "He that believeth in me, though he were dead, yet shall he live," quoting Christ in John 11:25. It also resonates with the line of the Miserere Psalm, "thou shalt make me hear joy and gladness; the bones that be humbled shall rejoice" (v8). Rouault's dead bones are luminous, seeds ready to awaken to new life.

Romania, 2005

The 18-hour journey home was almost over. Now, 9:30 p.m., it was a cool summer evening. I remember the window open still. Earlier it had kept at bay the full summer sun, and now let in a little dampness and some air to give a first shiver. It was the last stretch past Brailla, and next would be Galati. It all came over me: the time in the US seeing family and friends, eating peanut butter and Oreos, seeing friends buying homes, having more kids, settling into career paths. What are we doing?

Then the train began to bank and I imagined the city streets above the hill. The graveyard was just a few hundred feet beyond the tracks. The air on my face could have been carried past the grave of Annamaria and Lazarus. The face of Daniel, and of the street boys and "old man" who died on his own vomit underground came to mind, the slashed wrists and night thrashings taken by the boys just because a gang of teenagers knew they could get away with it. The litany of suffering went on in my head. In my semi-depressed state, it felt like a train curving back into hades.

Passing the graveyard on my right and on my left was the steel factory taking up about a quarter of the land area of the city. At that time in the evening, it was a glow and hum of lights, smoke and machines whose collective noise created a deep bass sound foundation. The plant was a big machine, and we were all part of it, a death machine spewing toxins into the watershed for the sake of profit, in the pursuit of world status as a steel producer.

It was from a distance a kind of charnel house, like the production of the dark powers in the Lord of the Rings, pillaging trees and spewing toxins. For me it represented vast overwhelming power that I was no match for. It was much like the suffering of youth living on the street, the kids who grew up in the orphanages without being touched, those kids infected with HIV/AIDS due to the reusing of needles and a disbelief in the science of the day, the unemployment and child abandonment, the exclusive educational system, to name a few. The vulnerable and weak seemed to have little but a prayer.

"In all things tears…," "he that believeth in me, though he were dead, yet shall he live." Rouault brings us to the ashes, the bones, the holocaust: we are but skulls waiting to die. When it seems plenty dark he takes the pilgrim another layer deeper into the charnel house of the soul, the place where the signs of hopelessness are lined up one after another, and the only power we possess is the power to trust a power greater than ourselves. We are in a prison cell, the doors have clanged shut, and the lights are out.

And in this place there is a great silence, a terrifying and perhaps pregnant silence. I may go back and forth from hope to despair in the course of seconds.

Around the edges of my eyes, tears would form but were too shy to drop. It felt like hour after hour, day after day. I knew I was doing things but this part, this grieving for my lost Lazarus part was the most present, making everything else feel less real. It is easy to jump to the end of the story when you know everyone will be happy again, but when it feels when you are in it like this might just be the rest of your life. You are miserable, half alive, half dead with your lost one. And then all of the other losses creep in, until you have a charnel house full of the skulls and bones collected and ignored in this room. To keep on living, you said you would stay away from this place, and yet you find yourself returning without realizing it.

Rouault's way is through the charnel, not around it. Sit there and be still and silent, just believe, breathe, be still, and when all you have is unbelief, stay still and breathe.

Eastern State Hospital, Kentucky, 2012

Getting back on the unit for my shift I found that Jack had stuffed something in his ear again. What that meant for the mental health assistants was that he was to be closely monitored. He was officially on "close," and would be shuffled from assistant to assistant for the duration of his risk status. Jack was a trauma survivor of physical and sexual abuse, like a high percentage of those in the psych hospital, according to some statistics.[63]

Jack had the double whammy of also having used recreational drugs to the point of significant brain damage, resulting in psychotic symptoms, most of which did not result in threatening behaviors. When I was assigned to stay within 3 feet of him for a couple of hours. I had the choice of trying to talk him out of his delusions, or to just play along. Just in his late 20's, he had a mostly pleasant demeanor, and liked to talk and interact. You never knew what you were going to get. One day while on "close," he was full of energy, and walked quickly up and down the halls for hours on end. The assistant had to keep up per policy of remaining three feet away at all times.

Another day he started telling me how I was homeless, (and I was not, if you weren't sure), and in need of his instructions on how to survive homelessness. He proceeded to give me step-by-step instructions on how to manage the need for a place to sleep, go to the bathroom, to avoid the police and to find food. It was as if he were caring for me as a friend or brother, coaching me through with all his hard-earned wisdom. There was a kind of richness in the conversation, in which he in the prison of his involuntary psychiatric hospital stay was able to express compassion in this delusional, but beautifully human way.

Another day he was not doing so well. He was not cooperating with staff and was taking his clothes off and trying to walk around naked. He was placed in a special watch room next to the nurses' station, where he could be kept out of view of the other patients and staff, maintaining some dignity in his psychotic state. Staff were assigned to sit outside the door and monitor him for suicidal or self-harm behaviors.

During my post guarding the door and monitoring his safety, I checked in and saw the sleeping mat on the floor and his clothes perfectly laid out—as if his body had magically disappeared, leaving the clothes behind. Hat, shirt, pants, and socks were meticulously arranged to look like a sleeping, flattened form. He was curled in the other corner of the room, asleep.

On one level it was a physical representation of the protective dissociation that many sexual abuse survivors experience. Jack's charnel house was represented by clothes emptied of their animating body. So Rouault gives us this image of death, but it resonates with our own lifeless empty parts; dried, worn, withered-away parts; parts that hold the place while we are often unconscious on the other side of the room; the skeletal structure without life.

Disconnection and disassociation from others lead to dehumanizing, disrespectful words and behaviors that attack the dignity of our fellow humans. Disconnection and disassociation from ourselves are at times the only way to survive attacks that would devastate our inner system, threatening it with collapse. However, the more disconnected from ourselves we remain, the more our inner system is locked in a cycle of disenfranchising parts that need healing and reconciliation. The separation of flesh from bones Rouault places before us, this *memento mori* contemplation of death may be about cosmic religious and theological themes he saw, but it also illuminates our own inner experience of parts that feel sealed away, lifeless bones longing for the return of flesh and vibrancy.

I would not argue that Rouault was thinking about this inner level of reality, but rather that his intuition about the human, theological and cosmic resonates on every level of the relational systems that we exist in, cosmic, social, interpersonal, and intrapersonal. The level we seem to have the most control over is our own inner or intrapersonal relational system.

GUIDED MEDITATION

Take a moment to find a place to be still and quiet. See if it feels ok to close your eyes and count 5 breaths. Check and see if you have emotional space to sit with this meditation.

Now can you key into your body as you engage with this image of Rouault's Charnell house? What do you notice arise in you as you see this image and take it in? Can you identify a part of you that can make you feel powerless at times? Are you aware of the kinds of situations that bring it to the surface?

Are there parts that react whenever the powerless feeling gets close or does come to the surface? Can you check in with those parts that worry about the potential effects of the powerlessness feeling part coming out?

Can you just see if they would be willing to relax for a few minutes and allow you to attend to the powerless feeling? Is there anything you need to do or say to make it feel safer to go there?

If you feel safe and curious about exploring your part that holds the powerless feeling go ahead and notice again, where it shows up in your body. See if Rouault's image or any other image or sensation helps you connect with the part. Can you get a sense for how old the part is? Has it been around for a while?

If you can notice some compassion towards this powerlessness holding part, go ahead and let it know you are here and you want to see and understand the experiences that made it start carrying these feelings for your system. If it opens up memories of powerlessness, really let it feel your presence and your current ability to be responsive. Let it know you survived those powerless times.

When it seems it has shared what it needs to, see if you can update it on how your life is different now? Perhaps how you are not powerless now as you once were.

If there is death or permanent loss involved in the stories, perhaps there is a spiritual existential perspective you now hold that can help this part. Often, just feeling your presence and being seen can help diminish the intensity of the powerless feelings.

When this inner reflection feels complete for you, take a few moments to return your attention to your breath and to the space around you. Perhaps spend some moments reflecting on the experience and take any notes on things you would like to explore further later or insights you want to hold onto.

To engage with the high intensity level audio version described in the introduction, scan the QR code or visit tinyurl.com/rouault-meditations.

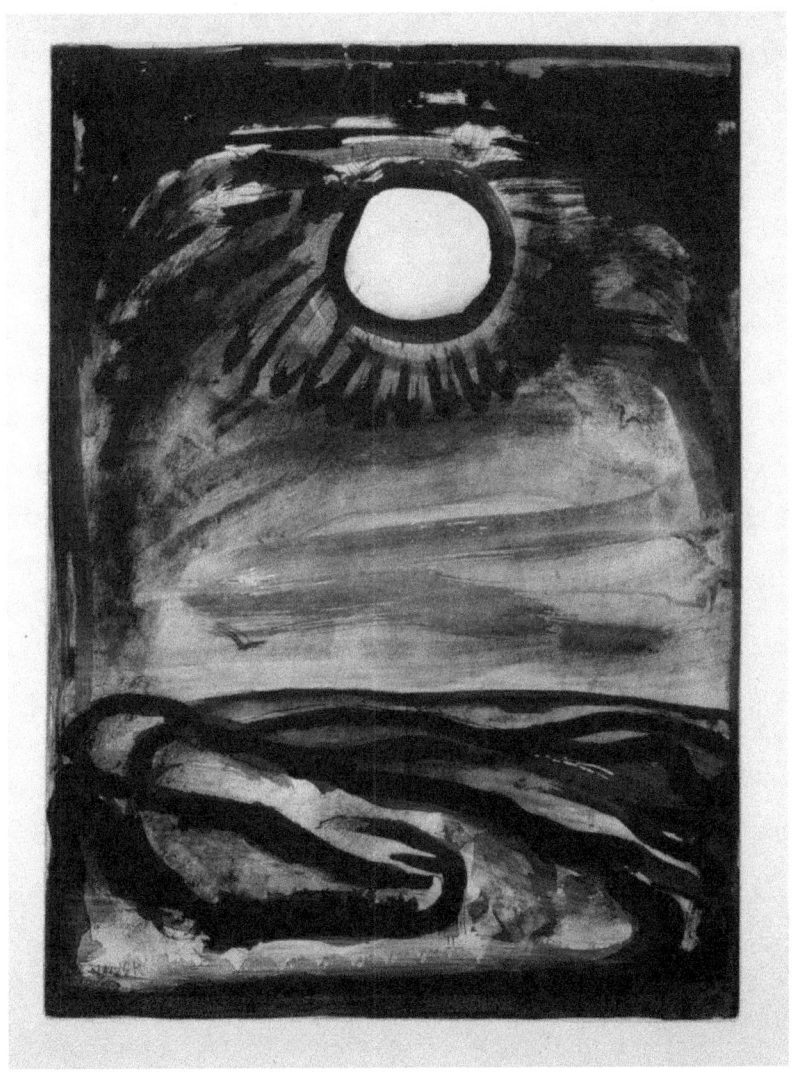

Plate 29

PLATE 29: SING

"Chantez Matines, le jour renait."
"Sing Matins, a new day is born."

In contrast with the stuffy, confining death space of the charnel house in the last image, this scene pulls the viewer out from an underworld of hopelessness and death to the open country air with the sun low in the sky. He gives us a sparse landscape, bare and atmospheric: a single bird flies in the distance and the viewer is on a winding path or road that meanders through the rolling fields. Rouault in his iconic style uses the high contrast of black brushed lines to push the appearance of a bright sun as much as possible. Everything is dark compared to this great light in the sky.

Rouault's stanza connects with the resurrection theme associated especially with the Matins Gospels sung every morning as part of the prayer cycle of hours by Catholics and observed by monks.

"Matins, the Catholic Encyclopedia says, was, the most important office of the day and for the variety and richness of its elements the most remarkable... after an invitatory psalm that served as an introduction to the whole Divine Office of the day, there followed twelve psalms and three readings on ordinary days, and eighteen psalms and nine readings on Sundays."[64]

This psalm begins all of the services but Matins as well...here are a couple of stanzas that seem to resonate with the spirit of this moment in the series,

Psalm 94/95 *Invitatory Psalm*
The Lord is a great king: come, let us adore him.
(repeat antiphon*)
Come, let us rejoice in the Lord,
  let us acclaim God our salvation.
Let us come before him proclaiming our thanks,
  let us acclaim him with songs.
  (repeat antiphon*)
For the Lord is a great God,
  a king above all gods.
For he holds the depths of the earth in his hands,

and the peaks of the mountains are his.
For the sea is his: he made it;
and his hands formed the dry land.

The morning light, matins light, becomes the resurrection light in Christian liturgics. Rouault has taken the viewer to the depths of isolation, terror and death, and now it is morning: a new day, a new sun, a luminous light, risen on the horizon of a cleared landscape, a road to be traveled, a bird to fly free within the distance. The fields seem to lie fertile and ready for a new planting; new year, new life and growth.

Russia, 1994

There was a joke that went around. The alcoholic was asked in the courtroom during a trial, "where were you the night of November 15th - January 15th?" I woke to what had been a shared hotel room for several weeks in the city of Naryan Mar in the arctic circle a couple of hours east of Murmansk. We were waiting for a cargo plane that would have room to fit us on the wooden benches under the windows, leaving the middle for the main cargo to be strapped down in the center of the plane.

It had been two months of darkness. It hardly seemed possible when they told me at first, but day by day the sun arched to a quarter of the way up the sky, peaking up for shorter and shorter times until the last wink on November 15th. It seemed not more than a couple of minutes of the rays of the sun reaching over the low hills beyond the Tuloma river outside of Murmansk.

After that the sky would look like the twilight before the sun rises, but for a couple of hours, as the sun skimmed below the horizon, sometimes it created incredible orange and rose-painted skies for hours at a time. By December 15th the sun seemed so shy that only between 10 a.m. and 2 p.m. did the sky lighten – and at that point it felt like it would be forever, and perhaps never be light again.

With so much dark, it made one want to sleep. By the end of the day, one felt weary with the work, straining one's eyes all the time to see – artificial light never really satisfied the thirst for light. We did some cross-country skiing, walked across the river, made trips into the city and enjoyed the Russian hospitality, but the unrelenting darkness took its toll.

Even to think back to that time, I feel the heaviness in my body as if gravity increased its pull when the sun stayed away.

On January 15th I woke in the Naryan Mar hotel, ice from condensation creeping into the room and bending towards the floor. Though I had forgotten the date, I had noticed that the midday brightness was lasting longer and longer. I stepped into my clothes, coat, and boots and headed out of the hotel on some errand.

The hotel to my right was followed by a series of four-story buildings to the end of the block. The other side of the street likewise was framed by a row of buildings. Looking up from the snow-covered street below, grey frost-bleached buildings to right and left, perfectly framed the most beautiful thing I had ever seen in my life.

A perfect ball of energy.

It reached its rays to the back of my eyes, filling every cone and rod with a rich warmth. My thirsty eyes drank deep and seemed to reach neurons long starved for stimulation.

Floating in the middle of the frame, the pale cadmium yellow ball on a white sky looked like a goldfish with perfect edges just above the horizon. It had not forgotten us forever. Like a dead electronic device finally plugged in, I felt new life surge into me.

"Sing Matins, a new day is born."

Romania, 2002

We said we would wait at least until the due date of Lazarus, our miscarried child, before trying again. The due date came with a slurry of grief and inner turmoil and sadness, the undeniable reality of what did not come to be in our arms. The consideration of trying to have another child came with its own slurry of emotions.

May 24, 2002 – *Journal Entry*

God help me. Yesterday we heard from a doctor that she thought her uterus was too small to carry a child to 6 months and would probably not survive if we lived in Romania. What the hell kind of diagnosis is that? "Congrats, you are pregnant, but you can't carry a full pregnancy." I just feel powerless and faithless.

She asks me to pray and I wipe the crumbs from the table and hope that it is enough faith to be a real prayer. My mouth is moving but my heart is terrified and full of doubt. I pray to help myself, not because I believe... I am scared. I am fearful of months of heaviness and pain. Of not having enough for my wife and of her being a constant reminder of my utter powerlessness and failure.

I am emotionally exhausted just thinking about it. Will we be forced by circumstance to move back to the States for a time? We really are powerless. I don't want to leave and start all over again. I don't want to say goodbye to kids. I want to have a baby, a healthy baby in my Galati community with all our problems and fights. God help me.

I am afraid to hope. It seems like a cruel joke, the death sentence on a new surprise life. And Rouault says, "Sing Matins, a new day is born."

Rouault's image does bear a bright light of hope, but it is in the midst of scumbled darkness. It is not an ignorance of the suffering, but a radical protest against the dark it comes to conquer. Rouault's hope is not delusion, but hope through darkness, embraced, suffered.

The sun is a heavenly body, a transcendent light, a hope that is above human powers of planning and ingenuity. This is a hope in a higher power, a spiritual underpinning that operates for our good. It is only from a mysterious disordered mess that real hope emerges.

Singing hope in the midst of darkness is different from the celebratory after-the-fact kind of song. Rouault's image says, "Sing Matins now, in hope of resurrection, restoration while things are yet dark, when you can't see it."

In the face of a polar night, of death and miscarriage, our illusions of power and control are mercilessly stripped away. Belief in a rising sun is an acknowledgement of a goodness we receive that is completely beyond our power to control. Religion can be used as just another attempt at control, by trying to get God to do your bidding. The spiritual truth is that we are in a world with pain, as well as a whole lot of beauty and goodness. There is no manipulating God. any more than one might manipulate the sun. What is in our power is the capacity for awe and gratitude, hope and faith that in the end the sun will rise again; that there will be an eschatological new day that puts an end to suffering.

"Sing Matins, a new day is born." In the Matins and liturgy, time is folded back on itself and the present is also the future tasted and seen.

David Bentley Hart writes:

> *"This amazement perhaps lies always just below the surface of our quotidian consciousness; but beauty stirs us from our habitual forgetfulness of the wonder of being. It grants us a particularly privileged awakening from our "fallenness" in ordinary awareness, re-minding us that the fullness of being, which far exceeds the moment of its disclosure, graciously condescends to show itself, again and again, in the finitude of an event: of a mere instance. In this experience, we are given a glimpse—again, with a feeling of wonder that restores us momentarily to something like the*

innocence of childhood—of being's kenosis in beings: that inexhaustible source that pours itself out in the gracious needlessness of creation. Beauty shines out in the midst of being as the sign and gift and ever-renewed revelation of what transcends discrete beings, exciting in us an eros for the source of all splendor and all delight. If, that is, we have eyes to see and ears to hear."[65]

Hiking alone in the Daniel Boone National Forest, I entered the deep silence of the woods in which only my footfalls and crinkling of my coat could be heard. I was struck again by this immediacy of presence to the natural world, enveloping me in its magical silent kingdom. It struck me that everything I touched and saw and smelled had names, were measured by precise instruments, categorized into flora and fauna, and searchable.

All of these labels, while useful in certain moments, become superfluous to the magic of breathing in the woods, seeing the light come through the trees, the ghostlike waterfall blowing in the breeze and the awe of standing under a monumental naturally formed stone arch. The silent beauty of Rouault's pieces carry this residue of mystery and magic, an engaging presence not definable by measuring the pigments or describing the shapes. This piece brings one into a wide-open space and invites the viewer to stand in awe at a new day.

Rouault hangs hope in the sky and gives us a road to walk in the dawn that has not fully shed the night. His landscape carries hope that is above and beyond how our individual lives play out. His kind of faith saw the fabric of humanity ultimately healed in the "fullness of being." This is a hope that survives a room full of skeletal remains and the decimation of war in the following series. Rouault's vision of suffering is comprehensive, preparing the road to the ridiculous hope for the poor, the wanderer, the orphan and widow, the convict, the lawyer and the judge, as well as to the woman in prostitution, or the clown. His hope scours to the bottom layers of despair, and invites downcast, ravaged castaways to lift an eye and let in the longed-for Matins light.

Kentucky 2021

Along with our other 2 children we just celebrated the 18th birthday of this beautiful boy, conceived in fragile hope.

GUIDED MEDITATION

Take a moment to find a place to be still and quiet. See if it feels ok to close your eyes and count 5 breaths. Check and see if you have emotional space to sit with this meditation.

What is stirred in you when you engage with this image? Is there a protective fear that arises when you consider hope? Can you consider the role of this fear to protect you from repeating a past episode of pain, suffering, or a dark abyss? Can you just honor for a moment how terrifying hope can be for this part of you that have felt and guarded from so much pain for so long?

If it fits for you, perhaps consider expressing gratitude for this part that has worked to keep your life going by avoiding anything that requires hope? Can you ask this part that protects against hope, what it would need in order to allow some hope to live more fully into an uncertain future? Is there a story this fear-of-hope part needs to tell you to feel understood? Are you in a place now where you can risk a little more hope?

If it feels ok, can you make some space for expansiveness and light? Are there signs of hope and change in your life you can embrace? Are there good things you are experiencing now in your life that you never dreamed of in the past? Perhaps things that felt hopeless that you got through? Can you bask in the light of the good and beautiful that has happened despite your struggles and the fact that everything isn't perfect?

Can you sense that you are on a journey, a path as in the image here? If it feels right see if you can get a general message into your inner system that you are on a path, you have a direction and that there is light now, presence now. If this works great. If there are protecting parts, just let them know you will work with them in time. Do you notice any shifts in your body as you do this? What is happening to your part that fears hope as it watches you experiment with some hope now?

When this inner reflection feels complete for you, take a few moments to return your attention to your breath and to the space around you. Perhaps spend some moments reflecting on the experience and take any notes on things you would like to explore further later or insights you want to hold onto.

To engage with the high intensity level audio version described in the introduction, scan the QR code or visit tinyurl.com/rouault-meditations.

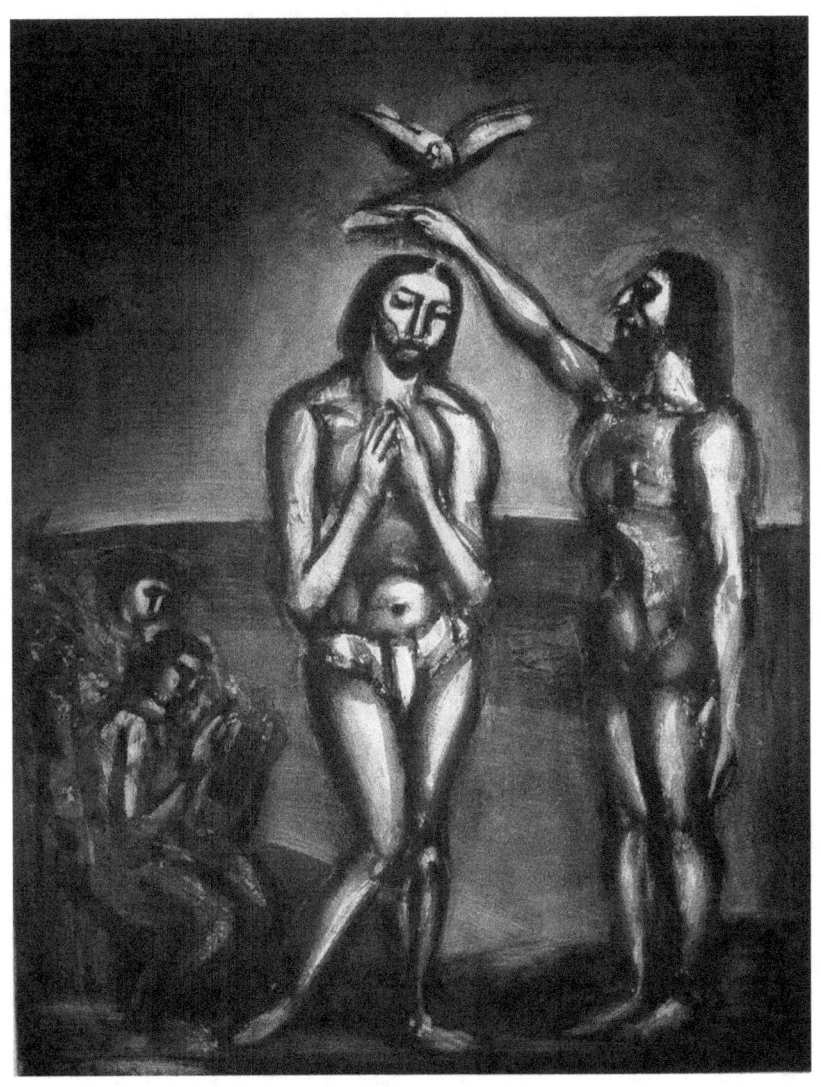

Plate 30

PLATE 30: BAPTISED

"Nous...c'est en sa mort que nous avons été baptisés"
"We...it is in His death that we have been baptized" (from Romans 6:3)

After we "Sing Matins," Rouault brings an image of the baptism of Christ. The baptism image is sandwiched between the sunrise stanza, "Sing Matins, a new day is born," and the crucifixion image associated with "love one another." This picture space is structured in a traditional iconographic arrangement for the baptism of Christ – or Theophany, as it is referred to in the Eastern Orthodox Church. In doing so, he invites the viewer to carry some of the historical ways of understanding the baptism to the image, while also perhaps accept the challenge of seeing it again for the first time in the context of the series.

His emphasis on making it speak directly to the viewer in the present moment is achieved by the first-person plural pronoun, "*We*...it is in His death that *we* have been baptized." He presses the viewer to consider themselves the subject of the image.

As with many of the other pieces in this series, the gorgeous modulation of lights and darks is carried throughout. There is always enough, but not too much. I have heard it said, from a friend who has had an ear in the New York art auctions, "The collectors buy the Picassos, but the artists want the Rouaults." Regardless of one's opinion about Rouault's religious beliefs, the truth he found, was won in a wrestling match with the materials and surfaces, like a farmer who plants and toils digging up the potatoes out of the ground. This, I believe, is what any artist can appreciate in Rouault's body of work. He is one who has entered the fight with brush and ink, paint and canvas, like someone wrestling a crocodile in a swamp and barely coming up with their life.

While this is not a painted surface, he approaches it in his characteristic painterly way: Christ central, John baptizing, dove descending, observed by angels. The figures to the left are perhaps angels bowing – perhaps referring to the Philippians kenotic hymn celebrating Christ, descending lower than the angels in taking on human flesh. Christ stands in a posture of humility, submitting to baptism by John.

Compact body and folded arms mimic the posture of one being prepared for death, corresponding with the poetic line, "...it is in his death..." Baptism in the Eastern Orthodox Churches and in certain Protestant denominations is done by immersion, a dramatic enactment of burial in water and resurrection to a new way of life. In the Catholic context, while sprinkling is the means of baptism, the meaning of the sacrament remains: entrance into the death of Christ and the rising with Him in His resurrection.

The baptism image as a concise summary of the previous journey – entry into the sufferings of the convict, the oppressed, the poor, the homeless, etc – is entrance into the death of Christ, the descent into the suffering of humankind. Like Orpheus, who descends and returns with his love, Christ descends into human flesh, into hades, and returns with the captives of hell as stated in the Eastern Orthodox paschal hymn, "Christ is risen from the dead, trampling down death by death, and upon those in the tombs bestowing life."

Rouault challenges the pilgrim at Plate 30, that being baptized into the death of Christ is also the empathic entrance into the sufferings of our fellow human beings. Simply put, Christ's journey is a compassionate entrance into every level of suffering humans have faced. To join Him, to be baptized into Christ, to die and rise in Him, is likewise to enter a life of agapic action to liberate every level of human experience, reconciling the broken and exiled parts. This is echoed simply in James as, "Pure and undefiled religion...is to visit the orphan and widow..." (James 1:27).

In the East this image and the feast is called Theophony, referring to the revealing of the Holy Trinity. Often there is a depiction of the voice of the father coming down from above. Here it is assumed from the context. The idea of this being also a revelation of the relational nature of God, three persons commingled but not confused, one God, adds force to the importance of the image.

This is one of the strongest examples – and much celebrated moments – in the gospels for clearly depicting the three persons of the godhead, Son, Spirit, and Father. The moment is characterized by condescension into the suffering and death of humanity. The Father and Spirit are with Christ, sending and empowering, and the compassion, the divine agape-apatheia, is illuminated in a dense theological moment.

God is love, and specifically an embodied compassion which descends into every corner of every part of every human suffering. This foreshadows the next image's stanza, "love one another." This love is perhaps the light illuminating every image in the series, the compassionate identification and descent into the sufferings of another – and perhaps into our own vulnerable suffering places.

Ion Bria, Romanian Orthodox theologian and priest who spent much of his career at the World Council of Churches, said one's Christian ecumenism could be seen in the level of acceptance of one another's Christian baptism.[66] Baptism in the Christian life is the initiation ceremony, the entry point in the journey, the way established by the apostles and Christ. It is the one sacrament that is held onto in almost every expression of Christ-following faith, from Orthodox, Catholic, and most of the different Protestant denominations.

Earlier in the history of Christianity, it was considered the second most important feast just after Easter. This was the revelation of the Trinity and the overflow of agape.

Romania, 2003

As my wife and I had been recently chrismated into the Romanian Orthodox church and now had a growing baby, it was time to baptize him. When I called home to the US and spoke with my parents about baptizing our infant, I had all kinds of ideas about what their reaction might be, since we had always gone to churches that only baptized kids once they were old enough to understand enough of what it meant. After I mentioned it to my mother, she responded with a story of how since she and my father had grown up Lutheran, my father had quietly baptized all the siblings as infants in the bathtub, "just in case Luther was right."

Orthodox Romanians tend to baptize their infants often even before leaving the hospital. A chapel just behind the main hospital serves as a thriving parish, and spiritual healing and sacrament station for those in the hospital.

The day of our son's baptism, we brought a lovely friend who agreed to be the godmother. She was the friend who was there to wash bloody sheets out after our miscarriage of Lazarus, brought us food and made coffee, kept us going when our heads were spinning with confusion and grief. It seemed only fitting that she be the godmother. A gathering of other friends joined us to help mark the day our "fingernail of a chance baby" was getting baptized.

When we got inside the church, it was already quite full of people we had not invited. There were eight other babies being baptized that midmorning. The church was well equipped with long tables along the side of the church, flexibility afforded by having no pews in the sanctuary, only around the edges of the church. The walls are covered in icons from bottom to top, frescoes covering the major feasts and events in the cycle of the church, with the highest Pantocrater icon in the dome all the way down to the local Romanian saints standing just a head higher than the congregants, a circle of saints almost at eye level.

The service started in the entry way of the church, the godparents standing in for the infant. Babies are taken from the parents and the godparents take over. As the father of my kid, this little liturgical separation was perhaps the most striking. This child is not my property, he is from me, yet separate from me. This is accentuated throughout the service, where the parents' only role is to give up the child and watch: watch the stripping of clothes till your infant is naked, watch as the priest holds him up, watch as he goes under the water, dunked completely in the water of the baptismal font.

There is some literal fear of death and drowning, even though the priest is trained and the infants are really only under the water for a split second. Water is a grave, it is certain death for an infant, and claims the lives of many in the world daily from drowning.

The infants are reclothed into brand-new clothes gifted by proud godparents, the old are discarded; a "new human" drawn out of the water gets new clothes. There are some prayers following, which culminate in the priest parading the newly baptized child around the holy altar. After the tour is done, the priest lays the child on the ground in front of the altar and leaves it there for the godparent to come and collect.

My helpless infant was just placed on the ground in front of the altar and my heart stopped.

This is not my property. This is God's child, made in His image, created by God, who will return to God. I am but guardian, custodian, curator, or caregiver, like a museum curator who holds the care of a priceless piece of art until another comes to continue the work of valuing and nurturing the priceless artifact.

Romania, 2006 - *Theophany*

Wandering to our neighborhood church on Theophany, the celebration of the baptism of Christ, one sees the crowds gathering. There are long plastic tables set up in lines in the courtyard of the church, with plastic decorative tablecloths and a random assortment of water-holding containers, from large pots to bottles and every shape in between. Each vessel is full of water already awaiting the service of the Blessing of the Waters.

I walk up in my hat and gloves, freezing cold already and cringing at being around this much water in the cold of mid winder. During the service water is blessed in the church, and the priest has a special water-sprinkling device used to hold water and evenly spray it out on the crowd up to 20 feet deep. The scene is all white from the snow, the cantor and priests all wear black and sing byzantine chants for the season, "When thou oh Lord was baptized in the Jordan..." They march around the water vessels praying, chanting, blessing and sprinkling the containers with the holy water, multiplying the holy water till there is enough for the whole community to put in bottles and carry home.

These little bottles end up on kitchen counters so they can be added to food and drinks. In this way the celebration of the baptism of Christ is the celebration of water being made holy and sending its divine healing properties to all corners of the earth. In a more basic way, it reminds the penitent that all water is holy, everything it touches is holy, the whole earth is sacred, as is the whole cosmos.

There are many interpretations of the baptism of Christ. One curious dynamic is that Christ refuses to baptize John, but rather insists on being baptized. Some early theologians saw this event being about Christ baptizing the element of *water* itself through his being baptized. These contemplatives see the connectedness of all water on the planet, and how at this moment God comes, submits to baptism, and sanctifies all water that will touch every corner of the earth.

In a similar way the work of Christ is seen as a victory over death, as sung in the Eastern Orthodox Paschal hymn, "Christ is risen from the dead trampling down death by death." Rather than focusing on substitutionary theories of salvation, here Christ is victor over death and is the new riverhead, as a river overflowing its banks finds a new path that will be followed from now on. Here water is changed, sanctified, and goes on sanctifying, starting something new that will change everything like the spread of an infection, only to spread life, wholeness and healing to the whole world, the whole cosmos.

"It is in His death we have been baptized." Death becomes a sacred meeting place, the absolute dark bottom of human experience. We include all of our experience, favorable and unfavorable alike, when we enter death, like cleaning the bottom of the trash can, usually hidden from view. In Rouault's baptism of Christ image, the importance of this divine identification with humanity in baptism – and eventually death – is highlighted. The presence of the Trinity is made sensible in the voice of the Father, Holy Spirit in the form of a dove, and the Son.

The idea is that somehow there are three persons, *hypostases*, and one essence, *ousia*.[67] These formulations have been debated over the centuries, but the idea remains in Christian orthodoxy that God is one and three without contradiction.

It is curious that modern psychological developments have evolved to conclude that human beings seem to be both one person, but also multiple parts at the same time, "Multiplicity of mind."[68] Richard Schwartz's Internal Family Systems model is perhaps the most pointed in exploiting this theory in his healing model.[69] Coming from a scientific, antireligious background, he was surprised to find that in working with all kinds of mental health struggles in clients, there always seemed to be internal aspects or "parts," seeking to do good (though often creating problems with their attempts), and a core essence, or in his language what he calls "Self."

This essence or core-self is recognized as showing up in therapy when there is a presence of compassion, curiosity, connectedness, calm, etc. The therapy is characterized by finding "Self," and helping the Self on a journey to find the lost and burdened exiled parts, restoring and healing them.

In this inner journey, a pattern that naturally develops, finding and healing the exiled parts, lost in a "black hole," or an "abyss of pain and darkness." These are images that repeatedly come up when working with this inner world, these young parts that have been shut away in shame.

When Rouault invites the viewer, "in His death," it is in this spirit of seeking and finding the lost exiles in society, and also in our own interior systems of parts, in which parts of us have been lost in death and despair. By the identification of God, Christ with death identifies with all lost and separated parts on every level of our inner and outer relational systems.

Upon entering into the death of Christ, we enter into the death and suffering of all humanity. We become one in death and one in resurrection. It is akin to rooting for a friend struggling with cancer for years and years, finally to have a clean bill of health. It is the identification in the struggle that joins us in the celebration of the overcoming.

Rouault by starting his poetic line with "We..." emphasizes the first-person plural pronoun by the separating ellipses from the rest of the line. The image is about Christ's baptism, but also about humanity's unity in suffering and the overcoming of death. This theme plays out throughout the series in Rouault's treatment of characters who could easily be treated with contempt.

Rouault seems to only see a "we" and never a "them." There is only "us."

GUIDED MEDITATION

Take a moment to find a place to be still and quiet. See if it feels ok to close your eyes and count 5 breaths. Check and see if you have emotional space to sit with this meditation.

What arises in your body as you consider openness to our shared human condition? Are there people groups who you struggle to admit to your circle? Are there categories of people, political allegiances that seem too far off, making it seem ok to strip them of their deserving of respect? Are there people in your life who have "gone too far," easy to write off as too something for care and consideration? Are there people unworthy of your empathy and understanding? Most of us have at least a short list. And do any of these people trigger parts of you that you dislike? Are there things you have done you hate or have attempted to be done with? Thoughts or impulses of your own you are afraid of?

Are there parts of you and your history that seem inexcusable and detestable? What are you afraid would happen if you were to even consider loving these enemies, or enemy parts of yourself? We often use suppression, avoidance and exiling of these parts of us only to find it does not cure or change them. By moving towards the demonized part, the enemy part, we can learn the intention underneath the unhelpful strategy. Once we understand the parts deeper intention there becomes space for more options that are more helpful.

See if you can just be curious for a few moments about the "enemy parts" in your system. Ask what it is trying to do for you by promoting its particular strategy. If you can appreciate the intention let the part know you see what it is trying to do and just ask it if it would be willing to try other things if it could meet the same need.

After doing that, just check if there is any more openness to considering that your social enemies may have positive intentions, common human desires underneath complicated behaviors. Don't be surprised if resistant parts arise. Try to be curious about the resistance because they always have good intentions too.

When this inner reflection feels complete for you, take a few moments to return your attention to your breath and to the space around you. Perhaps spend some moments reflecting on the experience and take any notes on things you would like to explore further later or insights you want to hold onto.

To engage with the high intensity level audio version described in the introduction, scan the QR code or visit tinyurl.com/rouault-meditations.

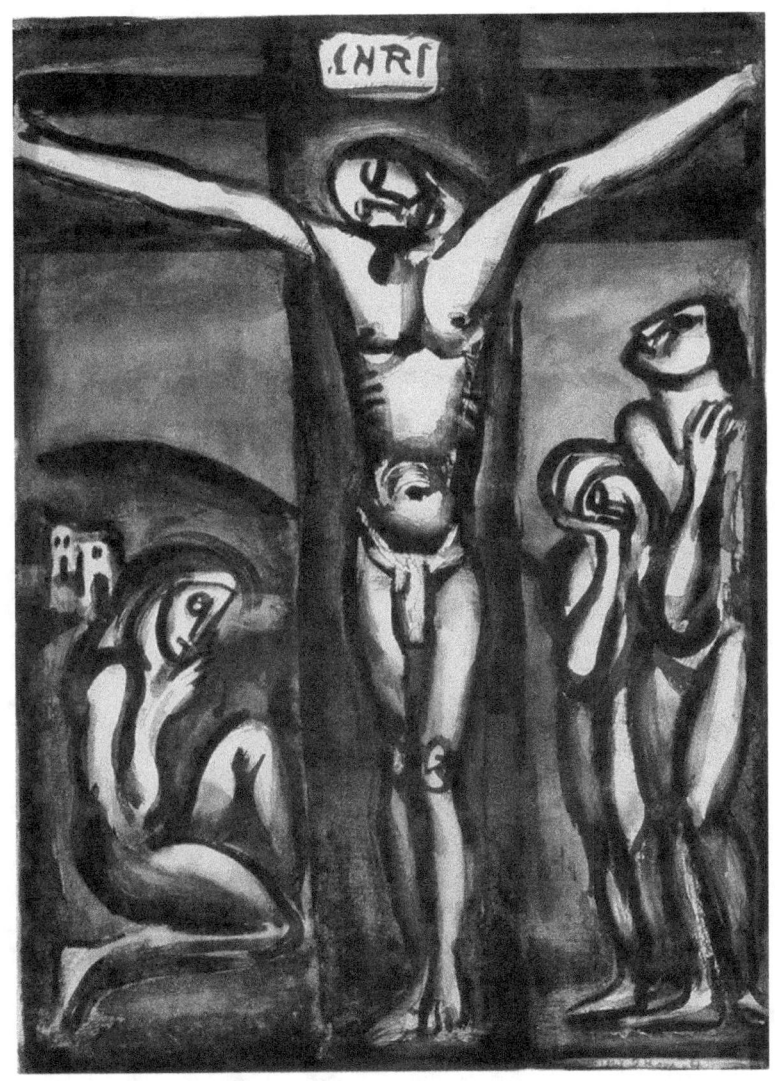

Plate 31

PLATE 31: LOVE ONE ANOTHER

"Aimez-vous les uns les autres."
"(I command to you) love one another."

Plate 31 presents the second crucifixion scene in the *Miserere* Series. The crucifixion scene in Plate 20 is connected with the courtroom drama, a simplified scene: Christ alone in a barren landscape. Plate 31 has a similar positioning of the body, Christ filling the picture plane head to toe and arm span width.

The hands again fall outside the edges of the frame. We have a simple landscape of a hill in the background, some buildings in the distance on the left, and three prominent figures standing neatly in the rectangles produced by the shape of the cross. Rouault uses eastern iconographic impulses that order space based on spiritual importance, rather than scientific perspective. In the relatively small area are packed four bodies, all very distinct from one another, but each with a direct purpose.

The composition is not dominated by the need to follow rules of linear perspective; but rather, line, shape, form, movement, and meaning directs the composition. The inner world, the intuitive emotional or psychological world of meaning and metaphor, is depicted directly without the cumbersome need to bow to naturalism.

This poetic line from the gospels associated with this piece is an imperative in the French not a mere suggestion; "Love one another. It references John 13:34, "A new commandment I give unto you, that ye love one another; as I have loved you, that ye also love one another" (KJV).

A grouping of people creates a space for this "love for one another" to be personal. The most prominent element perhaps is the sharing in suffering, compassion for the victim of crucifixion, the weeping and emotional collapse of deep mourning at the feet of loss, like having your heart torn from your body.

Kentucky, 1998

I was twenty years old, and trying to figure out where I was headed. Art was something that was always in my list of activities growing up. I won a scholarship at 13 to take a week-long workshop with an incredible artist named Bill Whitsett, who sat me down and looked through my drawings one by one. He searched through my pile of my drawings and pulled out the three I had done from life, brushing over the rest that were done from photographs. He pushed me uncomfortably close to the model for a week, drawing live portraits 6 hours a day.

The lights came on.

Drawing was about seeing what was actually there, not what you think was there. I remember struggling with the placement of an ear on the side of the model's face. My brain told me the top of the ear had to be somewhere near the eyes, but in fact they started closer to the mouth. I struggled with the enigma for a while, and finally complied with what I saw in front of me: I started the ear where it was relative to the rest of the face from my vantage point.

In wonder, I finished the drawing – and there it was, the portrait fit together, a single whole that looked like a real person. I found that as long as I could tie back the part of my brain that thinks it knows how things should look, and focus longer, ask how it really is in relation to the other parts, things began to ring true.

During my junior year of college, an exhibit of Georges Rouault's *Miserere* series came to the school where I was studying painting. Rouault's Plate 31 crucifixion scene was one of the images that arrested my attention in the small school gallery. A closet-sized gallery provided an intimate space, a sanctum to be with these rich black and white pieces. In this particular piece, Christ's hands extend beyond the edge of the print as if He holds the frame, almost as if He stands in a door frame.

Rouault has us in a different space altogether. Instead of Christ up high on a cross, high on a hill, Christ's feet are close to the ground, on the level of the mourners. Visually his mourners are under his arms spread like wings. Their suffering is visually contained in his suffering.

Things are not as you rationally think they should be, but intuitively are more than that. Spiritually the cross is never up, but down: down to the descent into hades, down to the lowest depths of human suffering. Rouault is a hyperrealist, depicting as accurately as possible the inner dimensions of experience. Rouault, quoting Gustave Moreau his teacher, said:

> *"Do you believe in God? I am asked. I believe only in God. In fact, I do not believe in what I touch, nor in what I see. I only believe in what I cannot see; solely in what I sense (sens). My mind and my reason seemed to me ephemeral and of a dubious reality. My inner consciousness (sentiment interiour) alone appears eternal and unquestionably certain."[70]*

After college I went to India, searching for a calling, a purpose, something I could do that had meaning. I found myself helping out at an orphanage with one hundred kids and a couple of staff people. I met a little 10-year-old girl named Lydia. She had an eye knocked sideways as an infant, and the staff were too embarrassed about it to get her the help she needed. When I met her, she struggled to keep her hair clean of lice, which meant having her head shaved. She had a delightful smile, engaging and playful. We bonded quickly.

One morning I came around the corner into the orphanage property, and she jumped into my arms. It was a very ordinary moment, and as I carried her around while greeting the others, she hung on – the ordinariness faded for a moment.

I found myself as if between two huge magnets, sensing a fundamental force; it was as if I could feel God's love for this outcast of the outcastes, this beat up orphan girl. It was bigger than me and the interior sense of things was invisible, but I was moved by it. Tears welled up as we just watched the others play.

God sees and hears. He knows the suffering of the poor, and in this moment I felt it. This little girl seemed to offer nothing. She had nothing to sacrifice, nothing to make God look good, but He loved her altogether.

At that same moment I could sense that all my pretentiously heroic acts were nothing before the love of God. All my "good choices," all my charitable acts, were strictly and forever irrelevant to this force; there was nothing I had ever done or could do in the future that had any bearing on this force of God's love for me.

Rouault's crucifixion image in Plate 31 is not a distant God-man crucified for those smart enough, devoted enough, pious enough to get it. Under the wing-like arms of Christ falls this love without boundaries.

There is a little structure in the background of the scene, also visually "under His wing." The structure reminds me of those simple homes of the poor around the world. It was the orphanage of the outcast Lydia and me in my true state, standing before this love of God, pure and always given to all, rich and poor alike.

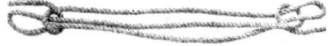

With the ubiquitous nature of the crucifix in Western culture, it is easy to overlook the fact that the cross was a form of capital punishment, a particularly hideous way of ridding the community of unwanted element, inspiring intense fear of finding oneself in the same deeply shameful position of being cast out, naked, and humiliated. Capital punishment is an ultimate exiling, an attempt to completely rid society of elements seen as beyond redemption, beyond repair, beyond reconciliation.

The electric chair, the firing squad, or, in the case in Romanian history that gave rise to the Dracula myth, "Vlad the Impaler," – who placed impaled bodies on stakes so all could see and fear – all reveal an impulse to exile whole peoples, and are responsible for some of the world's deepest wounds: the holocausts, genocides, and enslavements. It is always an attempt to purify and make peace by elimination of parts of humanity.

Inherently, it is also a warning to the internal systems of individuals to suppress any impulses which might evoke the same kind of punishment. Banishment and exile used as a strategy on the social and global levels happen on the intrapersonal level as well, the exiling or attempting to destroy or eliminate nefarious parts of ourselves. Demonizing the parts of us—crucifying the parts of us—that hold shame and guilt.

Plate 31 says we cannot exile, kill, or destroy without doing it to Christ Himself, who identifies here with each person who has ever been exiled, each part that has ever been banished, and each people group that has been targeted for genocide or slavery.

In contrast with the crucifix in Plate 20, with Christ alone above a barren landscape, here we have mourners packed into the spaces under the cross. The mourners suffer with, they hold the suffering space with Christ. "Love one another" is a sharing of empathic suffering, compassion by presence, emotional attunement, mourning, and grieving akin to sitting shiva in the Jewish tradition.

The focus in this image is a double compassion. First, the compassion of Christ in His total identification with the suffering of humankind, accepting humiliating public shameful death so that no exiled part of humanity can be outside of his comprehension and redemption. And the secondary compassion of the mourners who dare to stand with him in his shame and public death, risk being rejected and exiled themselves.

The alternative to exiling is healing and reconciliation, a new restoration.

As I attend to my inner world all these years later, I have returned to these moments of being confronted with holocausts. Early on, it was my Christian subcultures seeing abortion as a silent holocaust, as well as the conviction that people were dying every day without "saving knowledge of Jesus," and would spend eternity in hell. It was learning about the Nazi Holocaust in Germany. Later, I became enlightened to the holocaust of the native Americans, American enslavement, mass incarceration, sexism, and racism, not to mention the indiscriminate rape and pillage of our ecosystems.

Politics aside, these things override our natural longing for balance. I experienced these absolute urgencies as a teenager as reason enough to set aside balance and good sense. Either I sacrifice my desires entirely for the cause, or I am a terrible person who disregards the imminent tragedy of others.

This is the internal trap of the activist, leading to total burnout or apathy. I act out of terror of guilt and complicity, that part of me says, "You will not survive if somehow you contributed to the holocaust." This part drives hard until another part comes into rescue. Many times, it is the peace through alcohol or another pleasure and peace-seeking part that momentarily relieves the activist part of its duties.

The activist part seems to be the unassailably pure, good part. However, when explored with curiosity, this activist part, at least in me, is about seeking to avoid guilt, fear of disapproval, and even an avoidance of my own abyss of hopelessness and death and tragedy in my life. My self-righteous activist part means well but doesn't always have all the facts. It needs to know that even if I could be credited for rescuing 100 people from whichever tragedy, it would not increase or decrease my inherent worth and dignity as a human being. Guilt for the remaining millions would remain.

This activist part needs to know that it is expending a lot of energy avoiding guilt, rather than finding out what is actually effective; what ways I am gifted to help, and how I can contribute to the wellbeing of others out of unhurried compassion. The activist part has beautiful intentions but wastes a lot of energy and sets me up for burn out.

Agape-apatheia is the stuff we are made of, the activist part can rest in the apatheia of God, the calm, dispassion, ready and willing to help without compulsion from guilt or need to prove something. Work may be guided by what meets needs and what is effective versus what makes me feel less guilty.

Agape or compassion is our nature: when we peel back the fear driven activist parts, what is left is not neutral towards human suffering, it is active willingness, readiness, to help in a way that preserves the dignity of the helped without sacrificing the needs and betraying the gifts of the helper.

As in many traditional Eastern Orthodox crucifix images, Christ is seen not as a passive victim, with vivid veins and realistic blood, but rather willingly entering into human suffering, peaceful and calm and often with elegant, beautiful lines running along the edges of the body of Christ. Graceful visual lines parallel the spiritual meaning. Christ on the cross is another manifestation of agape and apatheia, dispassionate compassion. Rouault's Christ suffers with the suffering, willingly, without compulsion or coercion. He was not guilted into it, "for the joy set before Him" of reconciliation, healing and restoration.

In the context of this penitential *Miserere* series, built around personal change and reflection, I see Rouault believing that Christ suffers with all who suffer, and that to follow Him means to join Him in this kind of compassion for all who suffer.

"A new commandment I give unto you, That ye love one another; as I have loved you, that ye also love one another" (KJV).

GUIDED MEDITATION

Take a moment to find a place to be still and quiet. See if it feels ok to close your eyes and count 5 breaths. Check and see if you have emotional space to sit with this meditation.

If it fits for you, can you identify an activist part in you? A crusader for truth, a part that wants to be sure everyone understands how things really are? Notice where the part shows up in your body when it is ready to move out and make things happen.

Is there some kind of image or sensation or other way you notice your activist part? Notice how you are feeling towards this part of you? You may find some parts love it and other parts of you cringe at it. It may have gotten you in trouble in the past or gotten you positive recognition.

See if you can find some openness and curiosity towards it without too much evaluation. If so, can you ask it why it struggles to stand down at times when it might be more effective to wait and go slow? Ask it where the pressure comes from to act now? What is it trying to do?

If it feels genuine, can you share with this part some appreciation and also perspective on how if you can work together the energy it provides along with your deeper wisdom can get even better results, would it be willing to team up with you? See if there are any other hesitations it has to cooperating with you. Address them if you can, and end with some appreciation for its beautiful intentions.

When this inner reflection feels complete for you, take a few moments to return your attention to your breath and to the space around you. Perhaps spend some moments reflecting on the experience and take any notes on things you would like to explore further later or insights you want to hold onto.

To engage with the high intensity level audio version described in the introduction, scan the QR code or visit tinyurl.com/rouault-meditations.

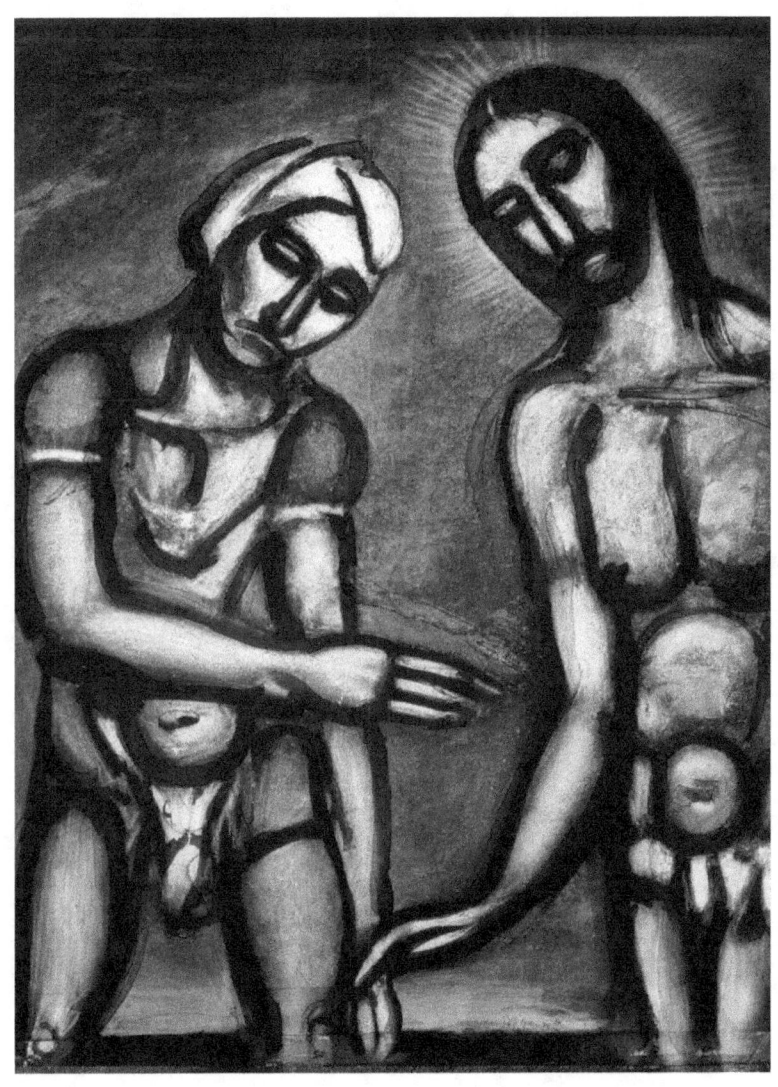

Plate 32

PLATE 32: RECOGNITION

"Seigneur, c'est vous, je vous reconnais."
"Lord, it is you, I recognize you."

Rouault narrows the focus from above the knees to the heads. Christ's left arm edges out of the print, His right arm hooks in like he is trying to steal a basketball. Thomas looks like he is going to gently jab the side of Christ. They gently bow to each other in the silent and very physical act, following the very awkward, "is it you?"

Thomas can't trust his own eyes. Christ humbly, gently, leans into the vulnerability of Thomas, asking the embarrassing question. There is a resonance between the fleshy bodies, carrying the same light emanating from Christ's halo. There is but a slight horizon line curving up into the visual plane, slightly bending space.

Their flesh bears the light while the landscape is dark in contrast. Christ once again offers his body; His compassion is embodied compassion. This is no purely intellectual faith, but a body-to-body encounter. Doubt is responded to with a revived corpse. Test it, place your hand in the wounds. See for yourself.

The work of Rouault becomes like a body: embodied lines, shapes and forms. His painting is stacked and caked oil paint, built up layers much like you might find under the easel. They are tortured canvases that he often worked on off and on over many years. Likewise in his printmaking process he worked and reworked his plates until they rang true. Almost like an archeological dig, he seemed to grope in the dark, searching and searching until he found the buried image that finally resonated with the internal and external world: historical, but also archetypal and true to human experience.

This particular image is the embodiment of bodies, which give form to the inner experience of being human, with the range of doubt, hope, disappointment, fear of further pain, communion, and recognition.

David Bentley Hart, discussing embodiment in a video dialogue, hits a resonant tone here:

> *"...In fact, it is understood that communion [and] community for finite spirits is an embodied reality. It is embodiment as such. But it is embodiment within a hierarchy of embodiment. It is embodiment within a spiritual community which is itself the greater body of the*

Protanthropos, the totus Christus (in Christian thought) or Adam Kadmon's cosmic expression."[71]

Part of Rouault's genius is his ability to strike notes that resonate on the fractal layers of experience or, in Hart's terms, the levels of the *"hierarchy of embodiment."* One may think of the experience of oneness in a congregation caught up in a moment together, the experience of corporate awe at a concert, the experience of a team that moves as one body on a field or court.

This image of Thomas carries innocence and simplicity, almost as a child might climb on an adult's lap, curious about a large mole on their face.

The action is a simple recognition of our need to see and to be seen, to reconcile with the change in the other, like a mother receiving back her child from war, "is it really you?"

Romania, 2001

When we announced the first pregnancy, Iulian and Bogdan said right away, "Let's take bets on whether it is a boy or a girl." They were two of the boys our community was working with in daily meetings to play soccer and share meals, hoping they would be able to let go of glue huffing and living on the street. More to get them off my back, I agreed. They both decided it was a boy, and I was then on the girl side of the bet.

A couple of months after the bet, I walked out of my apartment heavy with losing Lazarus three months into the pregnancy. The air was heavy; my head swam with the weight of the light from above and the glares from the city below. I walked across town to buy a box to fit the little body the size and color of a mouse, head, neck, fingers and toes, curved back in the fetal position.

I felt deserted by God and by community, and by our best friends, who were all traveling at the time. Phone calls were very expensive and difficult at the time, making it nearly impossible to get support from family back home. My youthful sense of invincibility and idea of God was murdered with the miscarriage our first pregnancy. I was devastated seeing the limp body of my first son.

A week or so later I needed to face the boys on the street again, "We lost the baby."

"When did it happen?

"Well, it was last week."

He put his head down looking at my feet. "So, was it a boy or a girl?"

"It was a boy" I said.

"I guess you owe me a pizza then. Remember our bet, I said it would be a boy."

Eventually we found a time and place to make good on the bet. We ended up in our new apartment we had just closed on but had not moved into yet. They walked into the apartment, and immediately it smelled like trench foot and shoe glue. You breathe it and are immediately conscious of trying not to react to it.

I flopped the pizza box on the floor of our new, yet still empty, apartment floor. The empty apartment felt like no one's place yet. The boys sat down on the clacking parquet floor, immediately filling the space, overcoming the unpleasant smells with their personality and humor. It was as if they had made it their place and welcomed me as their guest. We sat around leaning on the walls like kings.

They asked about his name, how old he was, what did he look like when I saw his little body. They asked these things as if they were the most natural questions like, "Where did you get those shoes?"

People kept telling us that the miscarriage was natural, that the body rejects a fetus that is malformed, that many miscarry their first pregnancy or that the system is cleaned out and getting the hormones straight. All these comments were like trying to move a dark cloud with a fly swatter. Hell, I lost my baby and lost the idea of a God who always made everything good for me. The cushion I was riding on disappeared. My little raft was deflating fast.

We sat and ate. We talked. We drank orange pop in old pickle jars. Now I realize these guys had invited me into their living room and were very comfortable dining with death in the room. I had entered the space in which they exist, live and breathe.

It seems as though they refuse to bathe and put on new clothes for long periods as a way to externalize this inner experience. The mangy dog stink they carry with them resonates with their feelings of cutting, sadness and abandonment, of being deserted by family, by God. If they could show how they feel by going to the south pole alone, they might just do it. Instead, they crawl into underground tunnels, in the dark, exiling themselves.

Now, we sat in the emptiness, the absence, together, the bare white walls and the memory of my child present in the room. Three people present to one another in the body, in a room, in a city on earth.

I, having felt abandoned by God, was now receiving communion with Him. He found someone who could sit with me in the ashes and just be with me there.

In Rouault's image, Christ is calmly present with Thomas in the doubt, the questioning. He is comfortable acknowledging the death, the suffering. I found dealing with grief and death to be very isolating, making most people very uncomfortable, squeamish, fearful of upsetting, afraid of saying the wrong thing. Thomas just dove in, and Christ said, "Go for it. Check out the death wounds if you need to".

The audacity to verbalize doubt was not offensive to Christ. It was met with presence, understanding, and grace; notice the arm of Christ in the center of the image forms a graceful "S" shape ending in a downturned hand like the sower. Also, the contrasting arm of Thomas, which is a downward jabbing arm, is almost a weapon in its straightness and rigidity, as if he attacks with his doubt, his questioning. And yet Christ responds with grace, confidence, and calm, receiving the doubt without defensiveness or attack.

Even in a resurrected, triumphant-over-death body, He submits to inspection, choses submission and self-emptying love. His kenosis doesn't end, but is the reflection of his very being, the natural action of apatheia-agape, compassion without compulsion.

As the miscarriage shattered my conceptions of a God who "makes everything good for me all the time," I was lost in a cloud of darkness for some time, not knowing how to move forward. And here the divine presence showed up in the wounded bodies of these boys saying, "I guess you owe me a pizza then, remember our bet, I said it would be a boy."

And we sat together acknowledging the very real, very painful loss of my first child and my first ideas of God, recognition led to communion and belonging.

The months following the miscarriage of our first pregnancy are now a blur of faded memories. I was in a fog, zombie-style moving through the motions. A doctor friend was with us in the cemetery in the shadow of the steel factory. I could see his little body that could fit into the palm of my hand as I placed it into a little carved box and buried it next to a little girl named Annamaria who had died of HIV/AIDS at 10 years old. It was an apocalyptic scene from a black and white Tarkovski film.

The songs that sustained me proved too thin a rope to hold the grief on my miscarried boy. The spontaneous prayers dried up, and the images of God I thought were unshakable burned. Like a phoenix from the ashes, I found myself holding an ancient prayer book. A book of prayers from the deserts and catacombs, the prayers of martyrs suffering gore and dismemberment. Blood and death would not cause these tested prayers to cease. I borrowed their words.

The dark sleep felt like a year. It felt like dragging my spirit along with my body, like a small child might drag an oversized stuffed bear. "Oh, heavenly king, spirit of truth, you are everywhere filling all things." Filling my hopelessness? My despair? My void? Filling my incapacity to get off the ground, to muster faith speech or meaning from meaninglessness?

We moved to a one-room apartment within view of the Danube River. I stand on 7th floor balcony. To the right, the swollen river bears the filth and wash and poisons shed from all the upriver towns. Despite the brown, there is still something majestic in the power of great water.

Straight ahead from the balcony is seen the towers of the church of Sfanta Precista, the church of the Virgin Mary in honor of her dormition. It remains one of the oldest churches in the city of Galati, dedicated in 1647. I could drag my ragged spirit to that threshold.

I entered the opening, and eight feet later I was inside the cave-like space, smaller on the inside than it looks on the outside. The antithesis of the great gothic cathedral's endeavor for an unearthly lit space, this church seemed to impinge down on the viewer, making a fairly large space feel like a cave, stable, or catacomb chamber.

Beyond that it was packed with the faithful. And at the shoulder level of the people started the full body icons of the local saints, frescoes solid as the fortress itself. Above them were more lines of saints well known and unknown from 15 centuries, and saints of the scriptures. Up higher were painted the narrative icons of all the great feasts: annunciation, baptism, transfiguration, and all the rest.

The walls prayed with their narratives of outpouring love, of the tenderness of the Mother of God, of Christ healing the blind man with a gentle touch. To the right in the front, an icon of the dormition of Mary, and above the altar Mary with her protecting veil; and in the highest dome above, the Pantocrator, Christ the uncreated creator of all.

Of all these visual wonders I was mostly aware of the golden light, the warmth of the mass of human energy negotiating tight quarters, and a priest with the large smile of someone about to tell a wonderful secret.

Over a year or two while we lived there in that neighborhood, this was my refuge. I was the paralytic carried on the faith of others, the words of others, and the songs of ancient people. They introduced me to Mary. The Virgin Mother whose spacious womb encapsulated the universe, held God made flesh and all of His children.

This womb was a fortress with eight-foot-thick walls to withstand the onslaughts of cannon fire, and tender enough to nurture my two-month-old miracle that came a year and a half after my miscarried boy. Mary held my first boy that slipped from our grasp while I held number two.

Though the walls were thick to the outside, on the inside the separation between heaven and earth was paper thin.

Dumitriu Staniloae, a Romanian Orthodox theologian, says idolatry is any fixing of the image of God, and that any true spiritual development is a continual iconoclasm in the sense of continual revisions of our false images of God toward a truer and truer image.[72] I wonder if Rouault was not in this series challenging himself to picture God, find the God behind our idolatrous images of who we would like God to be.

For the disciples, the Christ they imagined before the crucifixion was one of political power. Two disciples asked Jesus if they can sit on his right and left when he achieved this kind of power. For Thomas, there needed to be a recognition that his preconceived idea of Christ before the passion was really this same Christ that chose to conquer death through powerlessness, giving up, consenting to suffer all that is present in the kenotic hymn.

Thomas signed up for a religion of power, and ended up with a wounded, crucified savior who identifies with all the broken and lost, wounded parts of humanity. His wounds are also our wounds, the wounds of the whole humanity in need of healing.

Doubt may be an invitation to our next necessary iconoclasm, and experiencing of a new kind of reality, one that more accurately represents self-emptying love, compassion, and apatheia.

Rouault embodies the archetype of divine love and gentleness in this image wrought in his engraving materials of God embodied in Christ. Rouault demonstrates divine love and gentleness, to inspire the viewer to embody compassion to the communities, families, and relationships they are in, and also to offer compassion to the inner parts of themselves in need of compassion and care.

GUIDED MEDITATION

Take a moment to find a place to be still and quiet. See if it feels ok to close your eyes and count 5 breaths. Check and see if you have emotional space to sit with this meditation.

What gets in the way of acknowledging and appreciating your doubting parts? Whether self-doubts, doubts about others, or doubts about the goodness of the universe? Can you make room for them now for a moment? If not, what are you afraid will happen if you were to acknowledge your doubts? What are you afraid will happen if you make space and listen for a moment?

If you can, be present with your doubting part. Where does it show up in your body? Just see what you can notice about the doubting part, how and when does it show up for you? Is it more about doubting self, others or the universe?

As you focus on the doubting part, start to notice how you are feeling towards it. Are there other parts that criticize the doubting or bring up consequences of doubting, or have judgements about what it means that you doubt? See if these other parts will relax and allow you to get to know the doubting part. Is there some curiosity or openness towards it now?

Can you let your calm and compassion lead the way to offer room for the doubting part? If so, just approach the doubting part and invite it to share with you what it has been holding onto. See if you can just openly receive whatever the doubting part is stuck on, or what energizes the doubt. If it feels ok, ask it if it can share with you what it has felt like to hold doubt like this for so long. See if you can notice that you are not doubt, but that there is a part of you that doubts.

Can you ask this doubting part what it was needing when it began to flood with doubt? Is there some way that you can respond and offer the doubting part what it needed so desperately back then? Is there any other wisdom care or perspective you can give the doubting part, evidence you have now that maybe you didn't have back then?

Try to not hurry away, try to make room for this doubting part to really feel your presence, see that you are still alive, that you survived and are not alone. Can you let the doubting part know about your relationships, and especially about those who have been there for you even when they didn't have to, even when it was hard. Just notice how it feels to be with your doubting part in this way.

When this inner reflection feels complete for you, take a few moments to return your attention to your breath and to the space around you. Perhaps spend some moments reflecting on the experience and take any notes on things you would like to explore further later or insights you want to hold onto.

To engage with the high intensity level audio version described in the introduction, scan the QR code or visit tinyurl.com/rouault-meditations.

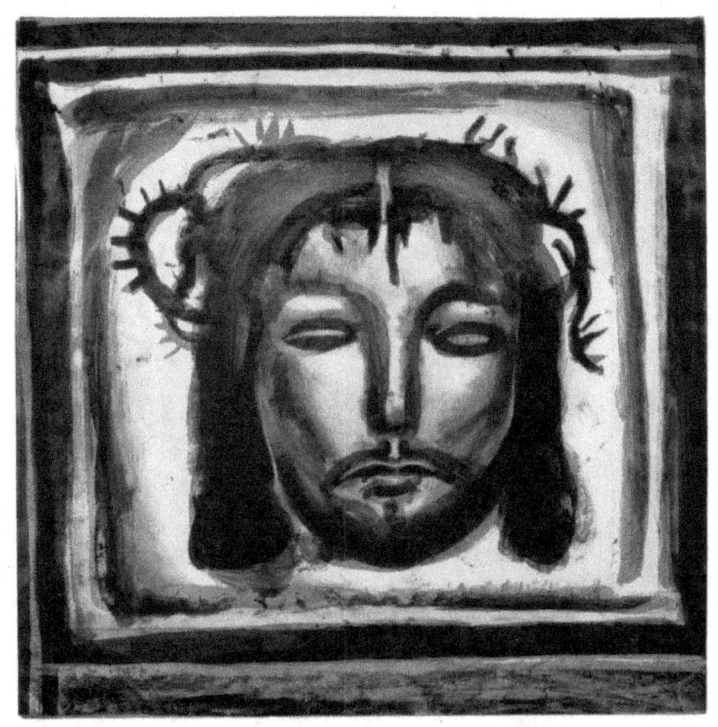

Plate 33

PLATE 33: VERONICA'S DELICATE LINEN

"et Veronique au tendre lin passé encore sur le chemin…"
"and Veronica with her delicate linen still goes (on the same path where she met Christ)…"

In this last plate completing the first cycle of the *Miserere* Series, number 33 fittingly corresponding to the number of years Christ lived before the crucifixion, Rouault offers a "face made without hands" image. This image refers to the tradition that Saint Veronica wiped the face of Christ during his journey to Golgotha. Tradition says that after wiping his face his portrait remained on the cloth, printed in his own blood. Rouault's painting, *"Carrying of Cross Under Veil of Veronica,"* (date unknown) depicts this story. Christ is seen carrying the cross, Veronica wiping his face, and above Christ is the cloth now imprinted with the image of his face.

It is perhaps notable in a series of engraving prints that this image of Christ was said to be quite literally "inked," and wiped and "printed" in his own blood on the handkerchief. Typically, the "made without hands" image is composed with a face alone, no neck or body as would be in this image.

Of all the plates so far, this is the first to be formatted as a square. Rouault frames the image in dark passages of deep blacks and contrasting lights, framing the piece to emphasize the contents in the middle. It is a frontal portrait with closed eyes, with almost the calm expression of a monk in meditation or the placidity of death. A crown of thorns interrupts the usual shape of the head; darks against lights make the thorns stand out framing, the head. Dark cheeks and mouth with blood streaming from the crown of the head and the hair, all create a harsh visual contrast making the portrait pop out.

One has a very different psychological reaction to a portrait with closed eyes versus open eyes. The viewer, placed in a voyeuristic position, has the feeling of seeing another without them seeing the viewer. Many standard Eastern Orthodox icons make the viewer the focus of the icon, a body to body, face to face, and eye to eye contact. This interaction of the viewer and the seen person is experienced as one directional. It is like watching a video conference with your camera off.

Aside from the clown image in Plate 8, Rouault does not place this viewer in this face-to-face position with the image. Ironically, his "Veronica" painting from 1947 uses this direct eye contact between viewer and portrait. By not using direct eye engagement, where the portrait is looking at you, Rouault maintains focus on the internal psychological churnings in the viewer's internal system. One is left alone with one's thoughts and reflections. Here as we look at a suffering God in the face, with His eyes closed, we can confront what is going on inside of us.

Rouault names Veronica in the associated poetic line, pulling the name out of history and connecting it to this image, which could have simply been referred to the image "made without hands."

The stanza associated with this image begs the question, what does it mean for Veronica to still be on the same path where she met Christ? This path could be understood as responsiveness to the suffering victim, moving in closer with comfort and compassion to offer nurturing, to not remain far from suffering but to get so close as to have one's handkerchief bloodied and ruined... or made holy.

She became known as Veronica, which in Greek means "honest image." This icon of icons is a prototype of images seeking to exact the true honest image of God in Christ. The icon in the Eastern tradition is focused not on perspectival accuracy but spiritual accuracy. As in the crucifixion, the graceful curve of the body more accurately depicts the spiritual reality of grace descending in the work of Christ.

Rouault was adamant that he creates images that are true. Before his entrance into the Catholic church and confession of faith, his religious paintings were naturalistic inspired by painters like Rembrandt. After his spiritual turning point, he sought to find a painterly form that embodied the spiritual and emotive vision of his faith and shifted into his heavier abstracted figures. Much in the spirit of the art of the eastern icon, naturalism steps aside so the inner truth of things can be given form. Images that ring true on spiritual, social, and psychological levels without compromise or shortcut are the result of the careful internal precision of his works. Rouault was looking for and finding convergences in the meeting place of several levels of experience at once.

The true image of Christ is that enfleshed God (John 1), made most clearly visible and transparent to His true nature by the act of suffering love in the service of reconciliation of all things. "Veronica's way" is the risky love of accompanying the suffering, getting dirty and even bloody, demonstrating compassion and vulnerability for the sake of human empathy and oneness in suffering, and eventually sharing in the resurrection and reconciliation of all things in Christ.

In this single image, Rouault condenses the movement of the entire first 33 plates and illuminates what seems like his understanding of God. Veronica, an "honest image" herself, in her compassionate act becomes another true living image of God, displaying compassion and mirroring Christ's action: *kenosis* in Greek, self-emptying, giving up power for empathy, connection, co-suffering.

If the series is about transformation and repentance, as the Miserere Psalm would suggest, here we have the final summary statement about what repentance and change would lead us towards. Plate 33 tells us of compassion, sharing in suffering for the sake of reconciliation, communion, *koinonia*: that all shall be saved and none left out. It is the way of Veronica and "her delicate linen," the simple acts of compassion and kindness.

While Christ's dramatic heroic compassion is demonstrated on a grand scale, in Veronica's act we see the honoring of tiny acts, small movements of humanity, empathy, kindness, and love. It does not have to be grand or notable. Veronica simply set aside fear long enough to wipe the face of a suffering victim. The act may have taken but a moment, and yet it is honored around the world. Any small act of kindness to any person is an act of compassion offered to Christ, the divine, mysteriously present in all people (Matthew 25:40).

It echoes the story of Mary washing the feet of Christ with her tears and His response, "Truly, I say to you, wherever this gospel is proclaimed in the whole world, what she has done will also be told in memory of her" (Matthew 26:13 ESV).

At a more basic level, Veronica saw His face and responded to it. Her response offers the face of Christ, the image of God's compassion for all, forever. Her compassion created an image of embodied compassion, which was imprinted on the cloth – becoming the physical face of compassion, "not made with hands."[73]

Romania, 2007

When we arrived, the boys were all laughing. Someone had called John's mother and told her that he was dead and in the underground tunnels. She found her way to one of his spots, climbed down into the tunnel and found him, like dead, but not dead.

He was drunk and asleep, and here she was told he was dead. She was irate, and it was the display of anger the other boys found so funny. As the retelling went, she grabbed him by the collar and pulled him to the surface, screaming at him all 5 blocks home, "Sewer rat, come on. You filthy rat, how dare you?"

John was well loved by the other kids, kind, empathetic, generous and ready to sing anyone a song. In some way he came to believe some version of being a "rat," struggling to find the hope that he could rise above the underground life into the world above. His inner image of himself was fit only for the streets and the sewers. While his mother could be aggressive, she could never match the internal violence of these beliefs about his true worth.

In the Romanian Orthodox liturgical life, Easter or Pascha is celebrated starting around midnight of Holy Saturday. The community gathers for prayers and a vigil service followed by a full liturgy after the candlelight has been received.

All of the lights in the church are out until one candle is lit at the altar, which is then passed from person to person until the church is full of light. One of my favorite moments of this experience is that suddenly each person's face is lit by their candle, much like the icons of the saints, each lit with a single candle. In the contrasting darkness all around everyone's face is radiant, 'honest images' of their true selves, revealing the luminous beauty of the divine. To see John and the other kids with us at the Easter midnight services was to see their radiance uncovered.

The story of Veronica is also one of moving towards shame. Much of human behavior is organized around the avoidance of shame and avoidance of being reminded of shameful memories in which we saw ourselves as bad. The way of Veronica can be seen as living into the courage and care to be present to shame, Christ's public humiliation of a death sentence. For us it may be to face our own shame and to be compassionate in the midst of the shame of others.

Part of the trap John lived in was the avoidance of feelings of shame by drowning them, only to wake up with more shame piled on.

Veronica's linen is a "delicate linen." She enters the place of shame, and tenderly, with care and respect of a delicate linen, sees and comprehends the suffering, registers it, acknowledges it. In the Internal Family Systems therapy model, this is a primary component of lasting healing, being witnessed in our shame while being seen and held as wonderful, as a divine image, as essentially good. The fear of shame, or protections against shame, are no longer needed because the true image has been seen and experienced. The story we told about why bad things happen is altered. The shame of felt badness is replaced with a new experience of being a human having done one's best in a difficult situation yet retaining beauty and dignity.

As I sat one day with a part of me that has sought desperately to please people, to never be seen as careless or insensitive, it led me back to the memories of that gravel parking lot from chapter 23 behind the American legion hall.

As I went inside, I found the 10-year-old boy that experienced this moment as being seen as bad, a careless kid. I could hear that experience, the deep sense of shame, of trying so hard to be good, but now feeling the hot judgement of grandpa, and the devastation as the sludge of shame settled into my system.

My people-pleasing protective part became more active, more vigilant, to prevent further breaches of shame. I introduced myself to that 10-year-old and asked about what it was like for him, what he felt and what he came to believe about himself from that experience. "To be loved you have to do everything right, all the time," echoed around inside.

My adult self could see the error in this, but that part had been alive and active for many years holding this belief. I could now go inside and take the 10-year-old by the hand, look him in the eyes, and let him know about those in my life who have loved me regardless of my failings.

There is then shock in his eyes, followed by a calm with the new perspective. And I could let him know that my grandfather had his own issues and was not intending to make any ultimate judgement of my value through his reaction.

"And what was he needing at that time that he did not get?" I ask the shame-holding part. He needed understanding that he was just being a kid, he was bored and exploring, playing – and yes, he could have been more careful, but things happen and they aren't the end of the world. And that he is loved and valuable, because he holds the inherent dignity of carrying the divine spark, and that nothing he could do would diminish or increase his value or belovedness.

So I hold his hand, look him in the eyes and tell him in words he can understand. He softens, relaxes into an embrace that I feel deeply in my chest. "You are wonderful to the core. There is no need to hide or be alone in shame anymore, I can help you anytime you feel bad or worry."

Tenderly, I enter my own system, find the wounded, shame-carrying one, wipe his face, hold him and bring him back from the dead, to bring more aliveness to my inner system.

When I open my eyes and come back to the present world, I find a new aliveness, fullness, and warmth, a new desire to care tenderly for those wounded and suffering around me. I hear echoes of 1 John 4:19, "We love because He first loved us."

For me there was one piece of work towards calming the protective people-pleasing part, healing the shame holding part it was protecting, freeing me some more to love without compulsion or fear, compassion without necessity, *apatheia- agape*. Perhaps this is Veronica's delicate linen. It is the fabric of calm compassion that connects us to ourselves, to divine love, and to one another across time and place to the end of time.

GUIDED MEDITATION

Take a moment to find a place to be still and quiet. See if it feels ok to close your eyes and count 5 breaths. Check and see if you have emotional space to sit with this meditation.

Can you make space to sit with some of those moments when you were touched by compassion? Even tiny gestures of care offered by people in your life. Can you remember the faces, the words, the feelings and body sensations when you felt the most embraced and seen.

Regardless of the multitude of parts we experience, the passions, pushes and pulls, out of balance part, can you focus on some of those moments when your compassion lead the way? What did it feel like in your body to give way to your essence, who you know yourself to be deep down, light, love?

You may notice inner critics arise, or parts that want you to stay humble and not acknowledge that you show love. Just ask them to relax and trust you that it won't go to your head, we are all made of this same compassion.

If they can relax, see if you can sit in that quality of calm love for a few minutes.

When it feels right bring to mind close friends and family members, and in a way that makes sense to you pray for mercy, healing and love.

Bring to mind acquaintances who you know to be suffering and pray mercy and love upon them.

If you are able, recall those you struggle to love and pray for mercy and goodness upon them as well.

Take a few more minutes to just sit in that quality of calm compassion.

When this inner reflection feels complete for you, take a few moments to return your attention to your breath and to the space around you. Perhaps spend some moments reflecting on the experience and take any notes on things you would like to explore further later or insights you want to hold onto.

To engage with the high intensity level audio version described in the introduction, scan the QR code or visit tinyurl.com/rouault-meditations.

AFTERWORD

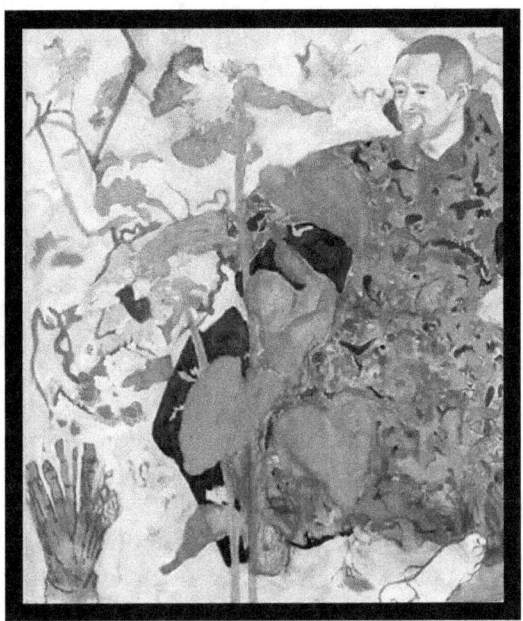

"He Who Sits in Death, Sees Life"
Joel Klepac, 2007 Oil on Canvas, 40" X 60"

This is the natural break in the *Miserere* series as it journeys on to Plate 58. My hope is that these reflections started you on your journey to spend time with the rest of the series, and that you write your own meditations, explore your own inner depths with Rouault; that the dark places holding hopelessness would no longer haunt you.

I started writing meditations on these pieces in an attempt to understand them better, and to use them to go inside and work through parts of myself in need of attention. I started with the crucifixion in Plate 31 I had encountered while in college. Another piece that struck me there in that little gallery was Plate 32, with Thomas. As I sat with these pieces and tried to understand what could reasonably be said from the visual data, they became trailheads for my own internal work. My hope is that Rouault's pieces, the descriptions of the pieces, and perhaps my own reflections would become a trailhead for your own work as well. While some may get squeamish about using art in this way, I can't help but believe deep reflection on the work was Rouault's driving hope for *Miserere*.

Though we cannot know the mind of the maker, the attempt to understand seems the highest form of flattery. I am more convinced of Rouault's compassionate gaze on his fellow humans. That he turned that

315

understand seems the highest form of flattery. I am more convinced of Rouault's compassionate gaze on his fellow humans. That he turned that compassion on himself I can hardly guess. Marchiori suggests, "Active contemplation has resolved his inner struggles. The peace of mind finally gained after so much meditation and so many experiences provided him during the last period of his life, from 1948 onwards, with a pictorial vision which at times attains supreme spiritual happiness."[74] Perhaps his children and grandchildren know better if he had peace within himself that could be felt by those around him. Some would say his late works suggest otherwise.[75]

Having the privilege to hear Rouault's grandson Phillipe Rouault share an intimate family history, I was impressed with the singularity of Rouault's vision. His vocation took him to the studio day in and day out, giving his spare time to only a very few friends, and spent his evenings with his children and grandchildren.

Working through these pieces, I am left with wonder at Rouault's ability to work hard and long, holding onto a vision and process that diverged from what others expected from artists in his day, standing up to the withering criticism of his fellow coreligionist, Léon Bloy, and developing a new religious aesthetic language misunderstood by both those inside and outside of the Catholic Church. As Venturi stated of the fauves painters, each, *"sacrifices tradition and realism in order to assert the rights of thought."* [76]

Rouault set out in the vast and treacherous ocean of intuition in order to assert those rights of thought, like Ahab of Moby Dick, to catch his beast and wrestle it to the end. The result of risking the deep intuitive waters with so little assurance of reaching his goal, of ever being understood, gives us this vision of humanity and divinity, compassion more luminous than we ever hoped. Rouault himself seems to have entered his own darkness touching into our shared darkness and came out with a new song; he dove to the depths of hades and came out with Euridice.

"He Who Sits in Death, Sees Life"

I began this painting above as I did with all of the *Sarcina* series (2006), with blind contour drawings in pencil and paint, filling them with lines that hinted at real life forms. A visiting friend came to my studio as I was working on it, and he ended up on the canvas in his sock hat looking a little menacing.

My methodology carries the hope of dialogue, a conversation between me and the canvas, the forms and metaphors that are surely inside of me but have not found voice. A sunflower was growing out the window of the studio and became a main character. And then my delightful friend – known to children around town as the red one, "Roshcatole" – came. If you walked with him, kids would shout his nickname from the apartment buildings, and his delightful welcoming smile became a joy to all of them. His portrait and figure entered the canvas and later my roughly drawn foot and paint brushes. His image sat in a rough-drawn chair similar to the background for over six months.

This painting annoyed me for a long time. I knew something was not right, but I did not know what. I carried the irritation in the back of my mind as I went on with my days working with kids, playing soccer on the street, doing art lessons and drum lessons.

Phillip Sherrard, in *The Sacred in Life and Art,* suggests that for a recovery of a truly sacred art we must return to "our proper dark," the dark of unknowing, of stumbling in the dark to find true forms once again. The artist must keep painting, digging, drawing and in the face of dissatisfaction let it fuel more seeking and groping in the dark. An art made from skill and technical competence is only that. Rouault had the boldness to enter the proper dark and faithfully fight his way through it to the beauty that only comes through darkness and death, an art that is in fact a kind of resurrection from the dead.

I believe it was on a walk home through the big open-air market that it came to me like a mosquito in my ear, "He who sits in death sees life," and I knew my joyful man needed to sit in a black chair. And with that the painting was done. I could hear the resonance of the truth of that in my experience of empathy of the suffering of others and my own suffering parts. It was a promise to my soul that inner work had a point, that outer suffering would someday be made right somehow, and that joy was the last word. That in the morning after the dark we wound sing matins together.

The dissonance of the painting's incompleteness helped me seek and listen for a deeper resonance. Beauty – the wisest of all therapists – drew me on, drew me in, and held me in its divine embrace. I thought I was making art, but it was making me.

I like to imagine that this experience was some tiny taste of the artistic feats of Georges Rouault, of bold entry into our proper dark, and persistence to see it through to beauty, to healing, to reconciliation and wholeness.

ACKNOWLEDGMENTS

Back in May of 2021 I sent Jim Forest an earlier version of the book, and from his sickbed just out of the hospital, he wrote these kind words, "I think it's a viable project — well written, beautiful, helpful, healing." Years earlier he offered generous responses to my questions about Orthodoxy and social justice and eventually invited me to write a few pieces for the Orthodox Peace Fellowship Journal *In Communion*. I remain grateful to him for encouraging me to write. Likewise, other cheerleaders along the way like Shawn Casselberry, Josh Fowler, Nancy Holloway, Elissa Morley, David Chronic, and Keith Barker need to be named. Also to Keith for helping turn slides into digital images. I appreciate others who waded through very rough drafts like Rick Durrance and Jess Coppedge. Thanks also to Wesley Vanderlugt and those who took part in the Gordon-Conwell Rouault Symposium in 2022 for their encouragement, SooYun Kang and William Dyrness among them. SooYun Kang kindly shared her deep knowledge of Rouault to help avoid catastrophic errors through her careful reading of the manuscript. Any historical errors remaining are all my own. My fellow IFS Practitioner Michael Learner graciously offered feedback on the meditations and suggested an audio version so readers could close their eyes. Thanks to Simeon Klepac who turned a small closet into a recording booth to make the audio recordings. Special thanks to Sandra Bowden for use of the digital images in the book, Terry Hibpshman for copy editing, and Jennifer and Shawn Casselberry for helping push this project over the finish line. Also, to those who have accompanied me on my IFS journey, especially Kevin Bellew, the Asbury practice group, and the Thursday practice group, this exploration is largely due to the safety and companionship you have provided. And to the kids and families in Romania who opened their homes and hearts to me, a stranger from a far country.

INDEX TO GUIDED MEDITATION THEMES
Parts Worked with in Each Chapter Guided Meditation

BIBLIOGRAPHY

Alfeyev, Hilarion. 2000. *The Spiritual World Of Isaac The Syrian (Cistercian Studies).* Cistercian Publications.

Bloy, Leon. 2017 . *Pilgrim of the Absolute.* Providence: Cluny Media.

Bria, Ion. 1996. *The Liturgy after the Liturgy: Mission and Witness from an Orthodox Perspective.* World Council of Churches.

Brown, Brene. 2010. *The Gifts of Imperfection: Let Go of Who You Think You're Supposed to Be and Embrace Who You Are.* Hazelden Publishing.

Brueggaman, Walter. 2001. *The Prophetic Imagination.* Philadelphia: Fortress Press.

Carter, Curtis L. 1998. "Georges Rouault's Miserere." Marquette University, 2 1.

Clément, Oliver. 2013. *Roots of Christian Mysticism: Texts from the Patristic Era with Commentary.* 2. New City Press.

Coakley, Sarah. 2013. *God, Sexuality, and the Self: An Essay 'On The Trinity'.* Cambridge University Press.

Davidson Galleries. n.d. "MISERERE: ARTIST'S PREFACE." *Davidson Galleries.* Accessed 4 23, 2021. https://www.davidsongalleries.com/collections/georges-rouault/medium_lithograph.

Doering, Bernard. 2004. *Truth Matters Essays in Honor of Jacques Maritain.* Edited by John G Trapani, Jr. American Maritain Association. https://maritain.nd.edu/ama/Truth/index.html.

Dyrness, William A. 1971. *Rouault A Vision of Suffering and Salvation.* 1st edition. William B. Eerdmans.

Flieger, Verlyn, and Douglas A Anderson, . 2014. *Tolkien on Fairy-Stories.* HarperCollins Publishers.

Hancock, Ian. 2002. *We are the Romani People.* Interface Collection edition. University Of Hertfordshire Press.

Hart, David Bentley. 2019. *That All Shall Be Saved: Heaven, Hell, and Universal Salvation.* Yale University Press.

—. 2017. *The Hidden and the Manifest: Essays in Theology and Metaphysics.* Eerdmans.

—. 2020. *Theological Territories: A David Bentley Hart Digest.* University of Notre Dame Press.

Kochanski, Martin. n.d. "The Office of Readings." *Universalis.* Accessed 4 28, 21. https://universalis.com/n-liturgy-readings.htm.

Marchiori, Giuseppe. 1965. *Rouault.* Reynal & Company.

Maritain, Jacques. 1974. *Creative Intuition in Art and Poetry.* Meridian Books.

Max Planck Society. 2013. *Compassion: Bridging Practice and Science.* 1.

Max Planck Society. http://www.compassion-training.org/?page=download&lang=en.

Merton, Thomas. 1968. *Conjectures of a Guilty Bystander.* Reissue edition. Image.

—. 1999. *Mystics and Zen Masters.* Reissue. Farrar, Straus and Giroux.

Miller, William R, and Stephen Rollnick. 2012. *Motivational Interviewing: Helping People Change.* 3. The Guilford Press.

Nouwen, Henri J. M. 1979. *The Wounded Healer: Ministry in Contemporary Society.* Image.

Oliver, Mary. 2019. *Upstream.* Reprint Edition. Penguin Books.

Rogers, Carl. 1989. *The Carl Rogers Reader.* Mariner Books.

Rosenberg, Marhsall B. 2015. *Nonviolent Communication: A Language of Life.* 3rd edition. Puddle Dancer Press.

Rouault, Georges. 1952. *Le Miserere de Georges Rouault.* Aux Editions du seuil. L'etoile filiante.

Rushdie, Salman. 2006. *Midnight's Children: A Novel.* 25th Anniversary edition. Random House Trade Paperbacks.

Schloesser, S. 2008. *Mystic Masque: Semblance and Reality in Georges Rouault, 1871-1958.* First ed. University of Chicago.

Schwartz, Richard C, and Martha Sweezy. 2019. *Internal Family Systems Therapy.* Second edition. The Guilford Press.

Sherrard, Philip. 1990. *The Sacred in Life and Art.* Galgonooza Press.

Siegel, Daniel J. 2011. *Mindsight: The New Science of Personal Transformation.* Bantam Books.

Smith, Huston. 1989. *Beyond the Post-Modern Mind.* Updtd&Revd. Quest Books.

Soby, James Thrall. 1945. *GEORGES ROUAULT: Paintings and Prints.* 1st edition. The Museum of Modern Art.

Sophrony, Archimandrite. 1974. *Wisdom from Mount Athos: The Writings of Staretz Silouan, 1866-1938.* Translated by Rosemary Edmonds. St. Vladimir's Seminary Press.

St. Maximos. 2003. *On the Cosmic Mystery of Jesus Christ.* Translated by Paul M Blowers and Robert Louis Wilken. St Vladimirs Seminary Pr.

Staniloae, Dumitru. 1998. *Orthodox Dogmatic Theology: The Experience of God, Vol. 1: Revelation and Knowledge of the Triune God.* Holy Cross Orthodox Press.

Taseel. 2021. "Transcriptions from the Q&A with David Bentley Hart — Discussing "Roland in Moonlight" from Ta'seel Commons with Hasan Azad and Esmé Partridge." *Copious Flowers.* April 8. https://copiousflowers.com/2021/04/14/transcriptions-from-the-qa-with-david-bentley-hart-discussing-roland-in-moonlight-from-taseel-commons-with-hasan-azad-and-esme-partridge/amp/.

Venturi, Lionello. 1939. "Rouault." *Parnassus* 11 (6): 5-13.
https://www.jstor.org/stable/771787.

Wikipedia. 2021. "Psalm 51." *Wikipedia.* March 19.
https://en.wikipedia.org/wiki/Psalm_51.

Wikipedia. 2020. "Winged Sun." *Wikipedia.* December 10.
https://en.wikipedia.org/wiki/Winged_sun.

Wofsy, Alan. 1976. *Georges Rouault: The Graphic Work. A Catalogue Raisonn é.* 1st edition. Alan Wofsy Fine Arts.

Wroe, Ann. 2012. "Ann Wroe's 'Orpheus': Why the Mythological Muse Haunts Us." *The Daily Beast.* 5 31.
https://www.thedailybeast.com/ann-wroes-orpheus-why-the-mythological-muse-haunts-us.

BOWDEN Collections

PRESENTS

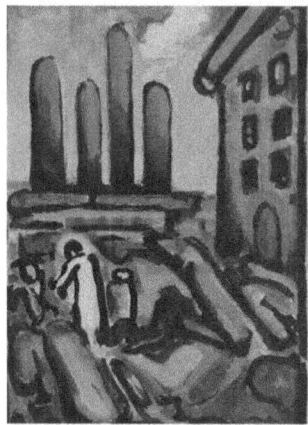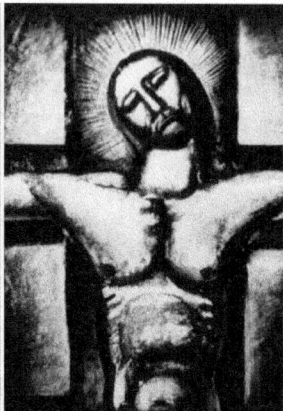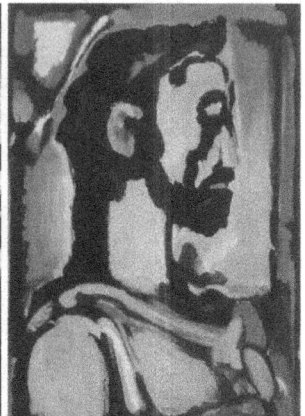

Georges Rouault
3 Traveling exhibitions

Miserere Series
All 58 intaglios from this remarkable
20th century suite

Seeing Christ in the Darkness:
Georges Rouault as Graphic Artist
41 prints from Miserere,
The Passion, Fleurs du Mal

Georges Rouault: A Steadfast Vision
23 prints from Miserere,
The Passion and Fleurs du Mal

Interior plates:

Miserere, Plates 1, c.1914-1918. Georges Rouault (French, 1871–1958). Aquatint with sugar lift, drypoint, burnisher, roulette; 22 3/4 x 16 1/4 inches. Bowden Collections
Miserere, Plates 2, c.1914-1918. Georges Rouault (French, 1871–1958). Aquatint with sugar lift, drypoint, burnisher, roulette; 22 3/4 x 16 1/4 inches. Bowden Collections
Miserere, Plates 3, c.1914-1918. Georges Rouault (French, 1871–1958). Aquatint with sugar lift, drypoint, burnisher, roulette; 22 3/4 x 16 1/4 inches. Bowden Collections
Miserere, Plates 4, c.1914-1918. Georges Rouault (French, 1871–1958). Aquatint with sugar lift, drypoint, burnisher, roulette; 22 3/4 x 16 1/4 inches. Bowden Collections
Miserere, Plates 5, c.1914-1918. Georges Rouault (French, 1871–1958). Aquatint with sugar lift, drypoint, burnisher, roulette; 22 3/4 x 16 1/4 inches. Bowden Collections
Miserere, Plates 6, c.1914-1918. Georges Rouault (French, 1871–1958). Aquatint with sugar lift, drypoint, burnisher, roulette; 22 3/4 x 16 1/4 inches. Bowden Collections
Miserere, Plates 7, c.1914-1918. Georges Rouault (French, 1871–1958). Aquatint with sugar lift, drypoint, burnisher, roulette; 22 3/4 x 16 1/4 inches. Bowden Collections
Miserere, Plates 8, c.1914-1918. Georges Rouault (French, 1871–1958). Aquatint with sugar lift, drypoint, burnisher, roulette; 22 3/4 x 16 1/4 inches. Bowden Collections
Miserere, Plates 9, c.1914-1918. Georges Rouault (French, 1871–1958). Aquatint with sugar lift, drypoint, burnisher, roulette; 22 3/4 x 16 1/4 inches. Bowden Collections
Miserere, Plates 10, c.1914-1918. Georges Rouault (French, 1871–1958). Aquatint with sugar lift, drypoint, burnisher, roulette; 22 3/4 x 16 1/4 inches. Bowden Collections
Miserere, Plates 11, c.1914-1918. Georges Rouault (French, 1871–1958). Aquatint with sugar lift, drypoint, burnisher, roulette; 22 3/4 x 16 1/4 inches. Bowden Collections
Miserere, Plates 12, c.1914-1918. Georges Rouault (French, 1871–1958). Aquatint with sugar lift, drypoint, burnisher, roulette; 22 3/4 x 16 1/4 inches. Bowden Collections

Miserere, Plates 13, c.1914-1918. Georges Rouault (French, 1871–1958). Aquatint with sugar lift, drypoint, burnisher, roulette; 22 3/4 x 16 1/4 inches. Bowden Collections

Miserere, Plates 14, c.1914-1918. Georges Rouault (French, 1871–1958). Aquatint with sugar lift, drypoint, burnisher, roulette; 22 3/4 x 16 1/4 inches. Bowden Collections

Miserere, Plates 14, c.1914-1918. Georges Rouault (French, 1871–1958). Aquatint with sugar lift, drypoint, burnisher, roulette; 22 3/4 x 16 1/4 inches. Bowden Collections

Miserere, Plates 15, c.1914-1918. Georges Rouault (French, 1871–1958). Aquatint with sugar lift, drypoint, burnisher, roulette; 22 3/4 x 16 1/4 inches. Bowden Collections

Miserere, Plates 16, c.1914-1918. Georges Rouault (French, 1871–1958). Aquatint with sugar lift, drypoint, burnisher, roulette; 22 3/4 x 16 1/4 inches. Bowden Collections

Miserere, Plates 17, c.1914-1918. Georges Rouault (French, 1871–1958). Aquatint with sugar lift, drypoint, burnisher, roulette; 22 3/4 x 16 1/4 inches. Bowden Collections

Miserere, Plates 18, c.1914-1918. Georges Rouault (French, 1871–1958). Aquatint with sugar lift, drypoint, burnisher, roulette; 22 3/4 x 16 1/4 inches. Bowden Collections

Miserere, Plates 19, c.1914-1918. Georges Rouault (French, 1871–1958). Aquatint with sugar lift, drypoint, burnisher, roulette; 22 3/4 x 16 1/4 inches. Bowden Collections

Miserere, Plates 20, c.1914-1918. Georges Rouault (French, 1871–1958). Aquatint with sugar lift, drypoint, burnisher, roulette; 22 3/4 x 16 1/4 inches. Bowden Collections

Miserere, Plates 21, c.1914-1918. Georges Rouault (French, 1871–1958). Aquatint with sugar lift, drypoint, burnisher, roulette; 22 3/4 x 16 1/4 inches. Bowden Collections

Miserere, Plates 22, c.1914-1918. Georges Rouault (French, 1871–1958). Aquatint with sugar lift, drypoint, burnisher, roulette; 22 3/4 x 16 1/4 inches. Bowden Collections

Miserere, Plates 23, c.1914-1918. Georges Rouault (French, 1871–1958). Aquatint with sugar lift, drypoint, burnisher, roulette; 22 3/4 x 16 1/4 inches. Bowden Collections

Miserere, Plates 24, c.1914-1918. Georges Rouault (French, 1871–1958). Aquatint with sugar lift, drypoint, burnisher, roulette; 22 3/4 x 16 1/4 inches. Bowden Collections

Miserere, Plates 25, c.1914-1918. Georges Rouault (French, 1871–1958). Aquatint with sugar lift, drypoint, burnisher, roulette; 22 3/4 x 16 1/4 inches. Bowden Collections

Miserere, Plates 26, c.1914-1918. Georges Rouault (French, 1871–1958). Aquatint with sugar lift, drypoint, burnisher, roulette; 22 3/4 x 16 1/4 inches. Bowden Collections

Miserere, Plates 27, c.1914-1918. Georges Rouault (French, 1871–1958). Aquatint with sugar lift, drypoint, burnisher, roulette; 22 3/4 x 16 1/4 inches. Bowden Collections

Miserere, Plates 28, c.1914-1918. Georges Rouault (French, 1871–1958). Aquatint with sugar lift, drypoint, burnisher, roulette; 22 3/4 x 16 1/4 inches. Bowden Collections

Miserere, Plates 29, c.1914-1918. Georges Rouault (French, 1871–1958). Aquatint with sugar lift, drypoint, burnisher, roulette; 22 3/4 x 16 1/4 inches. Bowden Collections

Miserere, Plates 30, c.1914-1918. Georges Rouault (French, 1871–1958). Aquatint with sugar lift, drypoint, burnisher, roulette; 22 3/4 x 16 1/4 inches. Bowden Collections

Miserere, Plates 31, c.1914-1918. Georges Rouault (French, 1871–1958). Aquatint with sugar lift, drypoint, burnisher, roulette; 22 3/4 x 16 1/4 inches. Bowden Collections

Miserere, Plates 32, c.1914-1918. Georges Rouault (French, 1871–1958). Aquatint with sugar lift, drypoint, burnisher, roulette; 22 3/4 x 16 1/4 inches. Bowden Collections

Miserere, Plates 33, c.1914-1918. Georges Rouault (French, 1871–1958). Aquatint with sugar lift, drypoint, burnisher, roulette; 22 3/4 x 16 1/4 inches. Bowden Collections

ENDNOTES

[1] See William Dyrness, *Rouault: A Vision of Suffering and Salvation*, Eerdmans (Grand Rapids: Michigan,1971).

[2] See cover image.

[3] Alfeyev Hilarion, *"The Spiritual World of Isaac the Syrian"* (Collegeville, Liturgical Press, 2000), 73.

[4] Doering, Bernard. *"Truth Matters Essays in Honor of Jacques Maritain"*. Edited by John G Trapani, Jr. American Maritain Association. 2004. https://maritain.nd.edu/ama/Truth/index.html., p17.

[5] Marchiori, Giuseppe. "Rouault". (New York Reynal & Company, 1965), 29.

[6] Source: public domain. https://www.babelio.com/auteur/Georges-Rouault/53581.

[7] For a detailed history see Soo Yun Kang *"Rouault in Perspective" (Newcastle: International Scholars Publications,* 2000).

[8] The "Miserere" Psalm (from its Latin name), referred to here in the Hebrew numbering. This places the psalm as 51, while the Greek (Septuagint or Vulgate) numbers the same psalm as Psalm 50. For example, the King James Version would refer to it as Psalm 51 whereas the Eastern Orthodox would use the Psalm 50 designation. Here I will use Psalm 51 or the Miserere Psalm for clarity.

[9] David Bentley Hart, The Hidden and the Manifest: Essays in Theology and Metaphysics. (Grand Rapids: Eerdmans, 2017), p45-69.

[10] Tania Singer, Olga M. Klimecki, Empathy and compassion, Current Biology, Volume 24, Issue 18, (2014): Pages R875-R878, https://doi.org/10.1016/j.cub.2014.06.054.

[11] Philip Sherrard. *The Sacred in Life and Art (Winchester:* Galgonooza Press. 1990).

[12] Merton, Thomas. *Conjectures of a Guilty Bystander*. (Garden City: Doubleday & Co, 1968), 140.

[13] Hart, D. Bentley. *"The 'Whole Humanity': Gregory of Nyssa's Critique of Slavery in Light of His Eschatology."* Scottish Journal of Theology 54, no. 1 (2001): 51-69. doi:10.1017/S0036930600051188.

[14] Roma are incorrectly referred to as gypsies, see Ian Hancock's *We are the Romani People*, 2002, xvii.

[15] See Marshall Rosenberg. *Nonviolent Communication: A Language of Life*. 3rd edition. (Encinitas, Puddle Dancer Press. 2015).

[16] Maritain, 1974.

[17] Schwartz and Sweezy, 2019.

[18] St. Maximos. 2003. On the Cosmic Mystery of Jesus Christ. Translated by Paul M Blowers and Robert Louis Wilken. St Vladimirs Seminary Pr.

[19] 'Mother of God' in Greek.

[20] "Contributing to the wellbeing of others" was felt by Marshall Rosenberg to be a primary human need.

[21] John 8:7 KJV.

[22] Borderline is a professional label for someone with complex trauma who has erratic relationships and struggles with trust due to repeated experiences of relationship trauma.

[23] Isaiah 3:15 NASB.

[24] Dyrness, *"Rouault: A Vision of Suffering and Salvation"*, p149.

[25] See James Loder's *"The Logic of the Spirit: Human Development in Theological Perspective"* (1998).

[26] See Thomas Merton's "New Seeds of Contemplation, 1961.

[27] Thomas Merton, *"Mystics and Zen Masters"*. (Reissue. Farrar, Straus and Giroux, 1999).

[28] Sophrony, 1974, 87.

[29] Mary Oliver, "Upstream," (Reprint Edition. Penguin Books. 2019), 84.

[30] See Max Planck Society, "Compassion: Bridging Practice and Science" 2013; and Schwartz & Sweezy, "Internal Family Systems", 2019.

[31] Evagrius Pontics, "The Practikos and Chapters on Prayer", (J. E. Bamberger, Trans. Cistercian Publications, 1970).

[32] Walter Brueggemann, "The Prophetic Imagination" (Philadelphia: Fortress Press, 2001), 59, 88.

[33] Merton, Conjectures of a Guilty Bystander, 1968.

[34] https://visforvintage.net/2013/06/07/history-of-pearls/

[35] Léon Bloy, *Pilgrim of the Absolute* trans. John Coleman & Harry Binsse (Providence: Cluny Media, 2017), 125.

[36] Luke 16.

[37] Luke 15.

[38] I Timothy 1:13.

[39] Soo Yun Kang (Art Historian) personal communication with author, July 2023.

[40] Kang, personal communication, 2023.

[41] Oliver, "Upstream", 89.

[42] See David Bentley Hart's essay in "Theological Territories" essay "An Introduction to Leon Bloy's Pilgrim of the Absolute".

[43] Kang, personal communication, 2023.

[44] Ibid.

[45] Romans 8:2.

[46] Ian Hancock, We are the Romani People (Interface Collection Edition. University of Hertfordshire Press) 2002.

[47] Quoted in Dyrness, Rouault, 149.

[48] Luke 19:40.

[49] Jacques Maritain, *Creative Intuition in Art and Poetry*. (Meridian Books. 1974).

[50] Doering, 2004, 215.

[51] Carter,1998, 4.

[52] Doering, 2004, 14.

[53] Ibid, 212.

[54] Ibid, 14.

[55] Compare to Honoré Daumier depictions of the poor like "The Beggars".

[56] Carter, 1998, 4.

[57] Schwartz & Sweezy, 2019.

[58] Carter, 4.

[59] Wroe, 2012.

[60] See J.R.R. Tolkien's <u>On Fairy Stories</u> for how this dynamic is part of the power of a narrative art.

[61] See *St. Jerome* by Carrivagio, *Magdalene with the Smoking Flame* by Georges de La Tour for example, or the many Vanitas still life paintings.

[62] Sophrony, 87.

[63] See NIH statistics at https://www.ncbi.nlm.nih.gov/pmc/articles/PMC2894717//.

[64] Kochanski, n.d.

[65] Hart 2020, 250.

[66] Bria, 1996.

[67] Clément, 2013, 355.

[68] Daniel Seigel also ascribes to multiplicity of mind.

[69] Schwartz & Sweezy, 2019.

[70] Dyrness, 1971, 27.

[71] Taseel, 2021, 1:10 min.

[72] Stanioae, 1998.

[73] See my paper "The Healing Poetics of Georges Rouault: Veils of Veronica" to be published 2024.

[74] Marchiori, 28.

[75] Kang, Personal Communication, 2023.

[76] Venturi, 11.

www.ingramcontent.com/pod-product-compliance
Lightning Source LLC
Chambersburg PA
CBHW070409290526
45791CB00005B/1692